MILTON FRIEDMAN

MILTON FRIEDMAN

A Biography

Lanny Ebenstein

To Rob

MILTON FRIEDMAN
Copyright © Lanny Ebenstein, 2007
All rights reserved. No part of this book may be used or reproduced in any manner
whatsoever without written permission except in the case of brief quotations
embodied in critical articles or reviews.

First published in 2007 by
PALGRAVE MACMILLAN™
175 Fifth Avenue, New York, N.Y. 10010 and
Houndmills, Basingstoke, Hampshire, England RG21 6XS
Companies and representatives throughout the world.

PALGRAVE MACMILLAN is the global academic imprint of the Palgrave
Macmillan division of St. Martin's Press, LLC and of Palgrave Macmillan Ltd.
Macmillan® is a registered trademark in the United States, United Kingdom and
other countries. Palgrave is a registered trademark in the European Union and
other countries.

ISBN-13: 978-1-4039-7627-7
ISBN-10: 1-4039-7627-9

Library of Congress Cataloging-in-Publication Data is available from the Library of
Congress.

A catalogue record of the book is available from the British Library.

Design by Letra Libre, Inc.

First edition: February 2007
10 9 8 7 6 5 4 3 2 1
Printed in the United States of America.

Inflation is always and everywhere a monetary phenomenon.

—*Inflation: Causes and Consequences*

We are as a people still free to choose which way we should go—whether to continue along the road we have been following to ever bigger government, or to call a halt and change direction.

—*Free to Choose*

CONTENTS

Preface   ix

Introduction   1

I. 1912 to 1946

1. Early Life   5
2. Undergraduate Years   13
3. University of Chicago and Columbia   19
4. Rose   31
5. World War II   41
6. Return to Academe   47

II. 1946 to 1976

7. Department of Economics   53
8. "Positive Economics"   63
9. Family   77
10. Professor   85
11. *A Theory of the Consumption Function*   97
12. Keynes   105
13. *A Monetary History of the United States*   113
14. Chicago School of Economics   129
15. *Capitalism and Freedom*   135
16. Travel and Goldwater   147

17. Colleagues 155
18. Public Intellectual and Policy Proposals 169
19. Nixon and the Nobel Prize 185

III. 1977 to 2006

20. *Free to Choose* 197
21. Reagan and International Influence 205
22. Hayek and the Role of Ideas 215
23. School Vouchers and Social Issues 223
24. Friedman Prize 231

Epilogue 241
Appendix 243
Bibliographical Essay 250
Notes 267
Index 285

PREFACE

The influence of Milton Friedman on our lives is significant. His contributions in economic theory and public policy have arguably added tens of trillions of dollars to world product over time. In this book I give an account of his life and provide an introduction to his work. Specifically, I focus on Friedman's work in economics and his advocacy of libertarian ideas and government reform. In general, chapters one to six cover his youth and early career; chapters seven to nineteen, his mature career as an economist at the University of Chicago; and chapters twenty to twenty-four, his life as a public figure and in old age. In addition, a recent interview with him is provided as an appendix, and the bibliographical essay provides an introduction to the secondary literature on Friedman.

Friedman lives his life for a purpose, the utilitarian goal of producing the greatest good for the greatest number while being happiest oneself. His political goal is the greatest freedom possible.

I interviewed Friedman five times in person between 2000 and 2005 for this book, and I interviewed him once in 1995 for my biography of Friedrich Hayek. Friedman and his wife, Rose, reviewed preliminary drafts of what are now the first four chapters here, and he reviewed preliminary drafts of remaining chapters. He also reviewed a semi-final version of the first nine chapters here. We have exchanged fifteen or so pieces of correspondence on this project since 2000.

This is not an official or authorized biography. Although Professor and Mrs. Friedman have made themselves available to me in a number of ways, it was not suggested by them or me that this would be an official biography.

Friedman has been open and candid in his responses to my questions. When I first interviewed him, I asked if he minded whether I taped the conversation. He replied, in words I have thought about many times since: "I have a single rule. What I say to one person, I say to everyone. I never say anything off the record."

Many good people assisted on this project. I thank first Milton and Rose Friedman and their children, Janet Martel and David Director Friedman, for agreeing to be interviewed and for reviewing material. I also had the opportunity to meet David's wife, Elizabeth, and to have a telephone conversation with Milton's nephew Alan Porter. Friedman's longtime secretary, Gloria Valentine, was encouraging and helpful. Others who gave interviews include Gary Becker, Anna Jacobson Schwartz, Lester Telser, Larry Sjaastad, Thomas Sowell, Sam Peltzman, Stephen Stigler, Larry Wimmer, John Turner, and the late D. Gale Johnson. Paul Samuelson sent a useful letter with reactions to some questions. For my biography of Hayek, I had the opportunity to interview W. Allen Wallis, Edwin Meese, and Ronald Coase, among others, and to talk briefly on the phone with Aaron Director.

I also thank in particular J. Daniel Hammond, Robert Leeson, and William Frazer for their work on Friedman; the University of California at Santa Barbara for use of its library and interlibrary loan program; the Hoover Institution on War, Revolution and Peace for use of its Friedman archive; the Intercollegiate Studies Institute and Young America's Foundation for participation in conferences on Friedman; the Liberty Fund for participation in a conference on Frank Knight; Walter Mead for encouragement and assistance; Tom Schrock for continuing advice; Mark Skousen for calling various articles to my attention; Joe Atwill and Curtis Ridling, and Cyndy

Phillips for reviewing the manuscript; and Nik Schiffmann and Lee Gientke for research contributions.

Finally, I thank Airié Stuart, my editor at Palgrave Macmillan, and Chris Chappell, Heidi Bogardus, Debby Manette, and Yasmin Mathew, all also at Palgrave, for their work in improving the manuscript.

Lanny Ebenstein
Santa Barbara, California
November 13, 2006

INTRODUCTION

ilton Friedman was one of the leading economists and political philosophers of the twentieth century. His influence stems from several sources. In addition to his intellect, he had a strong work ethic, an engaging personality, and an excellent sense of humor. He was an influential teacher because many have gained from him intellectually, professionally, and personally.

But Friedman's primary influence is not as a "teacher of economics," as he referred to himself during his many years at the University of Chicago, as significant as this role has been. His primary influence is as an economic theorist and public intellectual. In these capacities—as scholar and wise man—he has changed and continues to change the way that economists and many others view economic history and theory and the appropriate role of government.

Friedman has a clear view of the world, a view that he communicates forcefully and effectively. His ethical view of the world is enlightening, whether one agrees with it or not. It is the libertarian view that adults should be able to do as they wish so long as they are not harming anyone else. This viewpoint typically leads to advocacy of less government—virtually everywhere, at all times, and in every way.

He has also had great influence through his purely empirical, or scientific, work. To the extent that humanity has learned that inflation is always and everywhere a monetary phenomenon—that is, inflation depends on changes in the money supply—he has contributed to the understanding of economic activity and money in a way that few have.

His career has been amazing in length and scope. He published his first article in 1935, over seventy years ago. His teachers, including Jacob Viner and Frank Knight at the University of Chicago and Wesley Clair Mitchell at Columbia, were the leading American economists in the first half of the twentieth century. Friedman is typically associated with the University of Chicago, which he attended as a graduate student in the early 1930s and where he taught from 1946 to 1976. He was also vitally influenced by his graduate studies at Columbia and his work for the National Bureau of Economic Research in New York.

His most significant scholarly accomplishments were in monetary history and theory. In 1963 he coauthored, with Anna Jacobson Schwartz, *A Monetary History of the United States, 1867–1960*—a landmark work in the history of economic thought that changed the view that the Great Depression in the United States was mostly caused by real, as opposed to monetary, forces. This was a great accomplishment, undercutting much support for Keynesian, Marxian, and welfare-state outlooks.

Following the success of *A Monetary History,* Friedman turned increasingly to influencing public opinion directly, rather than at a remove through academia. Paradoxically, he emphasizes the importance of government. Although he opposes much government activity, he believes that the way to a better future will be through government reform. He remarks that it has always seemed unusual to him that people can be "so cynical, realistic, and negative about the effects of reform measures and yet . . . such ardent proponents of the 'right' reform measures."[1]

He achieved his peak influence in economics from the late 1950s through the 1970s and in the broader society from the late 1970s through the 1980s. He built on the success he achieved first in academia, later achieving influence and renown in society as a whole. The extent of his influence, both academically and popularly, is worldwide.

Friedman is best known as an advocate of libertarianism, the free market, and capitalism. Although his views were considered out of the mainstream when he first enunciated them half a century ago, now, if they do not yet represent the majority view, they are at least no longer the opinion of an isolated and beleaguered minority. He was, until his death in November 2006, a regular contributor to popular and scholarly debate; in recent years, he has focused on educational reform through school vouchers.

In the 1896 first edition of Inglis Palgrave's *Dictionary of Political Economy,* before the Russian Revolution in 1917, Karl Marx was described as a "distinguished socialistic theorist and agitator."[2] This, perhaps, is how Friedman would be most commonly considered today with respect to libertarianism—merely as a distinguished theorist and agitator. But in the same way that Marx became considered one of the great minds of the nineteenth century, Friedman may become so viewed with respect to the twentieth century, if libertarianism becomes the wave of the twenty-first century.

Whether libertarianism becomes the wave of this century is, of course, completely speculative. The future affects our interpretations of the past and present; therefore, our knowledge can never be complete or certain. To the extent that the twenty-first century moves in a libertarian direction, Friedman's ideas would become even more influential than they have been. "Our society," he believes, "is what we make of it."[3]

Part One

1912–1946

1

EARLY LIFE

ilton Friedman was born on July 31, 1912, in Brooklyn, New York, the fourth and last child and only son of Jeno Saul and Sarah Ethel Landau Friedman. Of his family's past, Milton knows very little. Jeno was born in 1878, and Sarah was born in 1881. Both his parents were from Beregszasz, Carpatho-Ruthenia, in the Hungarian part of the Austro-Hungarian Empire. At that time—with a population of perhaps 10,000, a quarter of whom were Jewish—Beregszasz would have been considered a midsize city.

Carpatho-Ruthenia was on the northeastern edge of Austria-Hungary, close to Russia, near what is now Poland. It is almost the geographical center of Europe.

There was a Jewish community in Hungary dating back to the Roman times, but to what extent it continued through the Dark Ages is not certain. The immigration of Jews to Hungary occurred in waves over hundreds of years, beginning in the eleventh century. Significant immigrations occurred from that time onward. Jewish émigrés largely came from southern and southwestern Europe (originally from Spain) to the northeast. Over time, a central area such as Hungary received immigrants from all directions. Almost all Hungarian Jews, including Friedman's family, were Ashkenazim.

At a young age, Jeno moved from Beregszasz to Budapest, the capital of Hungary, to live with a much older half-brother, the son of the same mother but of a different father. The surname of Jeno's brother was Friedman, and Jeno, who was always referred to as "Friedman's brother," soon adopted this as his own last name. Milton is no longer sure what his father's original last name was, but believes that it was Greenberg, Greenstein, or "Green something else."[1]

Milton knows even less about his mother's background in Hungary. Sarah, too, was a younger sibling. She had three older sisters who emigrated to the United States before she did, at age fourteen in 1895. Jeno had emigrated to the United States in 1894, at sixteen. Both Jeno and Sarah were young to emigrate without their parents, who never left Hungary and whom Milton never met. Jeno had few close family ties once he arrived in America, other than his own family.

Jeno and Sarah were schooled in Hungary. They were fluent in Hungarian and Yiddish when they came to the United States, and they soon became fluent in English. In addition, Jeno knew some German. Milton says that Beregszasz was a "fairly progressive, active community."[2] It apparently had a good educational system.

Jeno and Sarah were part of the great wave of emigration to the United States during the late nineteenth and early twentieth centuries. They left their past completely behind and became assimilated to the United States, which they saw as a land of opportunity in all ways, an attitude that they conveyed to their children. It could have been of Jeno and Sarah that Emma Lazarus wrote the words that are inscribed on the base of the Statue of Liberty—which they would have passed on arriving in the United States: "Give me your tired, your poor, your huddled masses yearning to breathe free."[3]

On arrival in America as teenagers, Jeno and Sarah went to work. Sarah became a seamstress in a sweatshop—an experience about which, Milton approvingly comments, he never heard her make a negative remark. Indeed, he favorably says of her experience: "In those distant pre-welfare-state days, immigrants were strictly on their own except for the assistance they could get from relatives and private charitable agencies."[4] Jeno and Sarah met in the extended

Jewish community in New York that had connections with Hungary and Bereg county. They married in the early years of the 1900s. Milton and his three older sisters—Tillie, Helen, and Ruth—were born between 1908 and 1912. Jeno was thirty-four and Sarah was thirty-one when he arrived.

Milton takes after Sarah in appearance, possessing her finer features. A picture of the family taken when he was five shows a very short, perhaps slightly stocky father with a dark complexion, dark hair, and a well-trimmed mustache. His mother was taller, fairer, and thinner than her husband, though diminutive herself. The family looks as if they have a hard life but are proud of who they are and whence they have come. Two of Milton's sisters have bows in their hair, and two are wearing sailor scarves. His oldest sister, Tillie, is at nine almost as tall as her father.

Milton remembers his family as "close." He remarks that his parents, "like so many immigrants of that time, were very poor. We never had a family income that by today's standards would have put us above the poverty level."[5] At the same time, "There was always enough to eat, and the family atmosphere was warm and supportive."[6] Though the family was poor by the standards of a later era, relatively speaking they were not among the poorest of their contemporaries.

The Friedmans spoke English in the home. They occasionally visited Sarah's sisters in Brooklyn but spent most of their time in each other's company. Milton was emotionally closest to his sister Ruthy, to whom he was closest in age.

When Milton was one, the family moved from Brooklyn to Rahway, New Jersey. Rahway is a small commuter and light industrial town about twenty miles from New York City that, while he was growing up, had a solidly lower-income and working-class population of about 15,000.

Milton describes his father's work activities variously as a petty trader and jobber—that is, he worked by the job (though not as a day laborer). In his capacity as a trader, Jeno purchased merchandise from manufacturers and sold it to retailers, sometimes from a slightly speculative perspective. "He never made much money,"[7] Milton remembers.

The Friedmans owned their own home/business in Rahway. In typical immigrant fashion, they had a store on the first floor, which Sarah ran while Jeno went to New York each day to work. The family lived on the second floor. Milton recalls exploring the attic as a child and coming across words written with smoke from a candle that led him to believe that the house had been used as a way station for runaway slaves before the Civil War—which, at the time, was a mere fifty-five or so years in the past.

Although he denies any precocity that made him stand out in his family, Milton once made a comment that may be partly autobiographical that "individuals who have exceptional mathematical ability get early deference, and develop great confidence in their ability to solve problems."[8] Despite what he says, he must have stood out as a result of his verbal dexterity alone. Nevertheless, he says that the only way he stood out in his family was that he was the only boy.

He began first grade a year early, at age five, in 1917 (he did not attend kindergarten). Although he says, "I believe that was standard then,"[9] it was not standard to begin first grade at five, and that he did so no doubt reflected his precocity. His early admission into first grade was particularly noteworthy because, being born at the end of July, he would have been young for his grade in any event.

Milton was a voracious reader and excellent student as a boy and teen. He read many of the books in the small Rahway public library originally founded by Andrew Carnegie. He has always been remarkably fluid, clear, and fast in oral and written verbal expression. In the middle of sixth grade, he was moved to seventh grade, making him two years younger than his peers. He recalls that he talked very loud—indeed, almost shouted—in class, so that when the proverb "Still water runs deep" came up in a lesson, his fellow students dubbed him "Shallow."[10]

His childhood and youth revolved around family, school, and faith, though there was only a small Jewish community of about a hundred families in Rahway. His parents were not particularly religious, and although by today's standards they would be considered Conservative (as opposed to Orthodox or Reform) Jews, they were reasonably progressive at the time. He attended Hebrew school with other boys after the regular school day was over to learn Hebrew for his bar mitzvah.

Milton remembers that he went through a "fanatically" religious phase until he was about twelve. Around that time he became involved with the Boy Scouts. At first, there was only a Christian scout group, until he and some others encouraged the organization of a Jewish troop. He remembers an event in the Christian group at which hot dogs were going to be served. He recalls "running away, running home, because otherwise I was going to have to eat non-kosher food."[11]

That he had an excessively religious phase as a young boy is noteworthy because it reflects the natural character of his mind— things have to be consistent; they have to be one way or the other. He tends to go the whole way intellectually or not at all, and seeks order and harmony in the universe. When he was unable to achieve this intellectual state through the logical observation of every detail of Orthodox Judaism in its dietary and other strictures, he dropped religion completely. He is naturally a rationalist and empiricist, and he came to see no point in religion. By the time of his bar mitzvah at thirteen, he had adopted a stance of "complete agnosticism."[12]

It is also noteworthy that as a boy he played a role in organizing a scout troop. This indicates another facet of his personality, leadership, and his ability to draw people to him. He has always had a remarkably exuberant personality. He remembers "many happy years of scouting"[13] as a youth. Among other extracurricular activities, he took violin lessons for a time as a child, to no effect, then or now. He is almost completely nonmusical, which is perhaps particularly unusual in his case because musical ability often is linked with high mathematical ability.

Milton began high school two years early, when he was twelve, in September 1924. He must have really stood out when he entered Rahway High School—tiny (five foot three inches in his prime, and shorter at twelve), one of the smartest kids, talkative, loud, and funny. He participated in the usual activities, including the chess team and as an assistant manager of the baseball team. He took part in a national oratorical contest on the Constitution sponsored by the *New York Times,* for which his name appeared in the paper and he received a medal.

The 1920s were the "Roaring '20s" in the United States. Millions of homes were built and businesses started. Manufacturing, economic productivity, and production climbed. Employment rates were high and rising. Retail stores, new conveniences, and many new amusements proliferated. Professional sports emerged. Agriculture declined in importance as a proportion of economic activity. Radio stations began broadcasting nationally, and by the end of the decade, three radio stations were an essential part of the national ethos.

The use of cars also significantly increased. One household in four owned a car in 1919. A decade later, this figure climbed to three in four, including the Friedmans. Milton remembers riding with his father when he was about fourteen. As his father was driving into the garage, the wheel hit a rock that had somehow gotten on the driveway. Milton was thrown forward through the windshield (in those days windshields were not unbreakable), which shattered, cutting his lip and leaving a slight scar he would have for the rest of his life.

With the mass ownership of cars, many more suburbs emerged around cities, and travel became easier. Skyscrapers rose in cities, including the Chrysler and Empire State buildings in New York.

Some would characterize the era as a more innocent time with respect to moral and family values, but Friedman rejects this description. For him, at least in retrospect, it was the era of Al Capone and crime engendered by Prohibition.

Milton graduated from high school in June 1928, a month shy of his sixteenth birthday. He had, he recalls, a "good grounding in language (two years of Latin), mathematics, and history,"[14] and was on good terms with his principal. His graduating class numbered about eighty—this would indicate that Rahway High School had about five hundred students. He thinks that he was salutatorian or valedictorian.

In recalling his development, he is impressed by the "lucky accidents" that have shaped his life. The first was to have been born in the United States. His "second major lucky accident was a high school teacher...[who] had a great love for geometry." The high school course in Euclidean geometry that Milton took instilled in him a "love and respect for and [an] interest in mathematics"[15] that has remained with him for his entire life, and influenced his early intention to major in math at college.

Milton remembers his parents as hardworking—they "had to be to make a living." He was "much closer" to his mother, who he describes as "sympathetic, kind, gentle," than to his father. In a sentiment expressed by many of their mother, he says that she would do "whatever she could for her children."[16] He remembers both his parents as very bright.

In the same way that he knows little of his family's past in Hungary, he possesses few vivid memories from his childhood and even youth. This may in part be because this was the most difficult time in life for him.

Jeno died of a heart attack in the summer of 1927 at age forty-nine. Milton had just turned fifteen, and was due to begin his senior year in high school. Jeno had been ill, apparently from heart trouble, for several years and had been taking medication for chest pains, so the family was to some extent prepared for his death. In retrospect, Milton does not attach much significance to the effect of his father's death on him. Asked in an interview about how Jeno's death influenced him, he replied, "I don't believe it did."[17]

After his father's death, Milton, notwithstanding his agnostic proclivities, fulfilled his mother's request that he say *kaddish* (a prayer of mourning) for eleven months and one day, a Jewish tradition. To do so, he had to travel to a neighboring community every day to find nine men with whom to pray. This daily travel concluded in the summer of 1928. Milton was, he recalls, "glad to see the year's end."[18]

2

UNDERGRADUATE YEARS

major turn in Friedman's life was enrolling in Rutgers University in the fall of 1928 at age sixteen. Much had changed for him in the preceding year, primarily due to the death of his father. The family of his childhood and early teen years was gone. Although he does not attribute much significance to the influence of his father's death on him, he also say it "must have"[1] affected his life.

Milton was the first member of his family to go to college, but he nonetheless remembers that it was "taken for granted"[2] that he would attend, no doubt because of his intellectual ability. As a result of his family's impecunious circumstances, particularly following Jeno's death, Milton was able to win a state tuition scholarship to attend Rutgers on the basis of high exam performance. He notes that a "class of competitive scholarships for financially needy students which [now] go not to those who score highest in the exams but to underachievers is a nice illustration of how our standards have been corrupted over the years."[3]

At Rutgers, Milton was first exposed to an academic environment and intellectual life. He enjoyed many extracurricular aspects of his undergraduate career, and he notes in retrospect the "many novels"[4] describing college life that he had read in high school. Friedman was introduced at Rutgers to the discipline that became his life's focus: economics.

When he attended Rutgers, it was a private school of about 2,000 students, and, as in high school, he must have been one of the youngest students when he enrolled. One of the oldest institutions of higher learning in the United States, Rutgers has attractive, ivy-covered buildings. In his day and until the present, there is a separate college for women.

Friedman has "nothing but good feelings"[5] about his undergraduate experience. His area of greatest success, and the activity he enjoys most, is intellectual endeavor. Once he enrolled at Rutgers, he was able to be with academic peers and pursue scholarly activities. He lived on campus in a dormitory during the school year—he wished to live away from home. New Brunswick, New Jersey, where Rutgers is located, was about a dozen miles from his home in Rahway.

Milton originally intended to major in mathematics in order to take advantage of his natural ability in this area. He thought that he might become an actuary, a statistician who calculates insurance. It was not until later in his undergraduate career that he decided to major in economics, a field with which he was barely acquainted when he enrolled in Rutgers.

When he started college, the Great Depression was a year away, and the economy was booming. Milton held a variety of jobs to pay for nontuition expenses, including working as a clerk and a waiter, and selling Fourth of July fireworks. He recalls of his experience waiting tables that he gained better insight into the importance of entrepreneurial abilities and skills. The restaurant at which he worked changed hands while he was employed there, and he experienced firsthand the difference between effective and ineffective management, a lesson that he has remembered throughout his life.

Friedman embarked on several entrepreneurial ventures while in college, including a summer school for high school students, which evolved from an earlier job of tutoring students. By the summers of 1930 and 1931, after his sophomore and junior years in college, the school ran for five weeks. He considers this summer school to have been an excellent experience for him personally, as well as financially profitable: "I truly learned something about pedagogy."[6] So high was the esteem in which he was held by his former teachers at Rahway High School that his grades for students were accepted without question.

More courses were required of college students when Friedman was an undergraduate than is the case today. He took about twelve semester classes a year—the standard now is closer to ten. He enrolled in many courses in math, French and German (two years each), English, American government, public speaking, chemistry, and history, as well as, starting in his junior year, several economics courses. He was also required to enroll in Reserve Officers' Training Corps, for which he marched carrying "antique World War I rifles."[7] He considered the ROTC a great waste of time.

At Rutgers, he was not as exceptional a student as one might expect. On an A to F four-point grade system, his average was 3.62—higher than now, after grade inflation, but still not all As. Nonetheless, he graduated Phi Beta Kappa, with high honors overall and honors in economics.

Friedman received his introduction to libertarian thought at Rutgers through John Stuart Mill's *On Liberty,* which he read as a freshman or sophomore. He considers this work the "most concise and clearest statement of the fundamental libertarian principle, 'The only purpose for which power can be rightfully exercised over any member of a civilized community, against his will, is to prevent harm to others.'"[8]

During his time at Rutgers, Friedman served as copyeditor of the student newspaper. He briefly entertained the idea of becoming a journalist. One headline he wrote that occasioned a good deal of mirth was after a Reverend Sockman spoke at the Rutgers chapel on sin: "Sockman Speaks of Sin in Chapel"[9]—that is, the sin of which the good reverend spoke was interpreted by some to have occurred in the chapel.

Friedman credits two instructors, Homer Jones and Arthur Burns, with stirring and nourishing his nascent interest in economics.

It was genuinely serendipitous that Burns and Jones were among his teachers, as Rutgers was a small and not especially prominent college when Friedman was a student. Burns went on to become the chairman of the Federal Reserve Board, and Jones became vice president of the St. Louis Federal Reserve Bank. Thus three of the most prominent figures in monetary theory and practice in the twentieth century—Friedman, Burns, and Jones—were all at Rutgers in the early 1930s.

Friedman took two courses with Jones, in principles of insurance and statistical methods. He remembers that Jones's "great forte" was to ask "interesting and probing questions, not accepting superficial answers, and retaining the attitude that we all have a great deal to learn." He also recalls Jones's "traits that exerted so great an influence on me in my teens: complete intellectual honesty; insistence on rigor of analysis; concern with facts; a drive for practical relevance; and, finally, perpetual questioning and reexamination of conventional wisdom."[10]

Jones introduced Friedman to what became one of his two greatest lifetime intellectual affiliations: the University of Chicago. The other was the National Bureau of Economic Research. Jones was a disciple of the Chicago libertarian economist and philosopher Frank Knight, of whom Friedman subsequently became a student. According to Friedman's friend Allen Wallis, Jones's influence on national economic policy at the St. Louis Federal Reserve Bank was as "great as anybody's."[11] Under Jones's leadership, the bank published economic data that was of great importance in making the case for a monetarist interpretation of economic activity—the idea that changes in the money supply are the most important determinant of national economic activity and, especially, of prices.

Of Arthur Burns, Friedman wrote that his "greatest indebtedness," apart from his parents, was "unquestionably" to Burns. He calls Burns "almost a surrogate father."[12] Burns was a good-looking, well-spoken man who made a great impression on others. Friedman says recently that Burns was an "extraordinary man" of "great personal power" and that he had a "first-class intellect" and "high standards"[13] in academic work. As a result of Burns's personal magnetism, during his career in public service it was said that wherever he sat was the head of the table. Richard Nixon, though he did not come to know the economist until Burns served as the chairman of President Eisenhower's Council of Economic Advisers in the 1950s, also had a very high opinion of him.

Friedman took one course with Burns at Rutgers, in business cycles. Burns was a student of Wesley Clair Mitchell, whose specialty was this field. Friedman says that this course, which was his real introduction to economic theory, "imparted standards of scholarship—attention to detail, concern with scrupulous accuracy, checking of sources, and above all, openness to criticism—that have affected the whole of my scientific work." The course ended with Friedman and another student going over a draft of Burns's doctoral dissertation "word for word, sentence by sentence."[14]

As with Jones, Burns's influence—which had a greater effect personally on Friedman than did that of Jones—was not primarily with respect to political philosophy or ideology (though both Burns and Jones were proponents of a free market). Rather, the two impressed on Friedman the importance of scholarship and the satisfaction that comes from doing it well. Also like Jones, Burns led Friedman to one of his two most significant lifetime intellectual affiliations, with the National Bureau of Economic Research. Burns subsequently became the bureau's director of research.

Burns was a mediocre chairman of the Federal Reserve Board. His chairmanship in the 1970s coincided with the worst monetary policy since the Great Depression. Inflation reached double digits and the whole period was one of significant aggregate price increases. Burns, like many of his era, did not fully subscribe to the quantity theory of money, whereby changes in the money supply are the primary source of changes in average prices. Rather, for Burns, as he expressed it in a seminar, "Excess government spending causes inflation."[15]

The gathering storm of the Great Depression hit during Friedman's sophomore through senior years at Rutgers. The course of the Great Depression—and Friedman's reinterpretation of it—will be discussed later. For now, it is appropriate to say that the depression was mostly the result of a significant monetary contraction fostered by the Federal Reserve System. The money supply declined by over one-third between 1929 and 1933, net national product dropped in real terms by more than one-third, and unemployment reached a quarter of the working population.

Nevertheless, Friedman was able to save several hundred dollars during his undergraduate years. He was always very effective in generating income. He also recalls that, a year or two later, in the depths of the Great Depression, his mother lent him some money to help with school expenses, which he subsequently repaid.

In his junior and senior years, he moved away from the idea of becoming an actuary and toward the idea of becoming an economist. He received two scholarships for graduate work in his senior year. One was from Brown, in math; the other, thanks to Jones, was from the University of Chicago, in economics. He decided to become an economist. Friedman explains: "Put yourself in 1932 with a quarter of the population unemployed. What was the important urgent problem? It was obviously economics and so there was never any hesitation on my part to study economics."[16]

3

UNIVERSITY OF CHICAGO
AND COLUMBIA

riedman left for Chicago in high spirits. After graduating from Rutgers in June 1932 with a bachelor's degree in economics, he spent the summer in Rahway, before enrolling at the University of Chicago in September to work on a master's degree in economics.

If his undergraduate years were his introduction to academic life, Friedman's graduate year at the University of Chicago in 1932–33 was when he firmly and unequivocally decided that the career of an academic economist would be his life pursuit. He says that intellectually, the year at Chicago was the most "stimulating time of my life."[1]

The University of Chicago was the brainchild of John D. Rockefeller, who gave the university approximately $35 million in its early years (an amount that would be equivalent to $1 billion today). Rockefeller intended for the university to be one of the great institutions of higher learning and research, and he succeeded admirably in this goal. As many Nobel laureates have been affiliated with the University of Chicago as with any other institution. It has been one of the world's leading universities since it opened its doors in 1892.

When Friedman enrolled in 1932, he was twenty years old and had not previously been west of Philadelphia. He must have felt that he had truly arrived. The original head of what was then the Department of Political Economy at Chicago (now the Department of Economics) was James Laurence Laughlin, a staunch economic conservative and follower of John Stuart Mill. Laughlin presided over a diverse and eclectic department. Thorstein Veblen—perhaps the most famous American economist (and possibly the most famous economist in the world) in the first quarter of the twentieth century—had been at Chicago first as a fellow and then as a member of the faculty. Wesley Mitchell, a student and then a young faculty member at Chicago, called its early Department of Political Economy "perhaps the most stimulating group of scholars in the country, certainly the group with the most varied traditions."[2]

The transition of the name of the department at Chicago, which occurred early in the twentieth century and reflected a broader trend at other colleges and universities, indicates the changing conception that economists had of their discipline. Economics emerged only in the eighteenth century in the English-speaking world primarily through the work of Adam Smith. Initially, it was nonquantitative and verbal—economics was not especially mathematical, and was public-policy oriented. Then, in the last decades of the nineteenth century and first decades of the twentieth, economists, in an attempt to be more scientific, eschewed the verbal approach and substituted mathematical formulas for verbal descriptions of economic activity, and became increasingly less directed toward public policy.

A milestone in the development of economics at Chicago came with the appointment of Jacob Viner in 1916, the year Laughlin retired. Viner was one of the leading American economists from the 1920s to 1940s. Born in Canada in 1892, he did graduate work at Harvard before going to Chicago to teach at age twenty-four. Viner was crucial in Friedman's development as an economist.

To Friedman, Viner conveyed the idea of economic theory as an integrated whole. Viner taught the coordination of economic activity through freely fluctuating prices, as opposed to, for example, through government direction. In a free market, capitalist system, buyers and sellers can exchange goods and services at the prices they desire. Changes in prices reflect changes in the supply of and demand for goods, thereby guiding production. If prices go up, other things being equal, more goods will be produced. If prices go down, the opposite will occur. Prices are an information-bestowing mechanism. Theoretically, Viner influenced Friedman more than anyone else, and it was from Viner that Friedman learned microeconomics.

Stories of Viner's toughness and even ferocity as a teacher were and remain legion. Paul Samuelson, an economics undergraduate at Chicago at the same time that Friedman was a graduate student and who received the Nobel Prize in Economics in 1971, recalls Viner's "famous" 301 course in economic theory. During it, students "sat tensely around the table."[3] If Viner called on a student three times and the student could not provide satisfactory answers, the student was out of the class.

Frank Knight was the other leading member in the department when Friedman was a graduate student. Born in 1885, Knight hailed from a rural Christian background but early became an atheist. The story is often told of how, at a young age, Knight gathered his younger siblings around him after they had all signed pledges in church to be faithful in attendance, and instructed them to burn them—saying that pledges made under duress are not binding.

Knight was, or became, more a philosopher than an economist. Over the course of his career he moved from technical economics to a philosophical and historical approach. Edward Shils, another Knight student in the early 1930s who later became a prominent sociologist at Chicago, remembered an address that Knight gave in the fall of 1932. Knight

> came in timorously yet defiantly. . . . He was wearing a dark woolen shirt, a somber necktie. He was bald and had a closely clipped, bristling little gray mustache. He wore silver-framed spectacles. His face was pink and round yet with nothing soft about it. He looked like a very intelligent little rodent. . . .

I can no longer recall what Knight said in any detail, but the main point of his lecture was an affirmation of the principles of liberalism— individual freedom, rational choice and action, rational discussion to settle political disagreements, the functioning of the competitive market as the most productive, the freest, and the socially most beneficial mode of organization of economic life.[4]

In a course with Knight in 1933 on the history of economic thought, Friedman wrote a paper called "Labor Theory of Value in the Classical School." While a piece of juvenilia, this paper is interesting for basic perspectives and the cast of mind it conveys:

An historical study of theoretical doctrine can be conducted from two fundamentally different points of view. The investigator can either analyze the doctrine with respect to its correctness and utility when applied to the contemporary economic scene, or he can consider it in the light of the historical situation under which it was developed. While the latter of these is probably fairer to the promulgators of the theory . . . , the former is much more likely to result in a valid doctrine, in a clearer understanding of the present, both from expository and control points of view. The distinction is the same as that between history that is mere description, and history whose object it is, by a study of the past to make possible a better understanding and control of the future.

I, for one, see little point in the history that aims solely to explain a theory in terms of the conditions existing at the time of its ascendancy. If there be such a thing as truth, how a theory arose has little to do with the truth of it. And to me the primary interest of the economist is to find out the truth.[5]

Even early on, Friedman was concerned with the truth to an unusually earnest extent. Moreover, he looked on economics as a practical discipline whose goal is to obtain better control of the future. Knight wrote a single word on the paper: "Good."[6]

Friedman remembered that when he went to Chicago in 1932,

the Economics Department had the deserved reputation of being one of the best in the country. The two stars of the department, Jacob Viner and Frank Knight, were joined by other eminent economists—Henry Schultz, Paul Douglas, Henry Simons, Lloyd Mints, Harry A. Millis,

John Nef. Each had his special strength and left a unique imprint on the students. Controversies among faculty members, mostly on an intellectual basis, helped to make the department an exciting place to study. . . . Equally important, a brilliant group of graduate students . . . exposed me to a cosmopolitan and vibrant intellectual atmosphere of a kind that I had never dreamed existed.[7]

Paul Douglas was among the best-known members of the Department of Economics. Very involved in Democratic politics, Douglas became a United States senator from Illinois in 1948 after service in World War II. A Franklin Delano Roosevelt Democrat, Douglas was for activist national government fiscal and regulatory policies and was interventionist in foreign affairs. He had a long-standing feud with Knight that ultimately ended in Knight's favor with Douglas's departure for politics. Like Viner and later Knight, Douglas became a president of the American Economic Association.

Lloyd Mints was a longtime faculty member at Chicago. Although not as exciting as other professors, he introduced the young Friedman to the quantity theory of money, whereby changes in the quantity of money in an economy are the largest source of changes in average prices. Mints was an admirer of Irving Fisher, the leading proponent of the quantity theory, whom Friedman calls "undoubtedly the greatest economist the U.S. has yet produced."[8]

Among the works that Mints assigned were John Maynard Keynes's 1923 *Tract on Monetary Reform*—which Friedman considers Keynes's best work—and Keynes's 1930 *Treatise on Money*. Friedman notes that Keynes was originally a monetarist and that only in his later work did Keynes downgrade monetary policy to guide an economy and raise fiscal policy in its place. In an interview published more than sixty-five years later, in 1999, Friedman said that Keynes always subscribed to the fundamental monetary equation, $MV = PT$ (the amount of money times the velocity it circulates equals prices times goods sold or transactions). In his later work, however, Keynes postulated significant changes in monetary velocity, with which Friedman does not agree.

Interviewer: Did you view your restatement [of monetary theory] . . . as a distinct break with Keynesian analysis?

Friedman: No. I didn't look at it in that way at all. I was just trying to set down what I thought was a reformulation of the quantity theory of money. Remember Keynes was a quantity theorist. Look at his *Monetary Reform.* . . . [It is] straight quantity theory. . . . So if you ask in what way was Keynes's liquidity preference theory [changes in monetary velocity] different from the quantity theory . . . , it was different only in the idea of having a liquidity trap [a decline in monetary velocity]. This was the only essential different idea. In my reformulation I don't have a liquidity trap.[9]

Friedman was a hardworking student and took copious notes in class and of works that he read. He took, for example, eighty-seven pages of notes on Keynes's *Treatise on Money.*

The member of the faculty at Chicago with whom Friedman had the most contact as a student, but of whom he had a very low opinion at the time, was Henry Schultz. Allen Wallis remembered Friedman as a grad student calling Schultz "the god damnedest, dumbest bastard I ever met." Schultz, a pioneer in mathematical economics and econometrics, had a statistical bent. Wallis also remembered going past Schultz's office and hearing Friedman remonstrate him, "But Mr. Schultz, don't you see?"[10] Friedman recalls of Schultz that, "at the time, I regarded the number of errors I found, and on occasion the difficulty he had in understanding the argument, as evidence of limited intellectual capacity."[11]

Henry Simons was the third leading figure in economics in the 1930s at Chicago, after Knight and Viner. A short-set, somewhat pudgy man, Simons was a Knight acolyte. After Simons's death, Aaron Director, a junior faculty member at Chicago in the first half of the 1930s and the older brother of Friedman's future wife, Rose, wrote: "Through his writings and more especially through his teaching at the University of Chicago, he was slowly establishing himself as the head of a 'school.'"[12] This statement, dating from 1947, is apparently the first printed reference to an intellectual or academic school of economics associated with the University of Chicago.

Simons did not publish much early in his career, which led to controversy in the Department of Economics over whether he should receive tenure. He ultimately became professor of economics in the University of Chicago Law School, a fruitful association between law and economics at Chicago that continues to this day. Friedman describes Simons as

> my teacher and my friend—and above all, a shaper of my ideas. No man can say precisely whence his beliefs and his values come—but there is no doubt that mine would be very different than they are if I had not had the good fortune to be exposed to Henry Simons. If . . . I express much disagreement with him, that, too, bespeaks his influence. He taught us that an objective, critical examination of a man's ideas is a truer tribute than slavish repetition of his formulas.[13]

Friedman received his master's degree in economics from Chicago at the end of the academic year in 1933. He did enough course work in math also to qualify for a master's in it. Although he had enjoyed his years as an undergraduate at Rutgers, here, at Chicago, he was in his element.

He decided to attend Columbia for his second year of graduate studies, in 1933–34, for several reasons. In the first place, he received an excellent fellowship stipend, $1,500, which paid his tuition and other expenses with money to spare. Second, he wanted to avail himself of the many opportunities New York offered. Third, he thought he would gain academically from a change of locale, notwithstanding that he enjoyed and had benefited so much from Chicago.

Friedman went to Columbia largely as a result of the friendship of Henry Schultz, who had been a student there, with Harold Hotelling, who taught at Columbia. Located in New York City, Columbia University is spread across a number of city blocks, now from 110th to 122nd Street, and beyond. Founded in 1754, it has had top law, medical, journalism, and engineering schools. Friedman was twenty-one when he enrolled in the fall of 1933.

Columbia and Chicago were perhaps the two leading American academic centers in economics in the mid-1930s. Columbia was home of the retired John Bates Clark—the most esteemed economist America had produced—Wesley Mitchell, Hotelling, and John Maurice Clark, son of John B. Clark. Like Mitchell, John Maurice Clark had studied and taught at Chicago.

Friedman says that Hotelling "undoubtedly influenced me most"[14] in the year at Columbia. Hotelling, primarily a mathematician, has been described by Kenneth Arrow, a student and future Nobel laureate, as a "creative thinker in both mathematical statistics and economics."[15] Friedman remembers Hotelling as "concise, rigorous, and lucid. . . . [H]e also had an extraordinary instinct for picking problems and making contributions of the greatest practical importance."[16]

Friedman describes the active leaders in economics at Columbia in this way: "Hotelling did for mathematical statistics what Jacob Viner had done for economic theory: revealed it to be an integrated logical whole, not a set of cook-book recipes. . . . Wesley C. Mitchell, John M. Clark and others exposed me to an institutional and empirical approach and a view of economic theory that differed sharply from the Chicago view. Here, too, an exceptional group of fellow students were the most effective teachers."[17]

"Institutional" is a difficult term to define in economics, as well as elsewhere in the social sciences. Institutionalism typically refers to a verbal, non-mathematical approach grounded in historical analysis.

Although economics at Chicago had an institutional flavor in its early years, this was not the case by the 1930s. Both Viner and Knight were theoreticians, not institutionalists. Both used geometry and, a bit more in Viner's case, mathematics in their approaches, but their theoretical methods did not utilize math as much as most economic theory has since their time. Both Viner and Knight talked about ideal worlds of theory as a way to understand the real world—Viner, in particular, emphasized that, to be relevant, economic theory must coincide with empirical events.

The approach at Columbia and at the nearby National Bureau of Economic Research, was not as much to describe economic activity in the realm of theory but more to measure actual economic activity. Much of Friedman's statistical approach was influenced by his year at Columbia and, even more so, by his work for the National Bureau, starting in 1937. The Columbia–National Bureau approach was empirical, quantitative, and statistical.

Among other courses Friedman took at Columbia was currency and credit with James Angell. Angell remembered Friedman a half-century later as "obviously extremely bright, contentious but polite; and I enjoyed his presence."[18]

Friedman lived in New York for the school year and saw his mother regularly but not frequently while at Columbia. He lived at home for the final time in the summer of 1934, at twenty-two, after his year at Columbia.

He enjoyed and benefited from his fellow students at Columbia. They included Moe Abramovitz, who became one of his best lifelong friends, and Austrian émigré Fritz Machlup. Like Friedman and a number of his other early friends, Abramovitz and Machlup later became presidents of the American Economic Association. Among the most valuable aspects of Friedman's year at Columbia were the contacts he developed that made a position with the National Bureau of Economic Research possible a few years later.

Friedman considered his year at Columbia to have been of substantial importance in his development, as it gave him a broader outlook than if he had studied exclusively at Chicago. He has said on a number of occasions that he benefited from studying at both universities. "I concluded," Friedman says, that "the ideal combination for a budding economist was a year of study at Chicago, which emphasized theory, followed by a year of study at Columbia, which emphasized institutional influences and empirical work."[19] Allen Wallis, who also attended both universities, agreed.

Friedman's master's thesis at the University of Chicago in 1933 was titled, "An Empirical Study of the Relationship Between Railroad Stock Prices and Railroad Earnings for the Period 1921–1931." The master's thesis, written when he was twenty, contains both stylistic and substantial comments that mark it as unmistakably his. It is an interesting document in part because it shows the influence of his Chicago professors on him, and their approach to economic theory, before he went to Columbia and acquired a more statistical method.

He begins his master's thesis on this note: "One of the most widespread of quasi-economic quests is the search for the inner springs of . . . stock prices. A very large proportion of these investigations assume a marked resemblance to the continual attempt to devise 'systems' with which to 'beat Monte Carlo,' to 'break the bank.' They result in the proposal of sure-fire prediction methods, which promise riches . . . By their very nature such formulations are but 'fools' gold.'"[20]

Friedman was at this time more deductive, rather than inductive, in his scientific approach than he later became, reflecting the methodology of his Columbia and National Bureau professors and colleagues. "A quantitative and statistical study can have validity and utility from a scientific point of view," he writes in his master's thesis, "only insofar as it either verifies, or disproves, deductive conclusions; or furnishes us with hypotheses on the basis of which we can conduct further theoretical analysis." He also says of the topic under consideration that "[s]uch an investigation must proceed by a thorough analysis of each of the various factors that may *a priori* be assumed to govern stock prices."[21] He later became much more inductive (reasoning from facts to theories, rather than deducing facts from theories) and quantitatively empirical in his approach to theory.

One of the conclusions that he reaches in his master's thesis is that there is "little or no relationship between the price of a stock and the earnings of any single month."[22] The idea that long-term expectations are more important than short-term ones in influencing economic behavior would later concern him in *A Theory of the Consumption Function.*

As we understand and know the past better, we are able to predict and thereby influence the future more effectively. One of the most interesting passages from "An Empirical Study of the Relationship Between Railroad Stock Prices and Railroad Earnings" is where, speaking of predictions based on historical data, he says:

> This statement implicitly assumes that the present, or better, the time period studied, is a representative sample of the time universe of which the future (more especially, the immediate future) is a part. This assumption is implicit in every statistical study that claims for its results any validity in the future or any generality of application. . . . To what extent it is true, while of the utmost importance, is a question that is exceedingly difficult to answer even in a particular case. Yet, until it is answered statistical results, used for the prediction of future events, can be accepted only conditionally. Unless, in fact, the past is part of the same universe as the future, statistical studies are futile . . .
>
> It goes without saying that no definite and final answer can ever be given. But I am convinced that an answer can be obtained significantly probable that reliance can be placed in it.[23]

There is no absolute prediction, as there is no absolute knowledge. The future is an open question, and the past is never completely known.

Friedman concludes his master's thesis on the Knightian sentiment: "The fundamental difference between what is ordinarily known as static economic theory and the economic theory concerned with movement through time is the introduction into the latter of uncertainty and the consequent substitution of anticipations for knowledge. Dynamic theory must proceed by an analysis of these anticipations. It must try to study and discover relatively constant modes of behavior with respect to anticipations, and by this method reduce the amount of pure uncertainty it has to handle."[24]

4

ROSE

he most important contact Milton made at the University of Chicago in 1932–33 was with his future wife, Rose Director. They met in Jacob Viner's Economics 301 class. Because Viner sat students alphabetically, they sat next to each other. It says much about Rose that, as a woman of twenty in 1932, she, too, was a graduate student in economics at Chicago. She had received her bachelor's degree in economics there the previous June.

Rose was born in late December 1911 in Charterisk, Russia (she does not know the exact date). Her family moved to the United States in the summer of 1914 just before the outbreak of World War I, settling in Portland, Oregon, where siblings of both of her parents had already moved. Rose's family was more religious than Milton's—she comments that she "grew up in a strictly Orthodox Jewish home."[1] Although Rose, like Milton, came at a young age to look on religious belief as superstition, she retains a more conservative orientation than he does.

Rose began school at a young age, apparently enrolling in kindergarten at four in the fall of 1916. Like Milton, she must have skipped at least one grade somewhere along the way, for she started high school, as he did, in September 1924, when she was twelve years old. She graduated from high school after the first half of her senior year, in January 1928, just after her sixteenth birthday.

Rose was the youngest child of five, with two sisters and two brothers. She was closest to her brother Aaron, who was nine years older than she, who she calls a "semi-sibling and semi-parent."[2] Aaron became a graduate student and junior faculty member at the University of Chicago, and it was because of Aaron that she enrolled there.

Rose notes that she had few close friends as an undergraduate at Chicago. She is a private person—she does not burden others with her personal problems. She also comments that, somewhat like Milton, she was very close to her mother while growing up. Unlike Milton, she is very musical. She is honest, straightforward, and bright.

It would be hard to imagine a more ideal partner for Milton than Rose. The same age, attractive, intelligent, an economist, Jewish, slightly shorter than he, and, particularly for a woman of her era, excellent in math, Rose was a great catch. One gathers that initially Milton was more attracted to her than she was to him. He says that on meeting Rose she was "shy, withdrawn, lovely, and extremely bright."[3]

Milton and Rose tell the story about going to the Chicago world fair at the end of the 1932–33 school year—their first real date. As they sat on a bench at the end of the day discussing plans for the future, Milton "attempted a goodnight kiss."[4] Rose, however, did not accept this opportunity. She then returned to Oregon for the summer, and he headed to Rahway and then to New York.

In 1933–34, Rose remained a graduate student at Chicago, while Milton attended Columbia. He returned to Chicago for the 1934–35 academic year as a research assistant to Henry Schultz and to cultivate his relationship with Rose. During that time they became much more of a couple than they had been.

In addition to developing his relationship with Rose, Milton met his closest lifetime friends, Allen Wallis and George Stigler, at Chicago in 1934–35. Neither man had been at Chicago before. Stigler and Wallis went on to become leading figures in academia and elsewhere over the course of their careers—Stigler received the Nobel

Prize in Economics in 1982, and Wallis, after a distinguished career in academia and government, became president and chancellor of the University of Rochester, New York.

Wallis remembered that he, Friedman, and Stigler frequently ate dinner together. These were "long, drawn-out sessions, with our jaws doing more talking than chewing. The dominant subject always was Frank Knight. What did he say and what did he mean?"[5] Rose provides this description of Knight and Viner, which sheds further light on them and her:

> Jacob Viner and Frank Knight were brilliant men who could hardly have differed more from one another. They alternated in teaching the first-year course in economic theory. Viner had an incisive and organized mind, was rigorous and not given to suffering fools gladly. Knight was far less organized, given more to philosophical and even sophistical reasoning. The same course was very different when taught by Knight than when taught by Viner. Many students, I among them, took the course from both men and learned from each.[6]

Milton had a low opinion of Henry Schultz during the year he worked as Schultz's research assistant. Schultz, though, generously wrote in a footnote in the work that became his magnum opus, *The Theory and Measurement of Demand* (1938): "I am profoundly grateful to Mr. Milton Friedman for invaluable assistance . . . and for permission to summarize a part of his unpublished paper on indifference curves."[7] Friedman later revised upward his opinion of Schultz's "tenacity, patience, and industry."[8]

As the 1934–35 academic year ended, Friedman needed a job. Allen Wallis had gone to Washington a few months earlier and obtained employment with the National Resources Committee. He was able to arrange a position for Friedman. So Milton "went to Washington, leaving the sheltered academic cloister at Chicago and the warmth of my close relationship with Rose."[9]

New Deal Washington, in which Friedman began to work in the second half of 1935, was a lively place. He writes that the "explosion of government, combined with the paucity of academic and business jobs, attracted the best and brightest . . . and enabled them to achieve positions of far greater responsibility than was possible under more static conditions. There was a sense of excitement and achievement in the air. We had the feeling . . . we were in at the birth of a new order that would lead to major changes in society."[10]

Friedman's early political views are not possible to trace with any certainty. He mentions them only infrequently, does not particularly recall them, and there are a few comments by others. His very lack of remembrance, though, indicates that politics was not as important to him as it would later become in his life. His family was not interested in politics or government.

His memories of his growing-up years before the Great Depression have significantly influenced him. He remembers firsthand a society in which government played a far smaller role than it does now. Always intellectually curious, he had read John Stuart Mill's *On Liberty* at Rutgers and was impressed by the essential libertarian idea that individuals should be able to do as they wish, so long as they are not harming anyone else. But it was a long way from this general philosophical position to advocating particular government policies.

As an undergraduate at Rutgers, Friedman moved into economics almost by accident, and it was only in his last year there that he really began to focus on economic issues. He was more a budding mathematician than an economist for most of his undergraduate years, and it is unlikely that he considered political issues much during that time. His interest in economics appears to have been stirred more by a desire to understand the economic events then occurring than by a desire to influence them.

The first presidential election that he could vote in was the 1936 race between Roosevelt and Alf Landon. He does not definitely remember for whom he voted, but thinks that it was Roosevelt. Allen Wallis recalled in an interview that, to the extent that Friedman had political views, he "went to Chicago as what he describes as a Norman Thomas–type socialist."[11] Norman Thomas was the Socialist Party candidate for president in each election from 1928 to 1948.

Friedman was not especially ideological or political in his twenties or even for much of his thirties. According to the economic historian William Frazer, "Recalling Friedman's Chicago year 1934–35 with Henry Schultz, Martin Bronfenbrenner [another Chicago student of the era] remembered Friedman mainly as a statistician rather than an economist, and Abba Lerner . . . recalled Friedman as being non-political in 1937."[12] According to Leonard Silk, who has also written on Friedman, early in his career Friedman seemed "more eager to be known as a first-class technician and objective social scientist than as a political crusader."[13]

Paul Samuelson remembers Friedman as a grad student as "not primarily a macroeconomist. Just a really smart guy ready to be into anything," noting that Friedman's Chicago teachers were "macroeconomists."[14]

Friedman expressed these views as late as a 1946 pamphlet with George Stigler opposing rent control: "For those, like us, who would like even more equality than there is at present . . . , it is surely better to attack directly existing inequalities in income and wealth at their source than to ration each of the hundreds of commodities and services that compose our standard of living."[15] In a 1948 article, Friedman wrote that among his long-run objectives was "substantial equality of economic power. . . . I should hope the community would desire to reduce inequality even further."[16] Friedman came to value equality much less later in his career.

Essentially, he supported the welfare but not the regulatory aspects of Roosevelt's New Deal. He favored jobs programs for the unemployed, but he did not support direct government intervention in running and directing the economy. Viner and others at Chicago had taught him the virtues of the price system too well for that to occur. In the same way that he later lost his enthusiasm for greater equality, over time Friedman lost the favor that he had once felt for more government welfare-type programs.

Economic data collection was much less sophisticated in the early 1930s than it has become. Indeed, it was really only starting with World War I that much of the data that we now take for granted with respect to national economic activity began to be compiled. Friedman's position on the National Resources Committee was to design and implement what was up to that time the largest national study of consumer income and purchases.

Friedman's work for the committee from 1935 to 1937 proved beneficial and providential. The main purpose of his work was to calculate a cost of living index. The study was his first foray into what became one of his primary career emphases, the consumption function—the relationship between consumption and income. During his years with the National Resources Committee, he learned much about practical aspects of data collection and interpretation. He also made contacts that made his employment for the National Bureau of Economic Research starting in 1937 possible.

Notwithstanding his work duties, his relationship with Rose remained uppermost on his mind. She had hoped, in 1935, to work in Washington but could not find employment there. She returned to Portland for the fall and winter before going back to Chicago in 1936 as a research assistant for Frank Knight. Knight wrote in a footnote to an article on the British economist David Ricardo that for a "general check on the argument and aid in connection with references, I have relied upon an able graduate assistant, Miss Rose Director, who has lately been working over the material intensively in connection with a more specialized study in the history of the theory of capital."[17]

The study in the history of capital theory was to be Rose's Ph.D. dissertation, which she did not complete. Instead, she went to Washington later in 1936 to be with Milton. Milton helped Rose to obtain employment there, which was not too easy because Rose had never officially become a citizen of the United States, which she did at this time. Rose worked for several government agencies, including the new Federal Deposit Insurance Corporation for Milton's old Rutgers instructor Homer Jones.

When Rose joined Milton in Washington in 1936, they were considering marriage. He makes reference in their memoirs to a canoe ride apparently in 1936 with a friend from Chicago, Leo Rosten, who also was then in Washington. Although Milton and Rose have been unwilling to give Rosten "as much credit as he claims," it was, according to Rosten, Milton writes, in the course of this canoeing excursion that he persuaded Milton to "pop the question to Rose."[18] Interestingly, while she mentions boyfriends other than Milton in their memoirs, he does not mention going out with anyone other than her. "He couldn't afford it,"[19] she offers as the explanation.

Friedman's first publication in economics, a review of a work titled *Cyclical Fluctuations in Commodity Stocks,* by Ralph Blodgett, appeared in October 1935. He here demonstrated his ability to engage in forthright criticism, a trait that he has retained all his life: "Mr. Blodgett's empirical conclusions as to the behavior of the stock series seem well established. But his theoretical explanation of the empirical results is largely vitiated by a basic misconception as to the nature of the relationship among stocks, production, and consumption."[20]

A more significant publication, which stemmed from his work for Schultz in Chicago, was a criticism of "Professor Pigou's Method for Measuring Elasticities of Demand from Budgetary Data," which appeared in the November 1935 edition of the *Quarterly Journal of Economics.* A largely mathematical presentation, "Professor Pigou's Method" was met by a reply from Pigou, who was one of the leading economists of the day, in the May 1936 edition of the *Quarterly Journal,* together with a rejoinder by Friedman. Over the next five years, Friedman had about a dozen articles and reviews, sometimes coauthored, published in major economic and mathematical journals, and he edited several government and academic works.

After two years in Washington, Friedman moved to New York, where he worked for the National Bureau of Economic Research. He first made significant contact with the bureau in early 1937, while still working for the National Resources Committee, attending the bureau's first meeting of the Conference on Research in Income and Wealth. The National Bureau played a major role in developing many data in the 1930s and 1940s concerning gross domestic product that have since been utilized extensively.

The expression that an institution is but the lengthened shadow of a man has been used to describe the relationship between Wesley Clair Mitchell and the National Bureau of Economic Research. Mitchell—not merely one of the leading economists, but one of the leading social scientists in the first half of the twentieth century—made contributions in several fields and to several institutions. His most significant association was with the National Bureau, where he served as director of research for many years.

In this capacity, Mitchell played a leading role in guiding the research programs of dozens of the best economists for decades. Most importantly, he influenced their methodology toward his empirical quantitative and statistical approach to the study and presentation of economic activity. Mitchell's primary field of individual research was business cycles, in which he wrote several of the leading works. His thought here influenced Friedman, who absorbed Mitchell's emphasis on lags in economic activity between causes and consequences into his own work—in Friedman's case, lags between changes in economic (especially monetary) policy and changes in economic activity. Policies take time to work their effects; effects are not instantaneous.

Friedman got to know Mitchell and his intellectual outlook better while working for the National Bureau between 1937 and 1940 than he did during his Columbia graduate student year. At the same time, his Columbia ties deepened as a result of his greater association with Mitchell and others at the National Bureau who were affiliated with the university. Friedman lectured part-time at Columbia and associated socially with many from the Columbia crowd.

At the National Bureau, Friedman served as research assistant to Columbia graduate Simon Kuznets, a Mitchell disciple, who had organized the Conference on Research in National Income and Wealth. Kuznets was one of Friedman's last mentors, along with Burns and Jones at Rutgers, Viner and Knight at Chicago, Hotelling at Columbia, and Mitchell at the National Bureau. Kuznets impressed on Friedman the value of Mitchell's quantitative and statistical approach. Some indication of Kuznets's early prominence is that John Maynard Keynes referred to him in his landmark *The General Theory of Employment, Interest, and Money,* published in 1936. Kuznets went on to receive the Nobel Prize in Economics in 1971, the third year that it was awarded.

While at the National Bureau, Friedman edited three volumes of proceedings from meetings of the Conference on Research in National Income and Wealth. (On the fiftieth anniversary of the conference, it was noted that he published the volumes in the same year that the conferences were held, a rare feat.) For Friedman, this experience "forc[ed] me to clarify my ideas about how one should go about empirical work. Because so much of the national income stuff was pure empiricism of the rawest kind."[21] There is, in his opinion, much virtue in working directly with data at the most fundamental and basic level in order to understand phenomena. It is through this process, so often repetitive and unfruitful—and which he did not appreciate earlier in part because his intellectual quickness obscured the value of such labor to him—that occasionally a new idea or modification of a previous outlook may occur.

After Friedman left Washington for New York in the fall of 1937 to work for the National Bureau, he and Rose made definite wedding plans. They married in 1938, according to Milton, when their "depression fears of where our livelihood would come from had been dissipated."[22] Rose's brother Aaron wrote her after they announced their engagement: "I would have welcomed any person you chose. In this case I have real pleasure in so doing. Milton is a fine person, whom I always liked. There is universal agreement on his very superior ability. . . . (Tell him I shall not hold his very strong New Deal leanings . . . against him.)"[23]

Milton and Rose were in constant contact during the ten months or so that he was in New York working for the National Bureau as she continued to live and work in Washington. They wrote each other about twice a week, and Milton traveled to Washington frequently to see her. With respect to contemporary social mores, Rose comments that once, several years into their relationship, they both attended the same conference, and it would have been "cheaper if we had stayed in one room but that never occurred to us!"[24] Milton comments: "It was a different world altogether."[25]

Milton and Rose married on June 25, 1938, in a small ceremony in New York. He would have preferred a strictly civil service, but she persuaded him to have a religious ceremony in respect of their parents' wishes. She was twenty-six and he would turn twenty-six in a month.

In a telegram that Milton sent Rose shortly before their wedding, he used a new kind of calendar: "DN—days before Nirvana."[26]

5

WORLD WAR II

he most fundamental change in Milton's life to date came when he and Rose married in June 1938. By this time they had known each other for close to six years, and the transition to married life had few difficulties.

Following the signing of the German-Soviet nonaggression pact on August 23, 1939, and the German invasion of Poland on September 1, England and France declared war on Germany on September 3, marking the beginning of World War II. Germany's invasion of Poland capped a long series of bellicose acts by Adolf Hitler, including renunciation of the Versailles Treaty, rearmament, annexation of Austria, and the occupation of Czechoslovakia.

The United States did not enter World War II for more than two years. During this time, Hitler achieved his greatest military successes: the conquest and occupation of Norway, Denmark, the Netherlands, Belgium, and France between April and June 1940.

Milton and Rose headed west to the University of Wisconsin at Madison for the 1940–41 academic year. He had obtained a visiting professorship in economics, his first significant academic position. Wisconsin was a leading university.

They traveled to Wisconsin in a Mercury convertible the summer before the school year was to start, enjoying the sights along the way. Unfortunately, the year at Wisconsin did not go well. Friedman enjoyed teaching students, but he became involved in a dispute between different factions in the economics department over whether he should receive tenure. Ultimately, the economics department, though not the school administration, opposed him for a tenured position. The chairman of the department, Edwin Witte, Friedman recalled years later, still smarting from the nonappointment, showed the "courage of a fish"[1] in the matter.

Nevertheless, Friedman was an effective and popular teacher. When he did not receive tenure, a group of students—led by Walter Heller, who later would become a chairman of the Council of Economic Advisers under presidents Kennedy and Johnson, and who was a professional but not a personal opponent of Friedman's—protested his departure. Friedman could have remained at Madison in a nontenured post, but he chose not to accept this opportunity.

Milton and Rose experienced one of the disappointments of their lives when, following the year in Wisconsin and a difficult labor, Rose delivered a stillborn baby. Rose recalls that "sharing the pain of both these experiences [the stillbirth and Milton's unhappy year in the economics department] seemed to bring Milton and me even closer than we already were. . . . [W]e were no longer children; suddenly we had grown up."[2] When Friedman began to teach at Madison in September 1940 he was just twenty-eight, younger than some of his graduate students.

Milton and Rose headed back to Washington, D.C., for his second tour of duty in the nation's capital, starting in the fall of 1941. His new position, with the Treasury Department, was in part a result of a work that he had begun earlier, *Taxing to Prevent Inflation,* coauthored with Carl Shoup and Ruth P. Mack, which was published in 1943. The chapter that Friedman wrote reveals that he was not a monetarist at this time. Inflation has, Friedman held, its "genesis in an increased volume of spending by consumers, business, and government"[3]; he made little reference to the effect of an increase in the money supply on inflation.

In his work for the Treasury Department from the fall of 1941 through March 1943, he was one of the top ten or so aides to Secretary of the Treasury, Henry Morgenthau, meeting with Morgenthau frequently and accompanying him to congressional hearings. Friedman also participated regularly in luncheon meetings with Marriner Eccles, chairman of the Federal Reserve Board. Friedman had, for more than three-quarters of a century, been interacting frequently with economic leaders in government and academia.

He calls his work for the Treasury Department from 1941 to 1943 "hectic, fascinating, and extremely instructive."[4] Friedman gained insight into the actual working of government. His popular exposition improved through writing speeches for his superiors (he notes that he sometimes wrote clichés that would have made him smirk if he had used them himself). Among other duties, he occasionally testified before congressional committees. In testimony before the House Ways and Means Committee on May 7, 1942, he talked extensively about inflation without mentioning "money" or "monetary policy."[5] The method that he recommended to prevent inflation was increased income taxation.

His wartime testimony is of interest in part because of how different his views are from his later beliefs. In the part of his testimony on "methods of avoiding inflation," he said:

> Inflation can be avoided only by reducing consumer spending to an approximate equality with the value at present prices of the goods and services that will be available for purchase. Increased taxes help to bring this about by reducing the amount consumers have available to spend. . . . Taxation is not, however, the only method being employed to combat inflation. Price control and rationing, control of consumers' credit, reduction in governmental spending, and war bond campaigns are the most important other methods that are now being employed.

The next line was the clincher: "But just as it does not seem feasible to prevent inflation by taxation alone, so these other methods cannot be relied upon in the absence of additional taxes."[6] Later he would support almost any tax cut, any time, for any reason, and see little connection between taxation and inflation.

The most significant project in which Friedman was involved while working for the Treasury Department was the successful transition of American income taxation from payment after the fact to withholding at the source, which remains the current system. Withholding at the source was implemented in order to help finance the war effort. Although some libertarians have since faulted him for his participation in this transition, Friedman's efforts were on behalf of a wartime measure to provide funds for the nation's military. Moreover, as he himself notes, withholding would have been implemented irrespective of his involvement.

Journalist Robert Sobel remarks that Friedman "seemed to blossom in Washington. . . . The wartime capital was an exciting place."[7] Milton and Rose's second stay in Washington, this time as a married couple, was capped by the birth of their daughter, Janet, on February 26, 1943, by cesarean section. Three days later, Milton took a new position, with the Statistical Research Group, a wartime government research entity headquartered in New York at Columbia University. Looking back, the only thing that he regrets about leaving the Treasury is that if he had stayed, he might have participated in the Bretton Woods conference in 1945, which shaped postwar international financial institutions.

The Statistical Research Group (SRG) was high in the nation's scientific brain trust. It was made up of eighteen principals and about forty supporting staff, although typically no more than about ten principals worked at a time. The SRG was headed by Friedman's close friend Allen Wallis, who later recalled that the SRG was "composed of what surely must be the most extraordinary group of statisticians ever organized."[8] Friedman says that the group was "probably the best statistical research group, the greatest collection of statisticians . . . ever assembled in one place."[9] A dozen members of the SRG would go on to become presidents of the Institute of Mathematical Statistics, the American Statistical Association, or the American Economic Association, among many other accomplishments and distinctions.

Friedman's work for the SRG was unlike anything else in his career. Essentially, he was an applied or practical mathematician, developing techniques for improving the effectiveness of war materiel. He was indirectly involved with the Manhattan Project. One of the projects on which he worked was to design a statistical procedure to ensure that the detonator for the atom bomb worked, though he did not know this purpose at the time. He thus helped to design the trigger for the atomic bomb. He visited Alamogordo, New Mexico—the base for Los Alamos (where the atom bomb was to be tested)—on assignment during the war, which gives an idea of his and the SRG's stature.

Other projects in which Friedman was involved at the SRG included advising on the optimal number of pellets in antiaircraft shells and work in sequential analysis. With respect to the pellets, he found it is more valuable to have more and smaller pellets in shells than fewer and larger ones. He also helped to design antiaircraft projectile fuses that proved useful in defending against Japanese bombers and in the Battle of the Bulge. During that battle, Friedman went to Washington, D.C. to meet with several high-ranking army officers who had flown in from Europe to discuss optimal settings on proximity fuses for air bursts of artillery shells.

The SRG's work in sequential analysis was the most lasting of its endeavors. James Berger writes in *The New Pulgrave: A Dictionary of Economics*: "The founder of sequential analysis is generally acknowledged to be Abraham Wald [another member of the SRG], with Milton Friedman and W. Allen Wallis providing substantial motivational and collaborative support."[10] Experiments can often be stopped when a certain amount of evidence is collected, but no one knows in advance when an experiment can be stopped because of the indeterminacy of the information to be gathered. Sequential analysis provides a tool whereby it can be known when to stop an experiment because sufficient information has been collected to determine the answer to the question being studied.

Friedman's work on sequential analysis was significant. He and Wallis discussed its possibilities at lunch one day. Wallis remembered that Friedman said it was "not unlikely . . . that the idea would prove a bigger one than either of us would hit on again in a lifetime."[11] Friedman coedited one work on sequential analysis as result of his involvement with the SRG, and wrote several influential papers in statistics and on utility with Jimmie Savage, an SRG member who joined the faculty at the University of Chicago after the war.

Friedman was one of the most productive and effective members of the SRG. He was continuously with the SRG as one of its several longest-term members. Of 572 reports, memoranda, and letters that it produced, he wrote 98, more than one-sixth. In responses in 1980 from thirteen of the fourteen living principals, he was one of the two individuals most frequently mentioned with respect to influence on the members of the SRG.

Milton and Rose's second child, David Director, was born on February 12, 1945. Milton and Rose saw his mother when they were in New York. Sarah delighted, of course, in seeing her grandchildren. Milton was thirty when Janet was born and thirty-two when David arrived.

World War II came to an abrupt end on August 15, 1945, after the atom bombings of Hiroshima and Nagasaki. It had generally been anticipated that the war against Japan could last years longer. Germany had surrendered in May 1945. Friedman calls his work for the SRG "among the most varied, interesting, and indeed exciting professional experiences I have ever had."[12]

6

RETURN TO ACADEME

As the war in Europe was winding down in the spring of 1945, Friedman sought an academic position for the fall. He wanted to leave the SRG and become a teacher. He had the opportunity to return to the National Bureau of Economic Research after the war, but this was not the career that he sought.

He focused early on a position at the University of Minnesota, where his friend George Stigler now taught. In a May 1945 letter, Friedman encouraged Stigler to emphasize the former's work in sequential analysis, which had just been declassified, in seeking a position for him. "I would have rather special competence to teach sequential," Friedman wrote, "and, if I came to Minnesota, Minnesota could be one of the first to reveal the secret weapon to an eager public."[1]

He was hired there for the 1945–46 academic year, largely through Stigler's efforts. Friedman and Stigler's friendship flourished as they shared an office. Stigler was a tall, thin man, with a sharp wit. In a reminiscence, Friedman says that Stigler could have been a successful comedian. Stigler stood a foot taller than Friedman, and when they were later together at the University of Chicago, they were referred to as "Mr. Micro" (Stigler) and "Mr. Macro" (Friedman), ostensibly reflecting their relative emphases in microeconomics and macroeconomics, but also surely a play on their respective heights.

They enjoyed playing tennis and bridge together, among many other activities—mostly teaching and talking economics.

Stigler first gained renown as a historian of economic thought. His dissertation, in the history of economic thought, was published in 1941 as *Production and Distribution Theories*. As Stigler's career progressed, he moved to other topics, including microeconomic theory and industrial organization. He was an excellent writing stylist, and received the Nobel Prize in Economics in 1982.

Stigler provided this picture of Friedman in his autobiography. When Friedman was a student at Chicago, he was "already a formidable intellectual figure; he not only could think very rigorously and originally, but was so fast in his mental processes."[2] Stigler also said, "It did not take long to recognize Milton's talents: he was logical, perceptive, quick to understand one's arguments—and quick to find their weaknesses."[3] Friedman recalls Stigler as fond of saying later, when Friedman became actively involved in politics: "Milton wants to change the world; I only want to understand it."[4]

Friedman enjoyed his year at Minnesota, which was unlike his earlier unhappy experience at Wisconsin. At the University of Minnesota, he found a congenial group of colleagues. He taught two courses a semester, one in statistics, the other in economics, primarily to undergraduate students.

Friedman received his Ph.D. in economics from Columbia in 1946, thirteen years after enrolling there. The delay was the result of unusual circumstances. Columbia at this time required that a candidate's dissertation be published before the degree would be awarded. A major controversy arose with respect to Friedman's dissertation, *Income from Independent Professional Practices,* which he co-wrote with Simon Kuznets of the National Bureau.

Kuznets wrote a preliminary manuscript, which Friedman completely rewrote between 1938 and 1941. The study covers five professional fields, including doctors and dentists. The average income of physicians at this time exceeded that of dentists by about one-third. Friedman and Kuznets argued that the reason for this difference was in part that the American Medial Association (AMA) hindered entrance to the medical profession, restricting the supply of doctors and thereby driving their price up.

Pursuant to the rules of the National Bureau, Friedman's and Kuznets's work was submitted to a committee of the board of directors, which included a pharmaceutical executive who strongly objected to what he perceived as criticism of the AMA. For three years, from 1941 to 1944, a debate raged within the National Bureau over whether the work should be published. Eventually it was, and Friedman has nothing but praise for the role that Wesley Mitchell, director of the bureau, played in the ultimate publication through his finesse and diplomacy.

Income from Independent Professional Practice bears the hallmarks of the National Bureau of Economic Research. It contains much statistical data, with many charts of information. It is a predecessor in style, though on a lesser scale, of Friedman's later great work affiliated with the National Bureau, *A Monetary History of the United States, 1867–1960.*

During the year at Minnesota, Friedman and Stigler coauthored a pamphlet on rent control for the New York–based libertarian Foundation for Economic Education, titled "Roofs or Ceilings?" The pamphlet was a polemic against rent control, which had emerged as a wartime measure. Friedman and Stigler argued that rent control leads to fewer rental units, lower-quality rental units, greater nonprice discrimination, and inefficient use of rental units. If controls were eliminated, the shortage of housing that developed during the war as resources were directed to other purposes would quickly end.

The pamphlet was attacked by academics and commentators who found its arguments inconsistent with the pro-government and pro-intervention tenor of the times. "Roofs or Ceilings?" "outraged the profession," according to Paul Samuelson. "That shows you where we were in our mentality in the immediate postwar period."[5] Robert Bangs wrote in the *American Economic Review*: "Removal of rent controls would not solve the housing problem, but it could easily contribute to a worsening inequality."[6] Half a million copies of the pamphlet were circulated by the National Association of Real Estate Boards, and it has been republished many times since.

Through 1945, Friedman was closer, geographically and in spirit, to the New York area than to Chicago. Rose remarks that they had "many friends in New York and led an active social life" there. Most of their friends were, like the Friedmans, in "the early years of marriage. Most, though not all, were classmates of Milton's from his year at Columbia."[7]

Although he is typically identified with Chicago, through his thirty-third birthday in 1945, Friedman had spent about twenty-six years, over three-quarters of his life, in the immediate New York area. Since graduating from Rahway High School, he had spent four years at Rutgers, one year at Columbia in graduate studies, about three years working for the National Bureau of Economic Research in New York, and about two years working for the Statistical Research Group there. Most of the rest of his time, a little less than four years, had been spent in Washington. He had spent less than two years in Chicago.

William Frazer makes the interesting observation that through "his graduate education, the SRG years, and in the early teaching assignments, Friedman functioned primarily as a mathematical statistician . . . but with some teaching in business cycle."[8] Robert Leeson offers further thoughts along these lines, saying that Friedman

> knows more about . . . statistics than most economists: he studied at Columbia . . . under the mathematical statistician Harold Hotelling (1933–34); he was a statistical assistant to Henry Schultz (1934–35); he worked with economic measurement and data analysis at the NBER (1937–40). . . . Friedman's early career either combined, or alternated between, mathematical statistics and economics. For most of the war years . . . he was exclusively concerned with mathematical statistics.[9]

In the same way that, through World War II, Friedman was more associated with Columbia and the National Bureau than with the

University of Chicago, he was more of a statistician than he would be later. Friedman himself comments that his statistical abilities reached their peak at the end of World War II.

Milton and Rose were happy in Minnesota and thought they would spend many years there. Toward the end of the 1945–46 academic year, however, the opportunity arose to teach at the University of Chicago. Stigler was initially offered the position there, but he failed his interview with the president of the university, Ernest Colwell. Since this incident has attracted some interest, it is worthwhile to delve into it a bit, though some of the analysis is speculative.

The conventional story is that the Department of Economics wanted Stigler, but the university administration, in the person of Colwell, turned him down because he was "too empirical."[10] According to Stephen Stigler, George's son, though, it was unlikely that Colwell would have denied a department request unless there was opposition in the department. This was particularly true because the main administrator at Chicago was the chancellor, Robert Hutchins, not Colwell.

The most dynamic element in the Department of Economics at Chicago at this time was the Cowles Commission of econometricians, which emphasized a severely mathematical approach to economics. It is possible, according to Stephen Stigler, that Jacob Marschak of the Cowles Commission, who held a joint appointment in the Department of Economics, felt that Stigler was not mathematical enough in his approach to be appointed to the position. This would be consistent with Friedrich Hayek's comment that he did not receive a position in the economics department at Chicago at about the same time because the "econometricians didn't want me"[11]—Hayek, too, was nonmathematical in his approach to economics.

There is a difference between a mathematical approach to economic theory and the use of statistics in the discussion of economic activity. Stigler did not emphasize either in his work at this time.

Whatever the reasons, Friedman was offered the position in Stigler's stead. In later years, Stigler joked that his failure to be appointed in 1946 constituted his "greatest service to Chicago,"[12] although he was very disappointed at the time. Friedman speculates that Stigler did not return to Chicago for a dozen years after 1946, though he had several opportunities to do so, because he was hurt by the rejection. Friedman thinks it reveals much about Stigler's "generosity of spirit—though it also says much about the value Stigler placed on his friendship with Friedman—that Friedman's receiving the position originally intended for Stigler never had the "slightest effect on the closeness of our friendship."[13]

Milton and Rose enjoyed Minnesota, but they looked forward even more to returning to Chicago. This would become, they write, "what we continue to regard as *our* university."[14]

Part Two

1946–1976

7

DEPARTMENT OF ECONOMICS

riedman began to teach in the Department of Economics at the University of Chicago in September 1946, beginning a decades-long association that was his most productive time as a scholar. He believes that "almost all important contributions of a scientist are made in the first ten years after he enters the discipline. Not the first ten years of his professional life; he may shift from one discipline to another. . . . I was reading over some preliminary professional papers in the 1950s, and I could see there the whole future of the next thirty years of work I did; it was all outlined. . . . The 1940s–1960s was when I did my most important economic work."[1]

Milton and Rose bought a large, three-story house near campus for $12,500. Both were now thirty-four. Their children, Janet and David, were three and one. Rose's brother, Aaron, and his wife, Katherine, lived for a time in a separate unit on the third floor.

The University of Chicago is one of the leading centers in the world in economics and many other disciplines. Friedman praises Chicago for its "intense and stimulating intellectual atmosphere. Concentration on ideas; intellectual discourse among equals judged by scholarly ability, not status; tolerance of unconventional ideas; interaction among scholars in different fields—these are the hallmarks"[2] of the university.

Chicago's faculty was then, as now, among the finest in the world. High academic standards have been followed in faculty selection and retention. Popular graduates of departments have not been offered positions unless they are also top academics. Tenure is not automatic and is not always proffered. Excellent ability and scholarship are required.

The economics department underwent great changes in the years before Friedman's appointment. The Chicago Department of Economics has never been especially large; it has typically had about twenty-five members. Its personnel had changed greatly from what it was when Friedman was a student. As discussed earlier, then it was led and dominated by Viner, Knight, Paul Douglas, Henry Schultz, Harry Millis, John Nef, and Lloyd Mints. Henry Simons and Aaron Director were junior faculty. When Friedman returned after an eleven-year absence, in 1946, only Knight, Mints, and Douglas remained and Douglas had turned his attention to politics and would soon depart. Viner had gone to Princeton; Schultz and Simons were dead; Millis had retired; Nef had moved to the Committee on Social Thought; and Knight was not as involved in departmental affairs as he had been in the early 1930s. Another economist from the 1930s, Simeon Leland, left the department in 1946; another, Chester Wright, was approaching retirement; and Theodore Yntema left the business school for the Ford Motor Company in 1949. With the changes that always occur in lower-level positions, by 1946 there had been almost a complete turnover in personnel.

The most noteworthy development in economics at Chicago after Friedman left in 1935 and before he returned in 1946 was the location of the Cowles Commission of econometricians there in 1939, in close contact and association with the Department of Economics. The Cowles Commission filled the void in statistics in Chicago's economics department left by Schultz's untimely death with his family in a car accident in 1938. In addition, the market socialist, mathematically inclined economist Oskar Lange was on the faculty from 1938 to 1945, when he returned to his native Poland to become an official in the new Communist government. With the joint appointment of Jacob Marschak to both the Cowles Commission and the economics department, and the appointment of, among others, Tjalling Koopmans to the commission, by the time Friedman returned, the economics department was headed in a politically liberal to radical and professionally econometric direction.

The Cowles Commission's mathematical approach both reflected and led a trend across the economics profession around the world: a greater focus on the idea that mathematical expression is the best way to depict and to understand economic activity. The commission's method was different from Friedman's in several ways. First, while both use math, Friedman's mathematical approach in much of his major work is statistical presentation of data rather than the formulaic presentation of economic theory favored by the commission. Second, Friedman insists that economic theory should be subjected to empirical corroboration through predictions of events in the sensory world; the commission lacked this sort of focus with respect to a criterion for determining the relevance of economic theory. In addition, Friedman came to possess a virtually extremist libertarian position. He is not an anarchist, but government would play a vastly diminished role in his optimal society. By way of contrast, the Cowles Commission was, as a group, somewhere between Keynes and Lange politically, with a number closer to Lange.

Notwithstanding the profusion of famous economists (present and future) at the University of Chicago in the great 1930s era, economics reached an even higher point there in the late 1940s and early 1950s as the economists of the Cowles Commission and those of Friedman's emerging group jostled for institutional predominance and control. In Friedman's first years on the faculty, no fewer than thirteen future Nobel laureates in economics and no fewer than a dozen current and future presidents of the American Economic Association passed through the halls of the Social Science Research Building, where the Department of Economics and the Cowles Commission were located on the fourth floor and where the economics department remains to this day.

Not all would agree that the better side ultimately won the struggle for institutional preeminence at Chicago. Indeed, many, perhaps most, economists think just the opposite. Many economists believe that in the development of economic theory, the approach of the Cowles Commission has ultimately proved more significant than the approach of Friedman and his allies, notwithstanding Friedman's acknowledged public prominence and influence on public policy and its discussion. According to Lester Telser, now the senior continuous member of the faculty in the Department of Economics, who came to Chicago as a research assistant on the Cowles Commission in 1952: "While Cowles was here, the economics of Chicago was unparalleled in the world. I would say it was the leading center in economics. No one else even came close."[3] The only comparable gathering of scholars, according to Telser, was the Niels Bohr Institute of Physics in Copenhagen. According to Nobel laureate Kenneth Arrow, who was also at Chicago with the Cowles Commission, a "truly exceptional group of people was assembled in Chicago during the late 1940s. I doubt that such a group could ever be put together again in economics."[4] Here Arrow is not referring to the economists of Friedman's perspective.

Friedman wrote that he, as well as the rest of the economics department, significantly benefited from the location of Cowles at Chicago. There were some joint appointments, and this as well as the presence on campus of the commission resulted in a "great deal of interaction between Cowles and the department." Friedman recalls the frequent Cowles seminars as "exciting events in which I and other members of our department participated regularly and actively. . . . Similarly Cowles staff participated in and contributed to departmental seminars." Also, Cowles sponsored lectures by visiting scholars that "enlivened the intellectual atmosphere." Friedman remarks that the economics department in part benefited from the Cowles Commission because the commission had "very different views"[5]—both of economics as a discipline and ideologically—than some in the department, including himself, had.

In a 2004 interview, Friedman said that there was "no personal animosity"[6] between himself and members of the Cowles Commis-

sion. Six decades before, in a February 1947 letter of recommendation for Cowles member Tjalling Koopmans, he wrote that Koopmans "has a real ability to get to the essentials of a problem and to
expound these essentials simply and lucidly. He is one of the leading
spirits in the development of the field of econometrics and is likely
to do important work in that field. Koopmans is a very good teacher
and has an extremely pleasant personality."[7]

Friedman was nonetheless instrumental in the ultimate departure of the Cowles Commission from Chicago to Yale in 1955. There
was some falling-out, or at least decline, in his relationship and that
of his allies at Chicago generally with Koopmans and the Cowles
Commission after Koopmans harshly criticized Arthur Burns and
Wesley Mitchell's 1946 National Bureau of Economic Research work,
Measuring Business Cycles. Koopmans's criticism, "Measurement
Without Theory," appeared in a prominent August 1947 review in
the *Review of Economic Statistics*, six months after Friedman's letter
of recommendation on Koopmans's behalf. In the review, Koopmans
argued that because Burns and Mitchell had no theory of a business
cycle, they had no determinate idea of what data to gather or hypotheses to test. In a contemporary conference comment, Friedman
made reference to the "desultory skirmishing between what have
been loosely designated as the National Bureau and the Cowles
Commission techniques of investigating business cycles."[8] Robert
Solow, who received the Nobel Prize in Economics in 1987, relates an
anecdote about the response to Cowles Commission member
Lawrence Klein's *Economic Fluctuations in the United States* (1950) at
a Cowles seminar, which gives an idea of relations between Friedman
and the commission: "There was formal discussion. Friedman concluded that the whole econometric model-building enterprise had
been shown to be worthless and congratulated the Cowles Commission on its self-immolation."[9]

According to a number of historians of economic thought, the
relationship between the Cowles Commission and the Department
of Economics at Chicago was less than harmonious. Melvin Reder

writes that starting in the later 1940s there was a "struggle for intellectual preeminence and institutional control between Friedman, Wallis and their adherents on one side, and the Cowles Commission and its supporters on the other. The struggle persisted into the early 1950s, ending only with . . . the departure of the Cowles Commission"[10] in 1955. William Frazer writes that by the mid-1940s, a "fairly intense struggle in the economics department at Chicago was under way between Frank Knight and his former students on one side and the Cowles Commission and its adherents on the other." Robert Leeson also shares this view.

Still, relations between the Department of Economics and the Cowles Commission could not have been all bad. Though not exactly classics, the following songs written by graduate students and performed at an economics department party in 1949 or so give an idea of the contrasting views of the commission and Friedman, and a flavor of their interaction.

The first song, to the tune of "The American Patriot," gives the Cowles view:

> We must be rigorous, we must be rigorous,
> We must fulfill our role.
> If we hesitate or equivocate
> We won't achieve our goal.
>> We must make our systems complicate
>> To make our models whole.
>> Econometrics brings about
>> Statistical control!
> Our esoteric seminars
> Bring statisticians by the score.
> But try to find economists
> Who don't think algebra's a chore.
>> Oh we must urge you most emphatically
>> To become more inclined mathematically
>> So that all that we've developed
>> May some day be applied.[12]

This song about Friedman is to the tune of Gilbert and Sullivan's "When I Was a Lad":

When I was a lad I served a term
Under the tutelage of A. F. Burns.
I read my Marshall completely through
From beginning to end and backwards too.
    I read my Marshall so carefully
    That now I am Professor at the U. of C.
    (Chorus) He read his Marshall so carefully
    That now he is Professor at the U. of C.
Of Keynesians I make mincemeat
Their battered arguments now line the street
I get them in their weakest assumption:
"What do you mean by consumption function?"
    They never gave an answer that satisfied me
    So now I am Professor at the U. of C.
    (Chorus) They never gave an answer that satisfied he
    So now he is Professor at the U. of C.[13]

It was not so much that there was, or was much, overt conflict between Friedman and his allies at Chicago and the Cowles Commission. It was that the two groups had incompatible views of the future—of economics, and of economics at the University of Chicago. Chicago could not sustain two entities as forceful and dynamic as Friedman and his allies and the Cowles Commission. That Friedman emerged as the leading figure at Chicago in the face of such competition says much about his intellect and personality.

Friedman replaced Viner in the Department of Economics. Like Viner, he became the department's most stringent grader. The department used Viner's, and then Friedman's, price theory course as a way to screen out graduate students who did not measure up to departmental standards. The department followed a relatively liberal policy with respect to admission, with the thought that many students would drop out in the first year or so.

Friedman has emphasized that neither historically nor in his time to the present has the political orientation of Chicago's Department of Economics been mostly free market. In a 1991 article on Laughlin, the first head of economics at Chicago, Friedman writes that the department had always had "prominent members who held these [free market] views and presented them effectively. But they were always a minority. The Department has been characterized by heterogeneity of policy views, not homogeneity."[14] What distinguished Chicago from elsewhere politically when Friedman was on the faculty and to the present was not the presence of market-oriented scholars at Chicago but rather their absence elsewhere.

Friedman remarked in 2004 with respect to the department's development: "Don't underestimate Ted Schultz."[15] The appointment of Theodore Schultz to the Department of Economics in 1943 and his elevation to chair shortly thereafter marked a key turning point. Schultz was an effective chair and Friedman ally in the crucial middle 1940s and early 1950s when the department was in transition, and he remained chair through the early 1960s. Schultz was an excellent administrator and scholar, and built consensus among the members of the faculty. He received the Nobel Prize in Economics in 1979. Among Friedman's closest colleagues and friends in his early years on the Chicago faulty were Aaron Director (in the law school); Allen Wallis (in the business school); Frank Knight, Lloyd Mints, Ted Schultz, D. Gale Johnson and H. Gregg Lewis (all in economics); and Jimmie Savage (in statistics); and later George Stigler (who returned to Chicago in 1958) and Al Harberger, in economics.

Friedman established himself early as a leader in the Department of Economics, heading faculty committees, teaching a full load, participating actively in department affairs, and involving himself in many extracurricular activities—in addition to conducting a very active scholarly research and publication program. He received the third John Bates Clark Medal in 1951, bestowed biannually by the American Economic Association to the top economist under the age of forty.

Friedman emphasizes that concern for intellectual quality alone is what has made Chicago a great university. He remarked in a 1974 talk to the university's board of trustees: "If we are to preserve our heritage, we must continue to insist that intellectual quality and intellectual quality alone be the basis of appointments to the faculty—

not political or social views, not personal attractiveness or sex or race, not grantsmanship, not even potential contribution to a balanced faculty. Balance and diversity have been and will continue to be valuable by-products of an undeviating emphasis on quality alone. They are not objectives to be sought directly." Among the reasons Chicago is eminent are its "tolerance for diversity, stress on scientific quality as the decisive criterion for appointments, and success in identifying and attracting future leaders of their profession." The goal should be "the objective pursuit of knowledge—to science in the broadest sense."[16]

8

"POSITIVE ECONOMICS"

ne of Friedman's main projects on arriving at the University of Chicago in September 1946 to teach was to write the essay that became "The Methodology of Positive Economics." This essay is perhaps his second most well-known academic work, after *A Monetary History of the United States, 1867–1960* (1963), and is sometimes referred to as the most cited paper in economic method—and sometimes in method generally—in the social sciences.

"The Methodology of Positive Economics" considers issues involved in creating a "positive science" of economics. Friedman's idea here is that there "can be, and in part is, a positive science"[1] of economics, in the same way that it is possible to come to universally (or almost universally) acknowledged statements about the truth and falsity of propositions in the natural sciences.

The essay begins with reference to a Keynes—not to John Maynard but to his father, John Neville, a noted economist in his own right. The elder Keynes distinguished between "positive" and "normative"[2] science. The former concerns what is; the latter, what should be. The fact/value distinction is basic. Without recognition of the difference between facts and values, little or no progress is possible either in the establishment of facts or in the achievement of values. Economic theory instead becomes a mishmash of stray empirical observations (sometimes referred to by Friedman as "casual empiricism"[3]), disjointed ethical goals, and largely irrelevant mathematicizing. Facts concern the empirical world; values concern normative choices. Positive economics concerns facts.

The fulcrum on which "The Methodology of Positive Economics" turns is prediction, which to Friedman is the defining point of science, its pith. It is not an overstatement of his views to say that where there is no prediction, there is no science. Prediction defines science: "The ultimate goal of a positive science is the development of a 'theory' ... that yields valid and meaningful ... predictions about phenomena not yet observed."[4]

Prediction in economics is vital, Friedman believes, because only if one knows the likely consequences of action can one recommend actions to follow. One's values must be implemented according to certain conceptions of the facts: "Any policy conclusion necessarily rests on a prediction about the consequences of doing one thing rather than another, a prediction that must be based ... on positive economics." Friedman gives as an example minimum wage legislation. Proponents of minimum wage legislation predict, or believe, that it results in less poverty through higher wages for laborers. Opponents believe or predict that it will cause more poverty through higher unemployment. "Agreement about the economic consequences of the legislation might not produce complete agreement about its desirability, ... [but] it would certainly go a long way to producing consensus."[5]

It is not enough to know that the goal of positive economics is prediction. One must also know how to achieve this goal. Here Friedman puts forward an idea that is more controversial than the fact/value distinction: Theories should be evaluated not on the basis of the realism of their assumptions but solely on the basis of the accuracy of their predictions. There is one, and only one, criterion in Friedman's view for the acceptance or rejection of a theory: its capacity to predict.

He holds that "[f]actual evidence can never 'prove' a hypothesis; it can only fail to disprove it, which is what we generally mean when we say, somewhat inexactly, that the hypothesis has been 'confirmed' by experience."[6] Truth can never be completely proved. The search for truth is an endless process of testing old and new hypotheses against new evidence. Truth is pieced together, step by step, in the process of observing. The truth is not a mountain peak that eventually will be conquered, high as it may be. Every discovery opens new areas of ignorance and inquiry. The more we know, the more we realize how little we know, and how much more there is to know. Truth is no more than a way station in an endless journey on an endless road. Our presumed knowledge can never be more than provisional and tentative. Friedman is a skeptic, in the tradition of Socrates and Hume.

Absolute knowledge of the sensory world is not possible, Friedman believes, and theories cannot be fully proved. Along these lines, he said in 1988: "If there be a truth, there's no way of knowing when you get it. . . . I'm looking for truth. But the question is, how do I know when I get it? . . . [T]he answer is, I never will. And therefore, no matter how much evidence I get, I never can have one hundred percent confidence that I have truth."[7]

"The Methodology of Positive Economics" had, Friedman recalls, a "long gestation."[8] It originally grew out of a 1946 review of a work by Oskar Lange and may perhaps be dated to a 1941 review of a work by Robert Triffin. A first draft, titled "The Relevance of Economics for Prediction and Policy,"[9] dates to the first months after Friedman began to teach at Chicago in September 1946.

Crucially, in his review of Lange's work, Friedman ties theories to facts in the sensory world: "[A] theory that has no implications that facts, potentially capable of being observed, can contradict is useless for prediction."[10] He thus rejects economic and other theorizing that is not based in experience. Unless there are facts, there cannot be theories about them. Unless theories make predictions about the sensory world, theories would be without value and predictions would be meaningless. Unless prediction is of the world, it ceases to be prediction. The essential point in scientific methodology is not that facts cannot ultimately be proved. It is that unless there are facts, no prediction is possible, and the methodology to establish scientific theories is prediction. Friedman tied methodology in the social sciences to prediction in a way that had not been done before.

He says of Lange's work that it is a "brilliant display of formal logic, abstract thinking, [and] complicated chains of deduction,"[11] but it nonetheless is of little value because it says nothing about the real world that facts could establish. Unless theories are in some way about real, empirical events—and make predictions about future empirical experience—they are simply barren mathematicizing, not contributions to knowledge. Friedman thinks that much of twentieth-century economic theory fell into this category. He opposes "descriptive realism"[12] not because empirical information regarding historical events is not valuable, but because what is really valuable in theory is empirical *prediction*. Much of practical economics is about policy; it should be possible to come to relative agreement about the effects of policies before they are implemented.

Friedman's methodological views grew out of discussions of certain contemporaneous issues in economics, such as the theory of monopolistic competition and questions as to whether businessmen produce to the point where marginal costs equal marginal revenues and whether firms seek to maximize profits.

To Friedman, models of empirical activity with fewer rather than more variables are best. Our minds are small. His methodology is in part a criticism of overly mathematical and geometric presentations of economic activity. Mathematical intelligence without the wisdom to apply it is of little worth, and mathematical intelligence was far more common in twentieth-century economic theory than economic wisdom. The important question in economic methodology is not how mathematically or geometrically complex or intricate a model is; the question is solely how accurately it predicts.

Frazer notes that Friedman's "mathematical and purely statistical skills reached a peak shortly after his war-related experiences"[13] with the Statistical Research Group (SRG). It is interesting that Friedman's views in methodology developed in his early years on the faculty at the University of Chicago, after his work for the SRG and when his contacts with the opposing views of the Cowles Commission were at their height. "The Methodology of Positive Economics" may in part be read as a criticism of the Cowles Commission approach, particularly with respect to Friedman's conception that the evaluation of theories should not be on the basis of the realism of their assumptions but on the accuracy of their predictions.

He considers the Cowles approach, and much of twentieth-century economic theory, to be excessively formal and mathematical—tautological in character rather than explanatory. Of his interaction with the Cowles Commission, Friedman says that he was "anything but a devotee, or a disciple of their belief that the way to understand the working of the world was to construct big econometric models. In fact, I was a major critic of the kind of thing they were doing in Chicago. I introduced the idea of testing their work against naïve models, naïve hypothesis, and so on."[14] His point is not that descriptive realism is irrelevant or undesirable, but that what matters about a theory is its capacity to predict.

Don Patinkin, a University of Chicago student in the early and mid-1940s and someone who was not always sympathetic to Friedman, told an anecdote about Friedman's participation in Cowles Commission seminars. One of Patinkin's most distinct memories was a seminar in which Friedman advanced "the simple but powerful suggestion that a minimum test for the predictive efficacy of an econometric model is that it do better than a 'naïve model' which stated that the future would be like the past." Patinkin often wondered whether Friedman "thought that up on the spur of the moment, as well he might."[15]

Individuals often differ about the way the world is. How can one determine whose view is the most likely to be correct? Friedman's argument is that prediction is the key. Theories should be tested by the accuracy of their empirical predictions—accuracy both as to the number of correct predictions and as to the precision of predictions. If some theories provide more, and more accurate, predictions (which are, of necessity, of the physical world and are sensory), these are better theories.

Friedman believes facts are important both in developing and in evaluating theories. Information enters hypotheses in at least two ways. Information helps to form theories; our understanding of the past shapes our conceptions of the future. At the same time, facts corroborate or discorroborate our tentative hypotheses with respect to the future as the future occurs. Moreover, because prediction is preeminently of the future, the issue of timing—when events will occur—is another important element of prediction.

In a 1979 letter, Friedman spoke of two major influences that underlie his methodology—Karl Popper and Jimmie Savage: "I have increasingly come to put greater emphasis on the second compared to the first. The thing that impresses me about Savage's analysis in his *Foundations of Statistics* and elsewhere is the emphasis on statistics, i.e., all scientific investigation, not as a search for truth in some abstract sense but rather as a mechanism which will produce agreement among people starting out with initially different views." Friedman goes on to say: "Savage's emphasis is on a methodology under which if two people disagree about something, instead of arguing endlessly about it, they discuss the question of whether there are a set of observations which would bring them into agreement. And the nature of the discussion is that A says to B, 'If we were to make such and such an experiment and you were to observe such and such, then I would agree that you are right and I'm wrong; and B makes a similar statement."[16]

Friedman's work in statistical theory is the most difficult in his corpus for the non-mathematician. In addition to his formative role in developing sequential analysis, he and Savage wrote several articles in the late 1940s and early 1950s that acquired considerable renown in the economics profession. These were "The Utility Analysis of Choices Involving Risk" in 1948 and "The Expected Utility Hypothesis and the Measurability of Utility" in 1952. Friedman emphasized the importance of prediction again in the latter: "The function of a scientific hypothesis is to enable us to 'predict' phenomena not yet observed, that is, to make statements about phenomena not yet observed."[17]

It is vital, in Friedman's view, that there be calm, rational discussion of controversial issues, recognizing that calmness, continual search for factual evidence, and the willingness to revise or modify one's views is the surest sign of the scientific outlook, the source of so much human advance and one of the defining elements of western civilization. The classical liberal and scientific attitude is one of wonderment. It is, in many respects, a child's view of the world—looking at the world with open eyes and no preconceptions. Friedman explains why theories emphasizing prediction are the right kind of theory: "We are imperfect human beings with incomplete understanding and the important thing is that we must economize . . . our small minds by getting at the essential elements."[18]

Friedman jokes that he is "so happily blessed with critics that I have been forced to adopt the general rule of not replying to them."[19] Although he does indeed often respond to critics, he has not done so about "The Methodology of Positive Economics." Unusually, he has adopted a policy of not responding to criticism of this essay, saying that he is "more interested in doing economics than in writing about how economics should be done."[20]

The larger work of which "The Methodology of Positive Economics" is the first part is *Essays in Positive Economics,* a 1953 collection that sealed Friedman's reputation in the economic profession. Among the other essays of particular interest in *Essays in Positive Economics* are: "A Monetary and Fiscal Framework for Economic Stability," "The Marshallian Demand Curve," "The Case for Flexible Exchange Rates," and "Comments on Monetary Policy."

"A Monetary and Fiscal Framework for Economic Stability" was Friedman's first sustained attempt to put forward a comprehensive program of government policy. Originally given as a lecture in 1947 and published as the lead article in the June 1948 *American Economic Review,* the essay is strongly influenced by Henry Simons. Friedman takes several of his proposals from Simons's *Economic Policy for a Free Society.* Indeed, the title of the essay sounds like a distant echo of Simons's "A Positive Program for Laissez-Faire:

Some Proposals for a Liberal Economic Policy." Like Simons, Friedman had several long-run objectives to which he would like the economic system to contribute: "political freedom, economic efficiency, and substantial equality of economic power."[21] The last of these, "substantial equality of economic power," has virtually disappeared from Friedman's writings over the years.

In "A Monetary and Fiscal Framework," he considers free private property capitalism to be the most suitable vehicle to achieve his goals, although he notes that others do not agree with this view. When the essay was published, most academic economists, political scientists, and other professional students of society—perhaps the vast majority—advocated a heavily state-influenced mixed economy, if not democratic socialism. The idea that government could manage and direct the economy better than a market order was current; it was, indeed, overwhelmingly prevalent. The Great Depression demonstrated, in the minds of most professional students of society, journalists as well as academics, that capitalism was a bankrupt economic system. Conventional wisdom held that the collectivist and command economies of Communist countries were more economically productive than those of what at the time was called "the West." The disadvantage of Communism was its political tyranny. Therefore, many, perhaps most, commentators viewed continuing capitalism as merely a transitional step, via the democratic process, to some form of socialism in which government would play a greatly expanded role in the direct management of economic production. Most commentators on society thought that this would be a much more efficient way economically to produce in a society, and, as well as being more just.

Although he retreated over the decades from a number of the specific proposals in "A Monetary and Fiscal Framework for Economic Stability," Friedman got the main point right, unlike so many of his fellow students of society at the time. Free private property capitalism is the most efficient and productive economic order yet discerned and leads to the most democratic and most civilly free societies. It was not with the ends of his liberal opponents that he initially disagreed; it was with their means to achieve these ends. His disagreement was essentially over positive economics. He held in a lecture: "When I come to the question of the dispute and difference I have made with modern liberals, the conclusion that I always reach is that the problem with the modern liberal is not that their hearts are soft, but that their heads are."[22]

Among the proposals Friedman advanced at this time that were most influenced by Simons was a 100 percent reserve requirement, whereby all institutions issuing money would be required to maintain reserves equal to 100 percent of deposits. Another policy that Friedman advocated in this essay that was influenced by Simons was a progressive income tax. That Friedman has deemphasized the 100 percent reserve requirement or discarded the progressive income tax over the decades indicates that Simons's direct, practical influence on him has waned.

Friedman hoped that "A Monetary and Fiscal Framework for Economic Stability" would generate controversy. He was disappointed by the "very little violent criticism" of it, he wrote in a November 1948 letter to Don Patinkin. He had been "expecting that someone would take a crack at it. . . . I shall certainly be disappointed if someone doesn't write a rejoinder."[23]

"The Marshallian Demand Curve" was originally published in the December 1949 edition of the *Journal of Political Economy*. Friedman notes in beginning this article his debt to Jacob Viner, "to whose penetrating discussion of the demand curve in his course in economic theory I can trace some of the central ideas and even details of this article."[24] Friedman circulated the essay to a number of colleagues in draft form for comments before its published version.

"The Marshallian Demand Curve" is an attempt to present a different interpretation of Marshall's views with respect to the demand curve than was then standard, particularly regarding a dynamic as opposed to a static conception of demand. In passing, Friedman makes reference to Marshall's overarching purpose in economic theory, also stating his own purpose, which is perhaps of most interest to readers today: "I shall use the conception that underlies Marshall's work, in which the primary emphasis is on positive economic analysis, on the forging of tools that can be used fairly directly in analyzing practical problems. Economic theory was to him an 'engine for the discovery of concrete truth.' 'Man's powers are limited: almost every one of nature's riddles is complex. He breaks it up, studies one bit at a time, and at last combines his partial solutions with a supreme effort of his whole small strength into some sort of an attempt at a solution of the whole riddle.'"[25] Like Marshall, Friedman focuses on facts and economic policy issues, not on theory itself, especially when not joined with practical relevance.

"The Case for Flexible Exchange Rates" is, with "The Methodology of Positive Economics," one of the two papers in *Essays in Positive Economics* that had not appeared prior to the volume's publication. When Friedman first put forward the idea of flexible international exchange rates—whereby the value of national currencies would vary in relation to one another as determined by the market—he was in a small minority. When he discussed the concept on a 1948 University of Chicago Round Table radio program with Donald Gordon, deputy governor of the Bank of Canada, Gordon had, according to Friedman, never "heard this solution put forth seriously."[26]

Friedman participated in many University of Chicago Round Table programs, which were some of the best-known radio discussion forums of the day. Through his participation in these round tables, broadcast nationally Sunday mornings, Friedman was introduced to the American public.

Few thought that the idea of flexible exchange rates had a chance of ever being implemented when Friedman first enunciated it. It is the error, conceit, and stumbling block of every generation that they believe that their ways of doing things, their beliefs, and their views are eternal and immutable—as if given from God to humans—even though this has not been the case for any preceding generation. Humanity can hardly be reminded enough, John Stuart Mill wrote in *On Liberty,* that "ages are no more infallible than individuals—every age having held many opinions which subsequent ages have deemed not only false but absurd."[27] Not infrequently, ideas Friedman advanced were ridiculed when he presented them, but subsequently became accepted.

According to Stigler, Friedman's work on flexible currency exchange rates had "substantial influence" on George Shultz, who, after teaching in the Graduate School of Business at the University of Chicago, became secretary of the departments of labor, treasury, and state. "When George was Secretary of the Treasury . . . under President Nixon," Stigler writes, "he allowed the foreign exchange value of the dollar to float, and I believe that Milton's arguments had contributed to that eminently desirable act."[28]

The expansion of international trade that flexible exchange rates has occasioned and the greater flexibility in meeting domestic economic concerns that flexible exchange rates allow are great sources of the prosperity and relative stability of world economic development since the early 1970s. Flexible exchange rates also reduce what previously was a major source of international friction—fixed exchange rates.

The importance that Friedman attaches to the expansion of international trade is hard to overstate. He rarely uses the word "destiny." One place he does use the term is when discussing free trade in *Capitalism and Freedom*. With respect to unilateral implementation of completely free international trade to and from the United States, he declares: "Let us live up to our destiny and set the pace not be reluctant followers."[29] Free trade is the central libertarian economic tenet. Free trade, at home and abroad, is essential to human freedom, economic plenty, and peace.

"Comments on Monetary Policy" is of interest for several reasons, not the least of which is the continuing development that it shows in Friedman's ideas on inflation. In a paper also included in *Essays in Positive Economics*, "Discussion of the Inflationary Gap," first published in 1942 when he worked for the Treasury Department, Friedman discussed inflation but made no reference to money or to monetary policy. In 1951's "Comments on Monetary Policy," he raises monetary policy to at least a coequal place with fiscal policy in controlling inflation. At the same time, his views were continuing to evolve. He saw, even in the later paper, a significant role for fiscal policy: "Monetary and fiscal measures are the only appropriate means of controlling inflation. . . . Monetary and fiscal measures are substitutes within a wide range."[30] In the coming years, Friedman would depart from the view that fiscal policy is of substantial importance in determining national economic activity and, particularly, in determining changes in average prices.

In "Comments on Monetary Policy," he presents a good description of his view of what public intellectuals should do: "The role of the economist in discussions of public policy seems to me to be to prescribe what should be done in the light of what can be done, politics aside, and not to predict what is 'politically feasible' and then to recommend it."[31] The economist should say what he believes is true, irrespective of political practicality. Friedman has been known throughout his career for putting forward unpopular ideas that were seen as having little chance of being implemented when he enunciated them.

The response to *Essays in Positive Economics* was favorable, though few (if any) agreed with all of its recommendations. "Stimulating, provocative, often infuriating, but well worth reading,"[32] Peter Newman wrote in the journal *Economica*. According to William Baumol in the *Review of Economics and Statistics:* "Certainly one of the most engrossing volumes that has appeared recently in economic theory."[33] Not all reviewers were as impressed. C. S. Soper wrote of the proposal in "A Monetary and Fiscal Framework for Economic Stability" that government expenditures would automatically increase through unemployment insurance and other means in recessions and decrease in better times, as tax receipts moved in the opposite direction, that "[b]uilt-in stabilization sounds very attractive, especially as the counter-effects occur just when needed, but such a pill would need plenty of jam as an accompaniment, governments being so loath to relinquish their freedom of action."[34]

Friedman considers his work in positive economics—in the presentation of economic facts—to be his primary intellectual contribution. He comments in a 2001 correspondence: "My contribution to the libertarian cause has not come on the level of values or the like but rather by empirical demonstration, . . . by advancing the science of economics and showing the relevance of those advances to the policy of economics."[35]

9

FAMILY

ose writes that "both Milton and I felt that children were an important part of a full and happy life."[1] Although it is often the case that children have somewhat idealized memories of growing up, Janet and David have nothing but good things to say about their parents.

Janet's birth in 1943 occasioned, of course, a significant change in routine for Milton and Rose. When he was younger, Milton's preferred time to work was midnight to 4:00 A.M. or so. As he assumed parental responsibilities, his schedule moved in a more conventional direction. His work for the Statistical Research Group during the war was secret, so he could not talk with Rose about it. This must, to some small extent, have discombobulated him, for he always likes to talk about what he is doing, what is happening right now. Rose provides these recollections of their earliest time as parents:

> We could not . . . discuss what he was doing except on the most general and superficial level. Our talk was about what was going on in the world . . . and, most important, how our daughter spent her day. The statistical work that Milton did at home involved keeping detailed records and charts of her weight, how much formula she consumed (an important item, since she was not a big eater), . . . her physical and . . . intellectual progress. . . .
>
> Even after all these years, I vividly remember Milton's trying to keep her awake for her 10 o'clock feeding by tickling her toes while I tried desperately to get her to nurse. . . . Looking back, it is hard to

believe that one infant kept me busy all day and her father occupied, in one way or another, every evening.[2]

David's arrival two years later completed the family. Milton and Rose apparently hoped to have at least one child of each gender. David was Rose's third pregnancy.

The Friedmans were a close family—open, honest, and, perhaps somewhat surprisingly, physically demonstrative in their affection for one another. They know one another's strengths and weaknesses full well. One does not gather the impression that there were or are too many secrets in the Friedman household. They are all too honest and too intelligent for that.

Milton's basic schedule at Chicago in the late 1940s through the 1950s had him teaching three of its four quarters each year. The family generally left Chicago for the summer, vacationing a couple of summers in Vermont and then for the rest of the time in New Hampshire. He did "much if not most"[3] of his research and writing during these summer vacations. Several friends and economists, including Arthur and Helen Burns, had nearby summer homes. Dartmouth was not far away, so Friedman had access to research facilities.

Jan and David attended the lab school at the University of Chicago, which featured an eclectic and diverse student body, many of whom were drawn from the families of faculty and university students from around the world. In addition, the school enrolled lower-socioeconomic neighborhood students, particularly African Americans. It was an early integrated school.

The school was located on the campus of the university, a few blocks from where the Friedmans lived. Jan and David attended it for their entire school careers before college, with the exception of when the family was not in Chicago for the school year. David skipped first grade. Stephen Stigler remembers that when his family returned to Chicago in 1958 and he did not know many people, he took Jan to the lab high school prom.

The Friedmans' residence at 5731 Kenwood Avenue was home while the children were growing up. On a residential tree-lined

street, the brick house is similar to most others in the neighborhood and was built at the time of the Chicago World's Fair of 1893,
which was held nearby. The house is tall, thin, and deep, set back
about thirty to forty feet from the street. The yard behind the
house is narrow but long and with tall trees. The Friedmans rented
out the third floor, which had two separate apartments with their
own entrances.

A concrete walkway leads to the front door, which one walks up
several brick steps to enter. There is a stylish overhang immediately
above the front door and a small entry room. Immediately to the
right is a large living room, with a fireplace and picture window. The
kitchen is on the ground floor, and Milton had a workshop in the
basement where he did woodwork, a favorite form of relaxation.
Bedrooms are upstairs, and Milton's office at home was in an extension of his and Rose's bedroom that may originally have been a separate room. She must have tolerated his paperwork clutter; he is
known for his messy desk. The home contains many books, magazines, and journals, and some artwork, but it is not crowded with
material possessions.

The Friedmans' home was about a seven-minute walk from the
Social Science Research Building where the economics department is
located. Milton typically walked to work. The house is within a block
of 57th Street, a small commercial district with restaurants and
shops. Various libraries at the University of Chicago are a short walk
away. Many colleagues lived in the immediate vicinity. The house
and location were almost ideal, although by the 1950s safety issues
detracted from what would have otherwise been almost utopia. In
1955 the residence was burglarized and Rose was almost assaulted
while Milton was in India on a consulting assignment; thereafter, he
rarely traveled alone.

While Milton and Rose praise Robert Maynard Hutchins,
Chicago's mercurial president and chancellor from 1929 to 1951, this
view is not shared by all. The University of Chicago was, in fact, in
something of a slump, relatively speaking, when Hutchins departed.

Among the issues facing the campus in the 1950s was change in the adjacent Hyde Park–Kenwood residential area, where the Friedmans and many faculty lived. The increasing proportion of African American residents in a lower socioeconomic bracket, and increasing black-white tension, mirrored larger trends in the nation as a whole. The university ultimately responded by purchasing property in the immediate vicinity of the campus and gentrifying the area with both staff and middle-class African Americans.

The Friedmans went on several extended stays away from Chicago as a family in the 1950s, in addition to their regular summer vacations to New England. The family spent the fall of 1950 in Paris, where Milton was a consultant for a Marshall Plan agency. In this capacity he advised on the Schuman Plan, which established the six-nation European Coal and Steel Community, the original predecessor of the European Union. He basically opposed the Schuman Plan, on the grounds that it could lead to greater government control of the economy. In addition to this work as a consultant, he advised the West German government on exchange rate issues, which was the basis of his paper "The Case for Flexible Exchange Rates" that appeared in *Essays in Positive Economics.* Rose recalls that she and Milton were "astonished"[4] at how much French their children learned in their three months in France.

Milton received a Fulbright fellowship to spend the 1953–54 academic year as a visiting fellow at Cambridge University, the citadel of Keynesianism, where John Maynard Keynes had lived and where many of his former students and colleagues continued to teach. Jan and David turned eleven and nine during this year abroad. Friedman's understanding of Keynes and his work, and British life, developed during this Cambridge sojourn. In discussing Friedman's monetary views, Robert Solow makes an interesting reference to Friedman's opposition to "English Keynesian economics,"[5] which was even more inclined than its American cousin to view money as of little importance in determining economic activity and the price level. As in much of American and British English, there are subtle differences in meaning in economics terminology. The Friedmans traveled throughout much of Europe during breaks in the Cambridge schedule, with Milton often lecturing along the way.

Three years after the British adventure, in 1957–1958, the family traveled again for the school year, to the Center for Advanced Study in Palo Alto, California. This year, during which the children turned fifteen and thirteen, was another pleasant experience. Milton enjoyed the intellectual environment of the multidisciplinary center, which allowed scholars complete freedom to pursue activities of their choice—and regular poker games with, among others, George Stigler, also a fellow at the center that year. While on the West Coast the family visited Rose's parents in Oregon among other side trips and excursions.

The annual summer trips to New England were a highlight when Jan and David were growing up. The family's home in New Hampshire was a rustic dwelling, with a large porch and stone columns on either side of a wide stairway. Milton did most of his work in a separate building that had been the studio of the previous owner, an artist. Many friends visited the Friedmans during the summers.

A couple of anecdotes are illustrative of the summer vacations. One year Milton replaced some lead pipe and then melted the scrap into an army of soldiers for David. He had a little extra time, and thought it would be a good father-son experience and fun to try his hand at a little metallurgy. Another time Jan and a little friend came running back in tears to Milton because they had been chased off the property of a neighbor who had accused them of trespassing.

The following provides some idea of the Friedman's family circumstances while Jan and David were teens. Once, when the family was traveling across country by train, Milton gave Jan and David the choice of a room with berths or the difference in cash between the price of the room and the price of riding in coach. The children chose to sit up in coach for two days. Perhaps some indication of Jan's and David's personalities was Milton's comment—in the 1962 preface to *Capitalism and Freedom*, when they were nineteen and seventeen—on their "willingness to accept nothing on faith."[6]

Notwithstanding the family's travels and regular New England summer vacations, Chicago was home while Jan and David were growing up. David remembers the discipline his father practiced: "When I was very little and if I got mad at my sister . . . and locked myself in my room, my father would come to the door and say, 'Making a mistake and not admitting it is only hurting yourself twice,' and then go away. . . . [M]y father . . . believed very strongly in a sort of freedom vis-à-vis children and letting them do things. . . . [He] influenced me mainly through ideas. . . . We spent a lot of time arguing about everything." David says of these arguments: "The question was who was right, not who was older." His father spent, in David's words, "a lot of time"[7] with him and his sister while they were growing up.

Jan says that when she was growing up, she had "no idea my father was influential or unusual." She does not recall listening to him on the University of Chicago Round Table programs. Her impression changed to some extent when she saw him participate in a debate when she was in her early teens. She was "very impressed," and thinks that much of his strength as a debater is that he was "so charming. He never makes the other person feel uncomfortable," even though he may possess strong differences of opinion. Jan has no recollection that the family particularly talked about economics around the dinner table. Rather, the conversation was about "what was going on in the world and general life."[8]

Jan and David were raised nonreligiously. They celebrated Christmas each year from a secular perspective, with the accoutrements of mid-twentieth-century America. They did not celebrate Jewish holidays. Of his father's religious beliefs, David says that "he doesn't believe in God but cannot be certain God does not exist." David also says that his father is "not particularly socially conservative for his generation."[9]

Milton's mother, Sarah, died in about 1955. One of his sisters died at a relatively young age. His sister Tillie, called "Toots," had two sons, one of whom became a university professor in mathematics, the other an attorney. Milton's sister Ruth also married and had two children.

Milton's nephew Alan Porter provides recollections of Milton's mother, whom he knew as a young boy in the early 1950s. Sarah Friedman was a very bright and hardworking woman who took care of herself after her husband passed away at an early age. She was well respected in the community and intelligent, and people came to her for advice.[10]

The Friedmans had two dogs when the kids were growing up—a fox terrier named Sparky and a Shetland sheepdog named Galadriel (called Gal) after the elfin queen in Tolkien's *Lord of the Rings*, which Jan and David read. They also had tropical fish.

Friedman occasionally mentions the family in his work. Though the references are few, not many other writers in the classical liberal tradition have enunciated such views as these: "As liberals, we take freedom of the individual, or perhaps the family, as our ultimate goal in judging social arrangements," and "[t]he ultimate operative unit in our society is the family."[11]

Milton and Rose had a remarkably long marriage. In June 2006, they celebrated their sixty-eighth wedding anniversary.

Friedman wrote in the preface to *The Optimum Quantity of Money and Other Essays* (1969): "My main indebtedness is to my wife . . . proximately, for undertaking the task of selecting the essays for this book . . . but, fundamentally, for creating a home that enabled the essays to be written."[13] He has dedicated two books to his children: *A Theory of the Consumption Function*, dedicated to them alone, and *Capitalism and Freedom*, dedicated "To Janet and David and their contemporaries who must carry the torch of liberty on its next lap."[14]

10

PROFESSOR

ne of the most important lessons that Friedman learned was from Wesley Clair Mitchell, who early taught and remonstrated him, "If you cannot state a proposition clearly and unambiguously, you do not understand it."[1] Friedman has repeated this lesson to many of his own students. Words matter.

He is, to a certain extent, a word extremist. Every word that he speaks or writes has to be, in some sense, true. He writes in a letter with respect to correcting a minor impression that might be conveyed that to make the change would be "making something into business which shouldn't."[2] The total impression that words convey is vital. Friedman's emphasis on exact expression sometimes leads to literalism. For example, discussing Lionel Robbins's 1934 work *The Great Depression,* he says (while disagreeing with the work substantively) that it is an "extraordinarily lucid and penetrating analysis of the depression from the Austrian point of view." He then quotes, in support and approvingly, a footnote from John Maynard Keynes about Robbins's work: "It is the distinction of Prof. Robbins that he, almost alone, continues to maintain a consistent scheme of thought, his practical recommendations belonging to the same system as his theory."[3] But in context, Keynes's comment about Robbins was sarcastic—Keynes thought that Robbins was off base.

Allen Wallis provided an example of Friedman's emphasis on exact verbal expression in describing Friedman and Jimmie Savage's relationship, which began at the Statistical Research Group and continued at the University of Chicago:

> From Friedman, Savage learned a great deal . . . about the use of the English language. While later he was grateful to Friedman, at the time he could not contain his exasperation. . . . Savage ridiculed as overpunctilious pedantry Friedman's insistence on changing such phrases as "in most applications" to "in many applications." Friedman maintained—correctly, of course—that "most" means more than half, and to know whether something is more than half would require statistical data that did not exist.
>
> The ultimate effect of this experience . . . was that Savage worked hard at developing his literary style. He became as meticulous in his choice of words as in his choice of mathematical notation . . . whether in a note scribbled on the margin of a manuscript, in a letter, or in a technical treatise.[4]

Yet another example of Friedman's focus on clear expression is in a footnote to a comment that Friedrich Hayek made on a lecture of his. After discussing the content of the comment, Friedman writes: "Unfortunately, I have not had the opportunity to investigate this point at all fully, so this reaction . . . is a tentative impression, not a documented conclusion."[5] Every word matters.

Friedman was an exacting, demanding teacher. This was reflected not merely in his approach to language but in his complete role as a teacher. He was a tough grader and strict in the classroom, though helpful and more gentle in personal contact.

During his years at Chicago, he taught graduate courses in price theory and, in the 1960s, monetary theory. He thought that he benefited from teaching a course outside of, but related to, his primary professional focus, which is why he taught price theory rather than monetary theory in the 1950s. His only teaching experience with undergraduates at Chicago was during his first few years on the faculty. He also led, starting in the early 1950s, an influential workshop in money and banking in which most of the students whose dissertations he supervised participated.

Friedman established himself as a leader on the faculty at Chicago from the outset. When he was a student there, Viner and

Knight taught graduate price theory. Friedman succeeded them both. James Buchanan, who received the Nobel Prize in Economics in 1986, took price theory from Friedman the first time that he taught it. Buchanan recalls Friedman's "dominating intellectual brilliance in argument and analysis," commenting, though, that this could relegate "the student to the role of fourth-best imitation." Buchanan adds: "I noted earlier how Friedman's analytic brilliance exerted a negating effect. . . . An event occurred early in my post-Chicago years that tended to erase this negative influence. . . . A relatively obscure scholar . . . located and exposed a logical error in one of Friedman's papers, an error that Friedman graciously acknowledged."[6]

The primary text that Friedman used in his price theory course for its first decade or so was Alfred Marshall's *Principles of Economics*, the last edition of which appeared in 1920. Friedman later replaced this work with a mimeographed version of lecture notes by two students of the price theory course. Friedman said in the late 1940s that Marshall's *Principles* was "still the best book available in economic theory. This is indeed a sad commentary on the economics of our time. Marshall's superiority is explained primarily by his approach to economics as contrasted with the modern approach. Marshall was interested in economics as a real problem rather than as a form of geometry. Economics to him was an engine of analysis, a tool to study the economic system as it actually works."[7] Also assigned in the course were selections from Edward Chamberlain's *Theory of Monopolistic Competition* and Friedrich Hayek's "Use of Knowledge in Society."

Friedman's *Price Theory* text, based on the students' lectures notes and published in 1962 and revised in 1972, undoubtedly gives a flavor of the course. Economics emerges as a result of scarcity: "An economic problem exists whenever *scarce* means are used to satisfy *alternative* ends. If the means are not scarce, there is no problem at all; there is Nirvana." He says that economics is a "social" science because it is concerned with issues that "involve the cooperation and interaction of different individuals." The major division in positive economics is "between *monetary* theory and *price* theory. Monetary theory deals with the level of prices in general, with cyclical and other fluctuations in total output, total employment, and the like. Price theory deals with the allocation of resources among different uses, the price of one item *relative* to another. . . . Professional jargon has come to designate monetary theory as *macroeconomics,* price theory as *microeconomics.*"[8]

Friedman led a faculty committee in the department in 1948–49 on how to improve the quality of student dissertations. He advocated shorter theses that professors would supervise in greater depth. His own policy encouraged students to write concisely: On exams, he graded only the first 1,000 or sometimes first 500 words of an essay.

In addition to and likely of greater significance than his price theory course was his workshop in money and banking. From this workshop much of his own work and that of his students in monetary history and theory emerged. Workshops at Chicago are different than seminars elsewhere because participants are expected to read before coming to class the paper that is to be discussed, allowing more in-depth discussion than possible when students read the work only in seminars, as occurs elsewhere. Friedman practiced a policy of "no representation without taxation"[9] in the workshop; students had to present papers in order to participate.

Gary Becker, who received the Nobel Prize in Economics in 1992, came to Chicago as a graduate student in 1951. Becker holds a unique place among Chicago economists: He is the last major figure to be a student of both Viner and Knight, though his contact with Viner was as an undergraduate at Princeton. Becker says that Friedman has had the "greatest influence on me of anyone I've studied with." He is a "great teacher," "outstanding," "intellectually the most exciting," a "tremendous debater," "quick," and a "novel thinker." There is "no question he was dominant" in the economics department during Becker's time there. From the perspective of graduate students, "It was Friedman's department, and it became increasingly so."[10]

According to Becker, in the course in price theory, Friedman provided "numerous illustrations and applications," which "helped students absorb Friedman's vision of economics as a tool for understanding the real world, not as a game played by clever academics." Becker adds that, for Friedman, "[t]heory was not an end in itself or a way to display pyrotechnics. Rather, the theory became worthwhile only insofar as it helped explain different aspects of the real world." In attending Friedman's classes, "[t]o me and others the main purpose of a meeting was to hear Friedman's comments on different subjects."[11]

Friedman did not attract all the top students, however. Becker continues: "Some students found the intensity of the course, the high standards demanded, and the bluntness of Friedman's comments on questions and written work too difficult to absorb. . . . Most students, however, found Friedman's approach an eye-opener, and were willing to put up with pressures and low grades to be exposed to his brilliant insights."[12]

Friedman chaired about seventy-five doctoral thesis committees in his years at Chicago—two or three a year, on average—more than any other professor. About two-thirds were on monetary topics.

D. Gale Johnson, who began to teach in economics at Chicago in 1944, recalled in 2001 that Friedman had a "tremendous following among students."[13] Lester Telser arrived at Chicago in 1952, and Friedman was his principal thesis supervisor. Telser remembers Friedman as a "very tough grader. I don't know how many As he gave." Telser recalls Friedman running the money and banking workshop "very strictly. Comments had to be pertinent to something in the paper." Friedman went through papers very methodically. As mentioned, papers had to be read before the workshop. Then, at the workshop, Friedman went through papers page by page, saying "Does anyone have comments on page 1?"[14] and so on.

Telser remembers that Friedman would dissect papers sentence by sentence. There were no visiting students in the workshop, only regular members. Only faculty who were directly responsible for particular students or who were involved in monetary theory attended. Telser remembers of students' papers: "God help you if you said something stupid or off the wall." The result was papers that were "greatly improved." Telser does not remember Friedman having a particularly good sense of humor in class. Once when Robert Mundell attended a workshop, Mundell made a joke about "permanent time" and "transitory time"[15]—a play on Friedman's use of permanent income and transitory income. Everyone laughed but Friedman.

Larry Sjaastaad became an economics student at Chicago in 1955. He remembers that Friedman had a "very strong" reputation among students, who would "flock to his classes." He "presented things with such clarity." As a faculty member, Sjaastaad occasionally sat in on Friedman's classes "just to hear him. He had a way of making complex things really simply, clarifying" them. Friedman is, Sjaastaad says, "fantastic in debates. He always won debates." Sjaastaad remembers a colleague once telling Friedman he should lose a debate, "just to show he was human." Friedman responded: "What, me lose a debate?"[16]

Friedman was a conscientious teacher who read and critiqued students' papers in depth, an activity that he does not particularly enjoy. He prepared well for class and did not give multiple-choice tests because he does not think that these are a good pedagogical technique, though this caused him more work in grading blue books. He knows how to encourage and coax the most from students, and his criticism is never cruel or malicious. He wants students to understand the world more accurately and completely, to understand their own and others' conceptions better. Becker recalls that Friedman frequently restated students' questions more clearly than the students did themselves.

Thomas Sowell, now the Rose and Milton Friedman Senior Fellow in Public Policy at the Hoover Institution at Stanford University, was a graduate student at Chicago from 1959 to 1961. Friedman was his adviser, and Sowell took his course in price theory. Sowell recalls

Friedman as a "wonderful human being, especially outside the class-room." He is a "great economist and saintly soul." He would "never go over students like a steamroller," as some academics do. Rather, he "planted a seed." He examined in great detail what students said and "forced you to confront your own sloppy thinking. There is nothing more important as a teacher." He "anticipates the other person's concerns and questions." Friedman made no attempt to convert students. He had a "polished classroom performance."[17]

Robert Lucas received the Nobel Prize in Economics in 1995. He came to Chicago as an undergraduate in 1955 and returned as an economics graduate student in 1960. He remembers Friedman as a "moral example" because of his commitment to the truth. He

> rarely lectured. His class discussions were often structured as debates, with student opinions or newspaper quotes serving to introduce a problem. . . . Then Friedman would lead us into a clear statement of the problem, considering alternative formulations as thoroughly as anyone in the class wanted to. Once formulated, the problem was quickly ana-lyzed . . . on the board. So we learned how to formulate a model, to think about and decide which features . . . to put at the center of the analysis. . . .
>
> The quality of discussions in Friedman's classes was unique in my experience. He did not call on students by name, . . . permitting me and many other classmates to experience the intensity of engaging Fried-man directly only vicariously. It was not dismissal that I feared—no graduate student would have been dismissed . . . —but the exposure of my confusion next to Friedman's quickness and clarity. He would en-gage a particular student in a dialogue, and once engaged no escape . . . was possible. Exit lines like "Well, I'll have to think about it" were no use: "Let's think about it now," Friedman would say.[18]

Other Nobel laureates in economics to date who were students at Chicago when Friedman taught there include Harry Markowitz, who received the prize in 1990; Myron Scholes, who received it in 1997; and James Heckman, who received it in 2000.

Friedman recalls his approach to students on their dissertations: "When I was advising doctoral students about their theses, they would come in and say . . . a lot's been done on . . . [a] subject. There is no subject on which there isn't more to be done."[19] In 1953 correspondence, he reveals a good understanding of deficiencies in the dissertation approach: "When the student turns to his thesis, he is largely thrown on his own. . . . [T]he guidance he gets is unsystematized and sporadic. Yet he is now expected . . . to meet absolute standards of quality; to make a 'contribution to knowledge.' . . . The result is understandably confusion, wasted motion, and an unnecessarily low quality of work."[20] He also commented at this time, in support of the workshop approach: "The capacity to do research cannot be taught; it can only be learned by exposure in the right environment and by experience with the actual doing of research."[21] He says as well, of the idea that first a student should do the research and then write up his dissertation: "There is no delusion more mistaken than the common one that first you do all the work and then you write it up. . . . You discover what you are doing and what you must do in the process of writing it up. There is no better way of forcing yourself to think through a problem than to write it."[22]

Friedman is ecumenical in his approach to knowledge. He does not think that only his own approach has value or potential value. Students should study "things that interest them, follow up their own insights and their own ideas. . . . I wouldn't want to discourage anybody from doing research in any area."[23] At the same time, he advised students to build on what had been done before them. He recognizes the provisional and tentative nature of all presumed knowledge, and therefore he does not overvalue creativity for its own sake. Rather, there is much to learn about what we presume to know, both in filling in infinite detail and in new conceptualizations and reconceptualizations of presumed known reality and experience.

Larry Wimmer studied at Chicago from 1960 to 1965. He remembers students holding Friedman "in awe." Wimmer says that Friedman "helped me as much as anyone else." He recalls Friedman telling him: "You can come to see me anytime you need help, but there's a price." The price was that Wimmer had to write twenty more pages of his dissertation. There was a significant difference in

Friedman's persona inside and outside of the classroom. In class, Wimmer remembers, he could be a "bulldog," and some students were almost terrified of his intellectual prowess. Outside of class, he was "kind, gentle, so helpful."[24]

Wimmer recalls Friedman's courses as "demanding." He did not "countenance any nonsense." No smoking was permitted in class. Friedman always introduced himself as a "teacher of economics." Wimmer remembers that "Mr. Friedman (that was his preferred title) did not preclude students from coming late, but he did impose a cost. Generally, he would stop lecturing while the student looked for and finally took a seat. The silence itself was a considerable cost to the student who was late. Occasionally, the silence would be followed by a comment before resuming his lecture. 'THAT is an example of an externality' was his favorite."[25]

Friedman could be stringent in criticism, particularly of students' papers. Economist Daniel Hammond refers to Friedman's "belief that frank and blunt criticism [i]s an indispensable ingredient in the recipe for effective scholarship."[26] Friedman wrote to one student in 1961 that a paper was "not worthy of you. . . . I am extremely sorry to be impelled to write in this vein. But it will do no good and only harm if I reply in innocuous phrases that conceal my frank judgment."[27] Friedman wrote another student that while his "paper shows signs of an enormous amount of reading and application, . . . the paper as a whole is so disjointed and disorganized that it is hard in brief compass to give criticism that will be useful."[28] He wrote a third student that his thesis was "too good to be presented in this shoddy form."[29] Hammond notes that "letters from Friedman to his students suggest that he put much time and effort into his students' work."[30]

Even in criticism, Friedman attempted to be positive. He wrote one student: "Nine times out of ten, sloppy writing reflects (and advertises) sloppy thinking. I predict with great confidence that in the process of making the exposition exact you will be led to discover unsatisfactory features of your analysis."[31]

As mentioned, Friedman was a tough grader. Of the seventeen graduate students who took the core written examination for the Ph.D. in 1959, for example, he passed eight, failed four, and gave a question mark to five. On a numerical basis with a maximum of 80, scores ranged from 56 to 17.[32] This grade distribution appears to be typical of the grade distribution in his classes at this time. Sowell remembers Friedman once congratulating him for receiving a B in his course. In response to Sowell's question of how many As there were, Friedman replied none.

One of the duties of a professor is to recommend students. Friedman wrote in an early letter of recommendation that is characteristic of many:

> I saw a fair amount of Mr. Schwartzman when he was a student. . . . He impressed me very favorably. He was a quiet, but thoughtful, intelligent and conscientious student. The work he did . . . showed evidence of care and a good deal of originality and understanding of the basic problems. I have little basis on which to judge his teaching ability, except his performance in class. This suggests that he would handle himself very well and would do a reasonably good job of explaining fairly complicated material to students.
>
> Mr. Schwartzman was always personally very pleasant and showed up very well in every way. I have no hesitancy in recommending him very highly to you.[33]

John Turner was a graduate student at Chicago in the early 1970s. Friedman was not his adviser, but Turner took his course in price theory. Turner recalls that he once sent Friedman a paper in which he quoted Friedman, and Friedman sent back a note saying that Turner had slightly misunderstood the point that he was making. Turner was impressed that Friedman would take the time to respond to a lower-level graduate student. Turner recalls that, notwithstanding his sternness in class and strictness as a grader, Friedman was known for writing exceptionally positive letters of recommendation.[34]

Paul Samuelson writes that "[as] a teacher, Milton Friedman achieves an A+ grade. . . . Typical reaction: At Princeton in 1951 an undergraduate star in economics was somewhat burned out. After Milton's first Chicago class the star was reborn. He literally 'couldn't wait for each successive class.' You can guess who is speaking [Gary Becker]. He speaks for many."[35]

Rose says of Milton's students that they would "remember his warm smile, his friendliness, his interest in the whole student not just in his class work. . . . Their children have heard him discussed with such warm feeling that they often think of him as a relative."[36] Milton believes that teaching a subject is the best way to learn it. By teaching, one becomes aware of gaps in one's knowledge. Also, having to express his thoughts to students improved his—especially popular—exposition. "Teaching," he believes, "is very much a two-way process."[37]

11

A THEORY OF THE CONSUMPTION FUNCTION

he 1950s were Friedman's salad days as a professor before he became a leading public figure in the 1960s. These were the happiest years in his life, as he and Rose raised their children and were leading figures in the brilliant intellectual atmosphere at Chicago. He was described in a 1950 *Fortune* magazine article on American economists: "Theorist, statistician, and political economist, he is one of the brightest lights among the young men of the orthodox classical school. His capacity for winning arguments is so dazzling that some of his opponents give him the Socratic name of gadfly."[1] This is among the first references to Friedman in the national popular media.

One of the central tenets of the Keynesian analysis that dominated economics from the late 1930s through the 1960s that Friedman challenged in *A Theory of the Consumption Function* is that the ratio of consumption to income declines as income rises. John Maynard Keynes's consumption function is a relationship between consumption and income. Keynes defined the propensity to consume as the fraction of an extra dollar of income that is spent on consumption. It is this propensity to consume that declines as income rises, not consumption as such, according to Keynes.

Keynes believed that the major cause of national economic activity at less than full employment in advanced economies was attempted excess saving for which investment opportunities did not exist. Essential to his view was that as an economy matures, desired savings exceed desired investment. As Keynes defined them, savings always equal investment after the fact. He argued that in developed economies, a failure to find investment opportunities would stymie the attempt to save. The result would be unemployment because money saved would not be spent on consumption. Economic equilibrium could occur at less than full employment and maximum output.

Keynes's *General Theory* is filled with references to the existence of and problems caused by excess saving as economics mature:

> The fundamental psychological law, upon which we are entitled to depend with great confidence . . . is that men are disposed . . . to increase their consumption as their income increases, but not by as much as the increase in their income.[2]
>
> [W]e take it as a fundamental . . . rule of any modern community that, when its real income is increased, it will not increase its consumption by an equal *absolute* amount.[3]
>
> In the United States . . . by 1929 the rapid capital expansion of the previous five years had led cumulatively to the setting up of sinking funds and depreciation allowances . . . on so huge a scale that an enormous volume of entirely new investment was required merely to absorb these financial provisions; and it became almost hopeless to find still more new investment on a sufficient scale to provide for such new saving as a wealthy community . . . would be disposed to set aside. This factor alone was probably sufficient to cause a slump.[4]

Much of Keynes's theoretical model revolves around the idea that, as an economy matures, the propensity to consume—the ratio of consumption to income—declines, an idea that has fundamental consequences for his system. It provides much of the basis and theoretical justification for the propositions that national governments should deficit-spend, especially during recessions, to pick up the slack in consumption to which excess saving leads, and that it is appropriate for national governments to tax high incomes and large estates. Keynes wrote in the *General Theory:* "[O]ur argument leads towards the conclusion that in contemporary conditions the growth of wealth, so far from being dependent on the abstinence of the rich, . . . is more likely to be impeded by it. One of the chief social justifications of great inequality of wealth is, therefore, removed. . . . This particularly affects our attitude toward death duties."[5]

Many of Keynes's interpreters emphasize that an essential feature of his system is that in developed economies, desired savings increase more than desired investment. According to Alvin Hansen, Keynes's chief academic popularizer in the United States: "Keynes laid great stress on the behavior of business concerns with respect to depreciation and other reserves and noted how importantly these practices affect the amount . . . of consumption in relation to national income. . . . If such 'financial provision *exceeds* the actual expenditure on current upkeep,' the effect is to add to net saving and to widen the gap between consumption and income." Hansen also thought that the "great contribution of Keynes' *General Theory* was the clear and specific formulation of the consumption function. This is an epochmaking contribution to the tools of economic analysis, analogous to, but even more important than, Marshall's discovery of the demand function."[6] Developed economies are, Hansen and other Keynesians believe, subject to long-term stagnation as a result of attempted excess savings.

According to Joseph Schumpeter, who was often considered with Keynes to have been one of the two leading contemporary economists in the first half of the twentieth century, Keynes's was a "doctrine that . . . can easily be made to say both that 'who tries to save destroys real capital' and that, via saving, 'the unequal distribution of income is the ultimate cause of unemployment.' *This* is what the Keynesian Revolution amounts to."[7] A declining average propensity to consume as economies mature provides much of the basis for core elements in the Keynesian public policy program: government deficit spending, high estate and progressive income taxation, and a major role for national government macromanagement of the economy.

A Theory of the Consumption Function, which Friedman considers his most technically proficient work, was published by the National Bureau of Economic Research in 1957. It is one of his major contributions to the academic discipline of economics as distinct from the realm of public policy. Others include his historical researches into relationships among money, prices, and economic activity; his restatement and extension of the quantity theory of money; his work in flexible international exchange rates; his concept of a natural rate of unemployment; his critique of a long-run Phillips curve; and his essay "The Methodology of Positive Economics." Essentially, in *A Theory of the Consumption Function,* Friedman rebuts Keynes's notion of a declining average propensity to consume as economies develop and societies become wealthier.

Friedman's approach in this work is to put hypotheses forward and to test them. He feels that this book most closely follows the method that he enunciated in "The Methodology of Positive Economics." Foremost among the empirical evidence to be confronted in *A Theory of the Consumption Function* is that as individual incomes rise, individuals tend to save more. Would not, therefore, savings tend to rise proportionately for an economy as a whole as it becomes more prosperous? An answer to this question was suggested by Dorothy Brady, a close Friedman friend, particularly of Rose—and Rose Friedman in a 1947 National Bureau publication, *Studies in Income and Wealth.*

Brady and Rose Friedman hypothesized that a "consumer unit's consumption depends not on its absolute income but on its position in the distribution of income among consumer units in its community."[8] That is, there is no declining average propensity to consume as economies develop. Just because individuals save more as they personally become wealthier does not mean that society as a whole does. Individuals save on the basis of their relative socioeconomic position, not their absolute one. As an economy develops, individuals at each real level of wealth save less than those with the same amount of wealth did previously.

Thus, one of the key empirical propositions on which Keynes built his system is not so. There is no declining propensity to consume as income generally rises. Rose played a more significant role in *A Theory of the Consumption Function* than in any of Milton's other technical work in economics. (In his work in public policy, Milton considers Rose an equal partner.) He remembers "many a pleasant summer evening discussing consumption data and theory in front of a blazing fire in a fireplace constructed of massive local stones"[9] at their summer home in New Hampshire.

Milton Friedman's work on *A Theory of the Consumption Function* extends back to his days at the National Resources Committee from 1935 to 1937, when he studied consumer income and purchases. The second source of the book was his work for his doctoral thesis, *Income from Independent Professional Practice*, where he introduced the idea of permanent income and transitory income, with "permanent income" being more or less analogous to expected income and "transitory income" being more or less analogous to windfall income or loss.

He begins *A Theory of the Consumption Function* by observing that the "relation between aggregate consumption or aggregate savings and aggregate income, generally termed the consumption function, has occupied a major role in economic thinking ever since Keynes made it a keystone of his theoretical structure in *The General Theory*." Significantly, the alternative view that Friedman put forward in this book "seems consistent with existing empirical evidence, and has observable implications"[10] that could be corroborated by additional evidence. Here, as elsewhere, his focus is empirical: Unless theories conform to the facts, they must be rejected.

Central to his revised presentation of the consumption function from the Keynesian analysis is the distinction between "permanent" and "transitory"[11] income. Individual spending is related to permanent income and is not related to transitory income. The distinction between permanent and transitory income is what allows Friedman to make his revised presentation of the consumption function. Savings do not disproportionately rise for the economy as a whole as income does. The disproportionate rise in savings is a statistical illusion generated by classifying people and their savings by their measured income. Individuals who are at the top of income distribution at any point in time tend to have positive transitory income, so their consumption is less than their measured income. Their savings result from the transitory nature of their income, not from its greater amount. For this reason, there is no tendency for economies as a whole to save more as incomes generally rise.

Similarly, individuals who are at the bottom of income distribution at any point in time tend to have negative transitory income, so their consumption is more than their measured income as they use savings. Their measured income is less than their permanent income. Transitory income in the economy as a whole is typically neither positive nor negative. It may be positive or negative and tends to average at zero, with total positive and negative transitory income balancing each other.

Savings are therefore not the detriment in either the long or the short run that Keynes thought them to be. Contrary to what Keynes believed, there is no tendency for economies proportionately to save more as they mature. The essentially underconsumptionist model of economic activity that Keynes put forward, whereby economic downturns are caused by inadequate consumer demand as economies develop, is in error. There is no reason, from an economic perspective, to discourage savings through high taxation of individuals with large incomes or estates. In addition, in the short run, a crucial ground for Keynesian government deficit spending is that during economic downturns, consumption declines with income. Actually, consumption declines less than income as individuals spend on the basis of higher permanent income rather than on the basis of lower transitory income. There is thus less reason to increase government spending in economic downturns.

Although interest in *A Theory of the Consumption Function* has been limited almost exclusively to professional economists, the work is not without practical significance. Economists Charles Rowley and Anne Rathbone write that although Keynesians

> argued that fiscal policy should be used even-handedly across the business cycle, countering recessions with budget deficits and booms with budget surpluses, the political system confounded such naïve expectations. The political incentives to maintain budget deficits during booms as well as slumps simply overwhelmed economic logic. Therefore, to the extent that Friedman's theory dampened economists' enthusiasm for an active fiscal policy, it thus helped to dampen the rate of growth of government.[12]

Friedman emphasizes the importance of the findings of *A Theory of the Consumption Function* in its final chapter. One of the major theoretical outcomes of Keynesian analysis is "the denial that the long-run equilibrium position of a free enterprise economy is . . . at full employment."[13] In Keynes's view, free private property capitalism is inherently unstable or nonmaximally productive because of excess saving as capitalist economies mature. In challenging this hypothesis, Friedman helped to pave the way academically for the intellectual rehabilitation of free private property capitalism from the 1960s to the present.

Friedman wrote in 2006 that, for the most part, *A Theory of the Consumption Function* "pertains to the history of economic thought. . . . [I]ts major elements are now embedded in the conventional wisdom of economists. Essentially everyone accepts the permanent income hypothesis with some variations and modifications. The language has made its way into the conventional language of economics; 'permanent' and 'transitory' are part of the lexicon." With respect to the question of the accuracy of Keynes's underlying proposition that there are fewer investment opportunities as economies mature, so that, particularly with oversaving, there would be long-term, secular stagnation, Friedman says that, in this case, there would not be unemployment but a lower rate of interest: The "end result would simply be a different interest rate, not unemployment."[14]

12

KEYNES

he ideas of John Maynard Keynes were triumphant in the economics profession in the 1950s and 1960s. Though Keynes was prominent, generally and in economics, around the world from the time of his *The Economic Consequences of the Peace* (1919) in which he attacked the Versailles Peace Treaty and its makers, he was not the all-dominant figure that he became in academic economics in the United States and elsewhere after World War II.

Keynes's *General Theory of Employment, Interest, and Money* appeared in 1936, but did not immediately attract much attention except from academic economists. From the late 1930s until 1945, all focus was on World War II. After the war through the 1970s, Keynesianism waxed and then waned as an academic and political perspective. When Friedman began to teach monetary theory instead of price theory at the University of Chicago in the early 1960s, chapters from Keynes's *Tract on Monetary Reform* and *General Theory* were included in the required readings. In the second course in the money sequence, Friedman required his students to read the entire *General Theory*.

"In the history of economics," John Kenneth Galbraith wrote, "the age of John Maynard Keynes gave way to the age of Milton Friedman."[1] It is an indication of the tendency of paradigms and views of the world to change and even to collapse that two economists who would have been considered in absolutely the first tier for half of the twentieth century (from about 1900 to 1930 and from 1950 to 1970), Thorstein Veblen and Galbraith, are now considered very differently. Though it is as certain as certain can be that the future will look on the present very differently than the present looks on itself, this is, for whatever reasons, among the most difficult of lessons to learn and to internalize. It is nonetheless among the most important. To live in an era is almost always to accept its unstated premises, assumptions, rationalizations, and beliefs. To look beyond the time in which one lives is one of the surest signs of greatness.

Friedman has looked beyond his era for much of his career. Consider, for example, the following passage from a 1963 article on him—presented not as conventional wisdom or established precept but as a radical new idea with little professional support: "In articles in economic journals, Friedman long has argued that most economists have been wrong in thinking that the U.S. free enterprise system shows a chronic tendency to instability that can be cured only by government fiscal action. He has maintained, instead, that our major economic troubles—including the depression of the 1930s—can be traced to mistaken monetary management."[2] Yesterday's heresy so often becomes tomorrow's dogma, just as yesterday's dogma so often becomes tomorrow's heresy. When Friedman first put forward many of his ideas, including those challenging the Keynesian consensus, he was in a very small minority.

He has a long career of controversy. He remarks in 2004:

> *Interviewer:* What was it like growing up in an academic environment in which your views ran counter to the status quo?
> *Friedman:* Well, it was wonderful! I enjoy argument.[3]

If one does not like the game, it is harder to play it. Part of Friedman's success comes from his liking the give-and-take of debate. He welcomes, even loves, the opportunity to present his views, knowing full well that many will disagree with them. He recognizes that it is almost inevitable that if one seeks to change the status quo, one must challenge it. This is usually not popular, certainly not universally and at least not at first. New ideas are often criticized, and those who put them forward are often ignored, particularly by those who consider themselves leaders in knowledge and opinion. Many times individuals are concerned more about their place in the hierarchy of opinion and knowledge than in the truth itself. Friedman attempts to give his allegiance to the truth, wherever it may lead.

He remarks of his willingness to consider divergent views, even from those many would consider cranks: "I have received literally thousands of missives from amateur economists professing to point out basic fallacies or brilliant insights. The bulk are obvious fallacies . . . But every once in a great while . . . there is an exception, and these compensate for the rest."[4] He knows from personal experience that the orthodox opinion in an area is often wrong—and is always incomplete. Concomitant with the ability to put one's unpopular ideas and views forward is the ability to revise or alter one's point of view, at least if one is to be successful. No one can be right all the time. Individuals who never admit that they are wrong are not always right; they just never admit errors. Friedman has never been one of these people.

He has expressed appreciation for Keynes as an economist and a person on many occasions. Among recent words of praise for the Cambridge don are these:

> *Interviewer:* Do you think Keynes's objective was to try to save capitalism?
> *Friedman:* No. Keynes's . . . objective like my objective was to contribute to the well being of society. I am a great admirer of Keynes. I think he was a great human being and a great economist. I don't agree with the particular hypothesis he offered about the Depression, but advances in every science come from people offering hypotheses that turn out to be wrong.[5]

Friedman remarked in 1951 on "two alternative languages" for discussing economic activity with respect to inflation—that of the quantity theory . . . [and] that of Keynesian analysis." He said, revealingly, that "since there is a high correlation between those who object to assigning monetary policy a major role and those who prefer to use Keynesian language, I shall myself use that language despite some doubts whether it is the more fruitful."[6] Friedman's granting monetary policy even an equal place with fiscal policy marked a departure from the general view of economists of his era. Keynes's mature opinion was that monetary policy is of little importance either in macro-managing an economy or in determining at least short-term and intermediate-term changes in aggregate prices. Friedman has used Keynesian language (that is, terminology and concepts) even though he disagrees with Keynesian analysis, because that was the language of most of his fellow economists in the 1950s and 1960s.

Some commentators have tied Friedman's use of the terminology of his opponents to his success. Robert Leeson, for example, writes: "One of the reasons for Friedman's successful assault on orthodoxy was his determination to construct his arguments in the *language* of his opponents."[7] This is a principle capable of more general application than to terminology alone, and includes research interests and observance of professional customs and etiquette.

Keynes, like Friedman, appreciated the virtues of capitalist civilization. Indeed, in *The Economic Consequences of the Peace*, Keynes wrote:

> What an extraordinary episode in the economic progress of man that age was which came to an end in August, 1914! . . . [L]ife offered conveniences, comforts, and amenities beyond the compass of the richest and most powerful monarchs of other ages. The inhabitant of London could order by telephone, sipping his morning tea in bed, the various products of the whole earth . . . He could secure . . . cheap and comfortable means of transit to any country or climate without passport and could then proceed abroad to foreign quarters. . . . But, most important of all, he regarded this state of affairs as normal, certain, and permanent. . . . The projects and policies of militarism and imperialism . . . were little more than the amusements of his daily newspaper, and appeared to exercise almost no influence at all on the ordinary course of social and economic life, the internationalization of which was nearly complete in practice.[8]

Friedman makes an almost parallel statement, which, one thinks, must have been influenced by Keynes:

The century from Waterloo to the First World War offers a striking example of the beneficial effects of free trade on the relations among nations. Britain was the leading nation in the world, and during the whole of that century, it had nearly complete free trade. Other nations . . . including the United States, adopted a similar policy. . . . People were in the main free to buy and sell goods from and to anyone, wherever he lived, whether in the same or a different country, at whatever terms were mutually agreeable. Perhaps even more surprising . . . , people were free to travel all over Europe and much of the rest of the world without a passport and without repeated customs inspection. . . . As a result, the century from Waterloo to the First World War was one of the most peaceful in human history.[9]

Unlike Friedman, Keynes lost faith in the attainment of this ideal in the twentieth century. Keynes thought that the economy of Great Britain particularly, but those of developed countries generally, had become rigid and stultified. "The forces of the nineteenth century have run their course and are exhausted,"[10] he felt. It was the duty of government to step in and fill the void that unfettered capitalism had previously filled.

Keynes expressly rejected socialism (common ownership of the means of economic production) and communism (common ownership of all property), favoring instead government intervention in a free market economy. As he expressed it in the *General Theory:*

> The result of filling in the gaps in the classical theory is not to dispose of the "Manchester [free market] System," but to indicate the nature of the environment which the free play of economic forces requires if it is to realize the full potentialities of production. The central controls necessary to ensure full employment will, of course, involve a large extension of the traditional functions of government. Furthermore, the modern classical theory has itself called attention to various conditions in which the free play of economic forces may need to be curbed or guided. But there will still remain a wide field for the exercise of private initiative and responsibility.[11]

In the 1920s and 1930s, as economic circumstances went from bad to worse in Great Britain (unlike the United States, Britain did not experience prosperity in the 1920s), Keynes increasingly supported a larger government role to macromanage the national economy. Key essential ideas in his new system were the relative bifurcation between changes in money supply and changes in prices, stress on immediate circumstances in setting policy, and a predominant role for government fiscal policy. Monetary policy was downgraded and fiscal policy was raised in its place.

Rather than heated denunciation, Friedman's battle against Keynes and Keynesianism has taken the form of patient, detailed exposition of theoretical issues and presentation of concrete facts that he thinks vitiate Keynes's analysis. Friedman has discussed Keynes on many occasions, including his 1970 Wincott Lecture in Great Britain, "The Counter-Revolution in Monetary Theory." "A counter-revolution must be preceded by two stages," Friedman says here, "an initial position from which there was a revolution, and the revolution. . . . It is convenient to have names to describe these positions. The initial position I shall call the quantity theory of money and associate it largely with the name of . . . Irving Fisher . . . The revolution was made by Keynes in the 1930s."[12]

Friedman says that Keynes started as a "quantity [of money] theorist," so the Keynesian "revolution was from, as it were, the governing body." Friedman emphasizes that for Keynes, in the fundamental monetary equation $MV = PT$ (where M is the quantity of money, V is its velocity or the rate at which it changes hands, P is prices, and T is transactions of goods and services), velocity is

> highly adaptable. If the quantity of money goes up, he [Keynes] said, what will happen is simply that the velocity or circulation of money will go down and nothing will happen on the other side of the equation to either prices or output. Correspondingly, if something pushes the right-hand side of the equation . . . up without an increase in the quantity of money, all that will happen will be that velocity will rise. In other words, . . . velocity is a will-of-the-wisp. It can move one way or the other in response to changes either in the quantity of money or in income. The quantity of money is therefore of minor importance.[13]

Keynes's and Friedman's primary difference is factual.

In 1951 Friedman and Roy Harrod, a close friend of Keynes and his first biographer, met at a conference of economists, congressmen, and business leaders to discuss whether it would be possible to check the inflation then coinciding with the Korean War. Harrod's recollections are of note:

> I was much impressed by the vigorous part played by Professor Friedman . . . . [H]e invited me to come into his seminar. It was quite a small class of some eight or ten people seated around a little oval table. Professor Friedman told me that he had reached a point where he was intending to deal with the velocity of circulation, and invited me to give my views on that subject. After I had done so, he proceeded, by some adroit amendments, of unimpeachable logic I need hardly say, to demonstrate that my views were very near his. I could not refute him, and yet I had an underlying feeling that my views were not in fact as near his as he made them out to be. I thought "My goodness, this is one of the most agile intellects I have ever met." And I have often thought since how fascinating it would have been to stage a debate between Friedman and Keynes.[14]

Friedman believes that Keynes's most original contribution to economic theory was his "emphasis on the conflict between the stability of prices and the stability of exchange."[15] Like Keynes, Friedman believes that domestic price stability is more important than international exchange rate stability, though he would like to see both. Indeed, he believes that the surest, and perhaps only, way to achieve stable international exchange rates would be for all nations to have stable domestic price levels. The goals of domestic price stability and international exchange rate stability are thus in the long run not in conflict but in harmony.

Friedman feels that a national economy is more stable than Keynesian analysis postulates. Investment (including by government in the form of deficit budgets) does not have nearly the multiplier effect on income that Keynes thought, whereby small changes in investment lead to large changes in income, nor do ups and downs in economic activity have as much effect on consumption as Keynes thought. Friedman believes that, if left alone, the market will generally perform its magic more effectively in producing wealth than government involvement could ever accomplish.

He does not subscribe to the doctrine of monopolistic competition, whereby market forces are precluded from working by producer collusion. According to Friedman, there is less economic basis for national government intervention in and management of an economy than Keynes thought. Monetary policy plays a much larger role in determining aggregate prices and economic activity, and fiscal policy plays a much smaller role.

To Friedman, the facts are ultimately of the most importance in economic as in other analysis. He believes that Keynes's crucial errors were empirical, not theoretical. He offers these views: "Keynes was a great economist, one of the greatest economists. . . . The *General Theory* offered a hypothesis about the way the world worked. Now, like every scientific hypothesis, it may be a very imaginative and thoughtful hypothesis. But it may be wrong. . . . I don't object to the hypothesis on theoretical grounds. I object because I think its predictions were not confirmed by reality, and that the evidence rejects it."[16]

13

A MONETARY HISTORY
OF THE UNITED STATES

riedman's major project from the late 1940s to the early 1960s was his magnum opus, with Anna Jacobson Schwartz, *A Monetary History of the United States, 1867–1960*. Published in 1963, this 800-page work was written for the National Bureau of Economic Research after Arthur Burns, who succeeded Wesley Mitchell as its director of research, asked Friedman to study monetary factors in economic activity.

A Theory of the Consumption Function and *A Monetary History of the United States* constitute Friedman's twin critique of Keynes and Keynesianism. The former work explains what did *not* happen in the Great Depression; the depression was not caused by excess saving and a declining marginal propensity to consume as economies develop. The latter work explains what *did* happen; the depression was primarily the result of inappropriate monetary policy that allowed the money supply to contract. Recognized immediately as a classic, *A Monetary History* has changed and continues to change the way that we look at the Great Depression and monetary history, theory, and policy.

In order to appreciate *A Monetary History*, it is vital to understand the view of the Great Depression that prevailed before its publication.

Friedman provides this, plus his own, contrasting view, in *Capitalism and Freedom,* published the year before *A Monetary History:*

> "Full employment" and "economic growth" have in the past few decades become primarily excuses for widening the extent of government intervention in economic affairs. A private free-enterprise economy, it is said, is inherently unstable. Left to itself, it will produce recurrent cycles of boom and bust. The government must therefore step in to keep things on an even keel. These arguments . . . were a major element giving rise to the New Deal. . . . The Great Depression . . . , far from being a sign of the inherent instability of the private enterprise system, is a testament to how much harm can be done by mistakes on the part of a few men when they wield vast power over the monetary system.[1]

Understandings of empirical events matter—and influence action—greatly.

Before *A Monetary History of the United States* appeared, the most common conception of the Great Depression was that it was caused by excesses in the capitalist system: Unscrupulous speculators buying stocks on margin forced prices up in an orgy of greed that inevitably ended in the great stock market crash of October 1929. Herbert Hoover's feeble attempts to right the growing imbalances in the economy were insufficient, Hoover being a capitalist of the old school. Only the ascension of Franklin Delano Roosevelt to the presidency in 1933 and his bold programs of recovery in the New Deal returned America to prosperity and strength leading up to and during World War II. Moreover, the Great Depression appeared to confirm Karl Marx's position as the great prophet and scientist of economic activity—and communism as the wave of the future. Marx predicted that capitalism would expire in a series of increasingly severe business contractions. Friedman's achievement is to contradict these interpretations and outlooks and to revivify the quantity theory of money, placing money at center stage in its influence on economic activity.

Research for *A Monetary History* began in 1948 as a three-year study for the National Bureau of Economic Research to investigate the "role of monetary and banking phenomena in producing cyclical fluctuations, intensifying or mitigating their severity, or determining their character,"[2] Friedman wrote at the time. He does not now believe that there is a business *cycle*, in the sense of regular, recurrent ups and downs in economic activity: "I really don't believe that there is a business cycle. . . . The notion of a business cycle is something of a regularly recurring phenomenon that is internally driven by the mechanics of the system. I don't believe there is a business cycle in that sense. I believe that there is a system that has certain response mechanisms and that system is subject over time to external random forces."[3] He is thus a follower of Eugen Slutzky's idea of random causes as the source of economic fluctuations. Friedman also now writes of his "skepticism about whether there is indeed an economic phenomenon justifying the designation 'cycle,' or whether the economic fluctuations glorified by that title are not merely reactions to a series of random shocks, along the lines of a famous 1927 article by Eugen Slutzky."[4] Economic fluctuations do not a business cycle make.

Early in his career, Friedman did not possess a particularly monetarist perspective of economic activity. Although Mints, from whom he learned monetary theory, possessed a Fisherian, quantity theory of money perspective, he was not empirical or statistical, and monetary theory was not Friedman's focus until the 1948 National Bureau study. When he taught a course on business cycles at the University of Wisconsin in 1940, he called them an "unsolved problem."[5] In a final exam question, he did not indicate that monetary explanations for economic fluctuations were his preferred method of analysis, as they later become—indeed, his focus appears to have been fiscal policy. In a study in the summer of 1941, he recommended increased taxation to prevent inflation.

When Friedman was at the Treasury Department from the fall of 1941 through the winter of 1943, he endorsed almost strictly fiscal analyses of the sources of changes in aggregate prices. In testimony before the House Ways and Means Committee in 1942, he talked extensively about inflation without mentioning money or monetary policy. Likewise, in a 1942 *American Economic Review* article, he neglected to mention monetary policy while discussing inflation.

His most recent consideration of monetary policy before he started his work for the National Bureau was "A Monetary and Fiscal Framework for Economic Stability," an article that appeared in 1948 and was influenced by Henry Simons. Friedman here made four specific public policy proposals for economic stability, only one of which mostly concerns monetary policy. (The others mostly concern fiscal policy.) He made reference to the "inflationary pressure of abnormally high government expenditures"[6]; only later did he come to emphasize that inflation is always and everywhere a monetary phenomenon. Simons was not, incidentally, a consistent monetarist, if he is considered to have been a monetarist at all. He wrote in 1936 in "Rules versus Authorities in Monetary Policy," speaking of the goal of price stabilization: "The task is certainly not one to be entrusted to banking authorities, with their limited powers and restricted techniques, as should be abundantly evident from recent experience. Ultimate control over the value of money lies in fiscal practices—in the spending, taxing, and borrowing operations of the central government. . . . [I]n an adequate scheme for price-level stabilization, the Treasury would be the primary administrative agency."[7] Later this would not be Friedman's view at all of the mechanism through which inflation occurs.

The first aspect of the project for the National Bureau was to collect data. Friedman remarked in a 1967 lecture that "we have all of us . . . had the experience of coming on a fact that suddenly illuminated an issue in a flash, showing us how wrong we had been and leading us to a fresh and very different opinion." For him, this includes the facts that have "primarily to do with the Great Depression."[8] New empirical understandings of the depression led him to change his theoretical views.

In an early 1949 memorandum, "Outline of Work in First Phase of Banking Study: Cyclical Behavior of the Quantity and Rate of Use of Circulating Medium," he provided a status report of findings on the basis of his and Schwartz's first nine months of work: "(1) the quantity of circulating medium responds sluggishly to cyclical movements . . . ; (2) this is true of both . . . [currency and deposits]; (3) both seem to react sharply if late, in major movements; (4) the rate of use (velocity of circulation) of the circulating medium conforms positively, velocity increasing during expansion phases and declining during contraction." He said, in one of his first written statements of the implications of these findings, that these "general conclusions differ widely from the assumptions about the behavior of the circulating medium implicit in most . . . discussions of the role of money in cyclical fluctuations. If valid they have important implications for the possible role of monetary factors in generating cyclical fluctuations and for the possible effectiveness of policies directed at promoting stability by controlling the volume of circulating medium."[9] Friedman the monetarist was beginning to emerge.

He and Schwartz worked for seven years compiling and building data, tracing the evolution and development of American monetary policy and its consequences for almost a century. Much of this information had not previously been collected, including monthly data on currency and deposits by state and type extending back to just after the Civil War. There is one consistent thread through the narrative of some 350,000 to 400,000 words, 33 tables, and 64 charts—a thread that Friedman and Schwartz identify at the beginning of *A Monetary History:* "the stock of money in the United States."[10] According to historian of economic thought Mark Skousen, one of the reasons for the preexisting "ignorance about the power of monetary policy is that the Fed did not publish money supply figures until Friedman and Schwartz developed M1 [currency plus demand deposits] and M2 [M1 plus time deposits] aggregates in their book."[11] Friedman says, "If the Federal Reserve System in 1929 to 1933 had been publishing statistics on the quantity of money, I don't believe that the Great Depression could have taken the course it did."[12] Information is power.

Friedman's account of the economic period from 1929 to 1933 in the United States—the period that he and Schwartz dub the "Great Contraction"[13]—was different from that of almost all their contemporaries. The preexisting consensus with respect to monetary policy during this period was that the Federal Reserve System had done almost all that it could to end the Great Depression and that monetary policy was relatively impotent to end the depression. Moreover, the consensus was that inappropriate monetary policy in the United States played little role in starting, lengthening, or deepening the depression, which emerged for reasons other than mistakes in monetary policy. Friedman and Schwartz's analysis is exactly the opposite. Friedman's factual view of the world came to differ from that of his earlier contemporaries by 180 degrees.

In chapter 7 of *A Monetary History,* "The Great Contraction, 1929–1933," he and Schwartz challenge the view that the Great Depression reflected inevitable defects in capitalism that it was the federal government's duty to cure. Rather:

> The Great Depression, like most other periods of severe unemployment, was produced by government mismanagement rather than by any inherent instability of the private economy. A governmentally established agency—the Federal Reserve System—had been assigned responsibility for monetary policy. In 1930 and 1931, it exercised this responsibility so ineptly as to convert what otherwise would have been a moderate contraction into a major catastrophe.[14]

As Friedman explains in his two major popular works, *Capitalism and Freedom* and *Free to Choose,* as well as in *A Monetary History,* before the 1920s, the United States had experienced great economic growth punctuated by occasional banking panics and short-term, sometimes sharp economic downturns. As the downturn started in the second half of 1929, there was nothing to indicate that it would become the system-transforming and catastrophic event it did. Although it might have been a significant recession between 1929 and 1931 or so, it would not have become the Great Depression had not inappropriate monetary policies been followed.

There are many myths surrounding the Great Depression, and it is important to be clear about some of them in order to better understand its significance. One of the first, and most important, of these myths is that the Great Depression started with an instantaneous crash—that the United States moved from positive economic growth to economic calamity overnight. This was not the case. While the stock market did experience a substantial decline between September (when it peaked) and November 1929, losing about one-third of its value—most notoriously on "Black Tuesday," October 29—the market had almost doubled in the previous year and a half. By way of comparison on October 19, 1987, the stock market lost almost 23 percent of its value in one day, and not even a recession, much less a depression, followed. Had not other events supervened, there was no reason for the Great Depression to follow the 1929 stock market crash. Indeed, over the following six months in 1929 and 1930, stocks recouped 20 percent of their losses and were higher than they had been less than two years before. Significantly, price-to-earnings ratios were not especially high when the stock market fell.

Moreover, before 1929, the U.S. economy had experienced sharp economic contractions unlike anything since the Great Depression. Following the inflationary recovery after World War I, the national economy went into a severe but short depression from the middle of 1920 to the middle of 1921. Between May 1920 and June 1921, wholesale prices dropped by 44 percent, the sharpest decline in U.S. history. More than 500 U.S. banks failed in 1921.

In the first year of the Great Depression, the gross national product (GNP) declined by 12.6 percent in the United States, a very high amount from the perspective of later generations but not out of line with experience up to that time. Similarly, the increase in unemployment, to 9 percent in 1930, was high but not unprecedented. In 1920–1921, unemployment reached 12 percent and GNP declined by 24 percent.

In the fall of 1930, the downturn took a further turn for the worse. Through October of that year, the American money supply had declined by only 2.6 percent. Then a raft of bank failures, mostly in midwestern and border states, shook confidence in the banking system. At this time, before deposit insurance, when a bank failed, its deposits disappeared. In November 1930, 256 banks failed, followed by 352 more in December—in particular, Friedman emphasizes, the Bank of the United States. Though private, the Bank of the United States possessed more prominence than it deserved because of its name; many thought that it was an official bank of the United States. Its failure—the largest of a commercial bank up to that time—was a major blow.

Instead of increasing the money supply, as it had done during past economic contractions and banking crises, the Federal Reserve allowed the stock of money to contract. Money supply fell by an additional 7 percent from 1930 to 1931, by 17 percent from 1931 to 1932, and by 12 percent from 1932 to 1933—unprecedented annual consecutive declines. These declines constituted the Great Contraction and were the primary source of the simultaneous deterioration of the U.S. economy. The Great Depression was an anomalous event.

After the first banking crisis in late 1930, the economy appeared to struggle to rebound during the first months of 1931. Industrial production rose in the first quarter of the year. The rate of decline in factory employment was the lowest it had been since August 1929. A lasting turnaround in the economy at this point was not, however, to be. The Federal Reserve responded, as it had thus far, with inactivity, passivity, and counterproductive measures. Friedman and Schwartz write: "The effects of returning confidence on the part of the public and the banks, which made for monetary expansion by raising the ratios of deposits to currency and reserves, were largely offset by a reduction in Federal Reserve credit outstanding"[15] The total stock of money changed little in the first quarter of 1931 and was in fact lower in March 1931 than in December 1930. The Great Depression continued and intensified.

Over the next two years, conditions went from bad to worse. The New Deal, an idea and phrase put forward by Franklin Roosevelt during his 1932 presidential campaign, was in large part what made the Great Depression so significant in retrospect, although it was the wrong cure for the wrong disease. Roosevelt's policies prolonged the depression and made it worse, and contributed to the very severe recession of 1937 to 1938—what came to be known as the "Roosevelt recession"—making the whole period from 1929 to 1939 one of transformational importance in society and in the economy. Moreover, that this decade of economic trial was followed by the even worse horrors of World War II led the whole period from 1929 to 1945 to be seen in retrospect as one seamless, awful era and resulted in a longer-term and more substantial increase in the role of government.

In March 1931, following the tentative positive stirrings in the economy, further demands on the banking system emerged. The public again started to withdraw deposits from banks, a cause whose negative effect on the money supply is multiplied because banks are subject to only partial reserve requirements. When their reserves are reduced substantially, they must call in loans and liquidate assets in order to generate cash. Between February and August 1931, commercial bank deposits declined by almost 7 percent of their total. This was more than in the entire period from August 1929 to February 1931.

Other domestic economic policies worsened the national and international economies. The Hawley-Smoot tariff in 1930 was reciprocated by higher tariffs elsewhere, discouraging international trade. Although at the time the United States engaged in less international trade than other countries did, the increase in American tariffs discouraged export-producing industries around the world, diminishing all economies. Furthermore, in this era when economic statistics were not as available and reliable as they have since become, the decline in international trade caused by the Hawley-Smoot tariff may have assumed psychological importance beyond its practical effects—similar to the psychological importance of the stock market crash and the fall of the Bank of the United States.

In May 1931 Austria's Kreditanstalt, its largest private bank, failed. At the time, Austria was a more important actor in world affairs than it would become after World War II. This bank failure led to reverberations particularly in Germany, which experienced bank closings in July. Then, in September 1931, as Friedman began his senior year at Rutgers, Britain went off the gold standard. Henceforward, the pound was no longer convertible into gold. The Federal Reserve Board's counterproductive reaction to these events was, two years into a very significant economic downturn, to raise interest rates to stem the flow of gold from the United States.

Most of the decline in the American money supply, as well as most bank failures, occurred after September 1931. In August and September, 463 commercial banks closed in the United States. In October, another 522 followed, and between November and January, 875 more—a total of 1,860 bank failures in the six months between August 1931 and January 1932.

Even at this point, had appropriate monetary policies been followed, the American economy could have stabilized at a higher level than it did. Friedman and Schwartz postulated the counter-factual circumstance, that following Britain's departure from the gold standard, the Federal Reserve engaged in substantial open market purchases of government securities. In this case, the money supply would not have contracted nearly as much, banking liquidity would have eased substantially, and there would have been significantly fewer bank failures. Instead, between August 1931 and January 1932, the national money supply declined at an annual rate of 31 percent. The economy was in free fall.

Then, in the spring of 1932, after strong pressure from Congress, the Federal Reserve engaged in large open-market purchases of government bonds, thereby stemming the decline in the stock of money. Once again, as in the beginning of 1931, it appeared that the economy might be close to turning a corner. Both the stock market and production rose. Personal income continued to decline, but at a much lower rate. Other economic indicators were modestly positive.

As was the case previously, however, a turnaround in 1932 was not to be. When Congress adjourned for the summer, the Federal Reserve ceased its more expansive monetary policy and economic decline continued. In addition, politics supervened. Roosevelt's election in November 1932 injected significant uncertainty into the economy.

It was natural that Hoover, who presided over the worst economic debacle in national history, would be thrown out of office in 1932, when Friedman as in his first year at Chicago. About one individual seeking work in four was unemployed, deflation was in the double digits, banks were failing by the hundreds and even thousands, and national output had declined by almost one-third since Hoover had taken office in 1929. Roosevelt won an electoral college landslide, 472 votes to 59, and swept large Democratic majorities into both houses of Congress. Uncertainty about the policies that the new administration would follow made economic circumstances more unstable. Bank failures resumed, the stock of money again began to decline, and by the time that Roosevelt took office in March 1933, about half of the states had declared banking holidays. Indeed, among Roosevelt's first actions after being sworn in was to proclaim a weeklong national banking holiday. When the holiday lifted, 5,000 banks did not reopen their doors.

Later aspects of the Great Depression confirm the potency of monetary policy. The recovery that began in 1933 was largely a result of an expanding money supply. The recession of 1937–1938 was caused mainly by doubling bank reserve requirements, which contracted the money supply. Economic expansion in World War II coincided with a very stimulative monetary policy.

The foregoing is now the generally accepted version among economists of the Great Depression's course in the United States. This was not always the case. The importance of *A Monetary History of the United States* is that it undercuts much of the basis for Keynesianism, the welfare state, and Marxism.

Keynes put forward a different picture of the causes and course of the Great Depression. Essentially, he looked to nonmonetary factors as its source and found them in sclerotic capitalism. According to Keynes, the investment opportunities that had existed in the nineteenth century no longer existed, and people were saving too much. To solve the problem, it was the responsibility of government to macromanage the economy. But if the depression was mostly caused by inappropriate monetary policy, as Friedman believes, rather than a consequence of decaying capitalism, as Keynes held, much of the justification for Keynesian intervention is lost. It is not that capitalism is inherently flawed. It is that it was not given the appropriate circumstances in which to flourish.

Much of the welfare state in the United States originated in the Great Depression. Because the reasons behind it were not understood at the time, the Depression led to vastly expanded government regulation of the economy and to many social programs, particularly at the national level. A misunderstanding of positive economies led to different policies than might have otherwise been adopted.

Friedman has never been, and is not now, doctrinaire with respect to government's role. He thinks that this role can and should vary over time and place. He is not an anarchist. Nonetheless, to oppose anarchism is not to endorse the welfare state. Apart from regulatory aspects of the welfare state (which originally were intended to boost the economy, a fact that is hard to remember now), many social welfare programs were begun because it was thought that free private property capitalism is inherently unstable, unreliable, and nonproductive. But if capitalism is, in fact, incredibly productive, much of the original justification for the welfare state is lost.

Concerning Marxism, the Great Depression seemed to many to confirm the theories and predictions of Karl Marx, who wrote in the *Communist Manifesto* of "commercial crises that by their periodical return put the existence of the entire bourgeois society on trial, each time more threateningly."[16] Many Marxists viewed the depression as the final crisis of capitalism. But again, if the Great Depression mostly reflected inappropriate monetary policy, Marx's status as a prophet and scientist is greatly reduced.

Friedman offers these thoughts on lessons of the Great Depression:

The major lesson of the Great Depression that has affected our lives is the wrong lesson, a misinterpretation of the Great Depression. There is no doubt that the major lesson [was] . . . you could not count on the private enterprise system to maintain prosperity and that you had to rely heavily on government to play a major role. If you take the period before 1929, so far as public opinion in general is concerned, government was regarded as a necessary evil. I think there was widespread support for the kind of views that Jefferson had expressed a century and a half earlier on the virtues of a small government and of limiting the role of government. The Great Depression changed that because the lesson that the public at large learned from the Great Depression was that it was the result of a failure of business, a failure of capitalism, . . . and that in order to be safe in the future they would have to rely much more heavily on government. That was the lesson that was in fact learned from the Depression. . . . [I]n my opinion, the lesson that should have been learned, the right lesson, was that government let them down. That it was mismanagement of the monetary system that produced it and not a failure of the market system.[17]

There has in recent years been a spate of popular and semipopular works challenging the view that the New Deal contributed to economic recovery and putting forward the opposing opinion that the New Deal was inimical to recovery. These works include, most prominently, David Kennedy's *Freedom from Fear: The American People in Depression and War, 1929–1945,* the ninth volume in the Oxford History of the United States, published in 1999. Although Kennedy does not mention Friedman other than in footnotes, Kennedy indicts the New Deal as a massive, counterproductive boondoggle. Other recent works in this line include Thomas Hall and David Ferguson's *The Great Depression: An International Disaster of Perverse Economic Policies* (1998), Gene Smiley's 2002 *Rethinking the Great Depression* and Jim Powell's 2003 *FDR's Folly: How Roosevelt and His New Deal Prolonged the Great Depression.*

Smiley writes: "Although various aspects of their analysis have been criticized, chapters 7–9 of Milton Friedman and Anna Jacobson Schwartz's classic study *A Monetary History of the United States,*

1867–1960 remain the starting point for studying the Great Depression and the recovery in the 1930s."[18] Friedman reviewed Powell's manuscript in draft and provided this promotional blurb: "Admirers of FDR credit his New Deal with restoring the American economy after the disastrous contraction of 1929–33. Truth to tell—as Powell demonstrates without a shadow of a doubt—the New Deal hampered recovery from the contraction, prolonged and added to unemployment, and set the stage for ever more intrusive and costly government."[19]

The reception of *A Monetary History of the United States,* almost exclusively from academics, was mostly enthusiastic regarding content and scholarship, while not agreeing with its policy. Allan Meltzer wrote in 1965:

> This volume is a delight to the economist. The book is clearly destined to be a classic, perhaps one of the few emerging in that role rather than growing into it. The reader cannot fail to be impressed by the size of the task to which the authors committed themselves, by the authors' ability to treat the broad sweep of a century of monetary history without being overcome by the mass of detail that they carefully examine, by the originality of the scholarship that is everywhere displayed, and by a host of other considerations. [20]

According to Harry Johnson: "The long-awaited monetary history of the United States by Friedman and Schwartz is in every sense of the term a monumental scholarly accomplishment. . . . The volume sets . . . a new standard for the writing of monetary history . . . It is, moreover, written in an eminently readable style."[21] James Tobin concluded a twenty-one-page review in the *American Economic Review* by saying: "This is one of those rare books that leave their mark on all future research on the subject."[22]

Not all of the professional response was positive. Schwartz emphasizes that the initial response to *A Monetary History*'s normative conclusions was hostile. She comments that the "reaction of the profession after the book was published was . . . we were some kind of nuts! Who believed that money had anything to do with the way the economy functioned? . . . It took a long time . . . until the message of *A Monetary History* became convincing to a large part of the profession."[23] As recently as 1987, only 7 percent of economics students at the Massachusetts Institute of Technology thought that inflation is primarily a monetary phenomenon (versus 84 percent at Chicago).[24]

Schwartz was three years younger than Friedman, and she was and remains a researcher at the National Bureau of Economic Research. She received her master's degree in economics from Columbia in 1935 and became a member of the National Bureau staff in 1941. Notwithstanding that she and Friedman were both at Columbia and in the National Bureau from the middle 1930s, they did not meet until World War II. Schwartz recalls that when Milton and Rose were in New York during the war and civilian production was limited, "they came to my door to borrow a stroller my oldest son had outgrown."[25] They had no further contact until Friedman resumed his connection with the National Bureau in the late 1940s. Their collaboration extends from *A Monetary History of the United States, 1867–1960* to *Monetary Statistics of the United States* in 1970 and *Monetary Trends in the United States and the United Kingdom* in 1982.

Schwartz says, in response to a question about the one particular "book, article, or person that did the most [in] shaping how you think as an economist": "Undoubtedly my contact with Friedman. He transformed my understanding of economics and it's because he is such a stimulating person to be with. You can't talk to him about anything without having a new idea as a result." She also says, "He could tell me 'No, that doesn't make sense,' and I could tell him 'No, I don't think that makes sense.'"[26]

In a 2004 symposium on *A Monetary History of the United States*, Friedman said that it is a

> source of real gratification that Anna Schwartz's and my book should be deemed worthy of a retrospective after forty years. The exhaustive research of the past forty years plus the additional forty years of history certainly require many modifications in detail in the story as we told it.

However, I believe that our major themes have held up remarkably well. The most controversial of those—our attribution to the Federal Reserve of a major share of the responsibility for the 1929–33 contraction—has become almost conventional wisdom. Money does matter.[27]

14

CHICAGO SCHOOL
OF ECONOMICS

he Chicago school of economics is frequently mentioned in discussions about Friedman, and especially since the view of the Chicago school here is somewhat different than his, it is appropriate to consider it. There was no "Chicago school of economics" when Friedman began to teach at the University of Chicago in 1946. This appellation derives almost exclusively, if not exclusively, from the period after World War II. No one has been able to locate a written reference to a "Chicago school of economics" before the postwar era—indeed, until the mid-1950s.

The Department of Economics at the University of Chicago has undergone four major periods of development. The first was the founding era, which coincided with James Laurence Laughlin's years in and as chairman of the department, from 1892 to 1916. The second was the era of Jacob Viner and Frank Knight, which began with Viner's appointment in 1916 and concluded with his departure in 1946. The third was the Friedman era, which should be seen as coterminous with the Chicago school of economics, which extended from his appointment to the faculty in 1946 to his retirement in 1976. Finally, there is the post-Friedman era, from

1977 to the present, which incorporates the work of Gary Becker, Robert Lucas, and others.

There have been "Chicago schools" in other disciplines, including law, political science, and sociology, and it is possible that there was some oral (as distinct from written) mention of a "Chicago school of economics" prior to the post–World War II era. Paul Samuelson writes: "By 1935 'Chicago School' was a familiar idiom."[1] According to Friedman: "I can't believe that if you could go through the American Economic Review . . . [for] the years '25 to '30 that you wouldn't find references to 'Chicago School.'"[2]

Nevertheless, Stigler wrote in his autobiography that he had "found no hints" of a distinctive Chicago school "before about 1950, and no widespread recognition of the school for another five years. . . . By the 1960s, however, the profession had widely agreed that there was a Chicago School of Economics. Edward H. Chamberlin had written a chapter on the Chicago School . . . in 1957, the earliest such explicit essay I have found."[3]

Chamberlin's chapter indicates that the idea of the Chicago school that later became prominent was not fixed in 1957. According to Chamberlin, the Chicago school "believes in 'competitive theory,' but such a belief is widely held and would not in itself distinguish a Chicago school. It is distinguished by the zeal with which the theory of monopolistic competition has been attacked. . . . I shall therefore call it the Chicago School of Anti-Monopolistic Competition."[4] Although criticism of the theory of monopolistic competition—the view that businesses are best considered to be monopolies and are able to obtain monopoly profits and charge monopoly prices—was certainly part of the Chicago school approach, in part through the work of Aaron Director, this was by no means the whole of what the Chicago school later became known for. Chamberlin's chapter indicates that the identity of the Chicago school was not yet fully formed in the popular academic mind in the late 1950s.

According to Stigler: "There was no Chicago School of Economics . . . at the end of World War II."[5] In response to the question of whether there was a "Chicago school of economics" when he taught there, Jacob Viner wrote in 1969: "It was not until after I left Chicago . . . that I began to hear rumors about a 'Chicago School' which was engaged in organized battle for laissez faire and the 'quantity theory of money' and against 'imperfect competition' theorizing and 'Keynesianism.' I remained skeptical . . . until I attended a conference sponsored by University of Chicago professors in 1951."[6]

Most significantly, in correspondence dating from 1945 or 1944, Henry Simons proposed an Institute of Political Economy at the University of Chicago that would bring together a group of "traditional liberal" or "libertarian" economists and that Chicago would be an appropriate location because its "economics still has some distinctively traditional-liberal connotations and some prestige." However, even at Chicago, traditional liberalism would "shortly be lost unless special measures are taken. . . . In the Department [of Economics] we are becoming a small minority."[7]

Friedman remarks in an interview that what made economics different at Chicago than elsewhere when he was a student was not political perspective, but "treating economics as a serious subject versus treating it as a branch of mathematics. . . . The fundamental difference between Chicago at that time and let's say Harvard was that, at Chicago, economics was a serious subject to be used in discussing real problems. . . . For Harvard, economics was an intellectual discipline on a par with mathematics. . . . It wasn't going to enable you to solve any problems."[8] Gary Becker shares this view with respect to Viner's "emphasis on the empirical relevance of microeconomic theory, . . . on the necessity of testing a theory with historical and other empirical evidence."[9] At the same time, Viner did not have Friedman's statistical empirical emphasis. According to Mark Skousen, Becker believes that "rigorous testing of theories with empirical data is Friedman's most important contribution to technical economics."[10]

D. Gale Johnson was a member of the economics faculty at Chicago from 1944 until his death in 2003, also serving as provost, and he was a student in economics at Chicago from approximately 1938 to 1940. When asked in 2001 whether the appellation "Chicago school of economics" was used in the 1930s, he replied:

> *Johnson:* I don't think the reference came until the 1950s.
> *Interviewer:* Why?
> *Johnson:* I suspect Friedman had a lot to do with it.[11]

Many agree that the phrase "Chicago school of economics" was not used until after World War II. According to Henry Spiegel, a well-read and judicious historian of economic thought: "At the time when Viner taught at Chicago, the designation 'Chicago School' was not yet a commonly used term."[12] No reference to the "Chicago school" has been found in histories of economic thought written before the mid-1950s, including Joseph Schumpeter's massive *History of Economic Analysis*, Joseph Dorfman's multivolume *The Economic Mind in American Civilization*, and Paul Homan's *Contemporary Economic Thought*. Similarly, there is apparently no reference to a "Chicago school" in the *American Economic Review* or *Journal of Political Economy* before the 1950s.

Friedman himself provides evidence that the name "Chicago school of economics" was not used before the postwar era. Writing in his memoirs about the first meeting of the Mont Pelerin Society, a group of libertarian-oriented academics and others, in 1947, he quoted journalist John Davenport as saying that these participants included a "sprinkling of what became known as the Chicago School"[13]—that is, they were not known as the Chicago school yet.

The Chicago school of economics is largely the Friedman school of economics; his positions and views are those associated with the school. Stigler wrote in his autobiography that the "origin of the school can be identified only if the central theses of the school are known. They were two: a policy position and a method of studying economics. The policy position was the more commonly recognized element of the school, and clearly Milton Friedman . . . was the primary architect." According to Stigler, Friedman influenced the policy positions of the Chicago school in these areas: "He revived the study of monetary economics, which had become moribund. He used the quantity theory . . . to launch a powerful attack on the Keynesian School. Second, he presented strong defenses of laissez-faire policies, and invented important new policy proposals." Stigler also notes that Friedman did "much empirical work to document money's strong historical role in American economic life."[14]

Melvin Reder, who was a student at Chicago in the early 1940s and later a faculty member there, and who has written several articles on the history of economics at Chicago, says that after Friedman became a member of the faculty, he "swiftly took over the intellectual leadership of one faction of the Department and energetically attacked the views and proposals of the others. His vigor in debate and the content of his arguments set the tone and public image of Chicago economics for at least a quarter century." Reder refers to a "Friedman Era" at Chicago in the 1950s and 1960s, when a "steady stream of papers on money, methodology, price theory, the consumption function, [and] public policy proposals . . . kept economists at Chicago and elsewhere busy reacting to various Friedman initiatives. Outside Chicago—and in this period I was an outsider— the force of Friedman's ideas was very strong; at Chicago, it must have been even stronger."[15]

Friedman's best presentation of economics at Chicago is contained in his remarks to the university board of trustees in 1974:

> To economists the world over, "Chicago" designates not a city, not even a University, but a "school." . . . In discussions of economic policy, "Chicago" stands for a belief in the efficacy of the free market as a means of organizing resources, for skepticism about government intervention into economic affairs, and for emphasis on the quantity of money as a key factor in producing inflation. In discussions of economic science, "Chicago" stands for an approach that takes seriously the use of economic theory as a tool for analyzing a startlingly wide range of concrete problems . . . ; for an approach that insists on the empirical testing of theoretical generalizations.[16]

15

CAPITALISM AND FREEDOM

riedman was at a peak in his academic career as *A Monetary History of the United States* was published in 1963. Although he would continue to contribute to economics as an academic discipline, never again would he challenge a historical understanding of the world on such a broad and comprehensive scale. After the book's publication, he increasingly moved in the direction of attempting to influence public opinion directly and through government leaders rather than at a remove through academia.

He transitioned over his career from a focus mostly on academic economics and teaching to involvement in public policy and advocacy. Although he was apolitical early in his career, he was involved in practical issues of government economic policy and study. Indeed, he originally become an economist and attended the University of Chicago as a student because of interest in and concern about conditions in the Great Depression. His early involvement in public policy began with his work for the National Resources Committee in New Deal Washington, continued through his work for the National Bureau of Economic Research in New York, and culminated in his work for the Treasury Department. Before he was thirty years old, he testified before the House Ways and Means Committee and worked diligently to implement income tax withholding at the source to help with World War II financing.

In 1946 Friedman and Stigler coauthored the anti–rent control polemic, "Roofs or Ceilings?" This pamphlet foreshadowed Friedman's later career as an economic writer for the general public. Friedman, Stigler, and others attended the first meeting in 1947 of what became the Mont Pelerin Society—an international association of classical liberal and libertarian academics and a few journalists and political figures—in Switzerland. This was Friedman's first trip outside of the United States. He considers his attendance at this meeting to have been important in his growing interest in public policy from an explicitly libertarian, or classical liberal, point of view. Others from Chicago to attend this meeting were Frank Knight, Aaron Director, and Friedrich Hayek. Hayek, the author of the 1944 international best-seller *The Road to Serfdom,* had organized the meeting. He joined the Committee on Social Thought at the University of Chicago in 1950, and Friedman attended his seminar frequently; it became another source of his expanding interest in the philosophical foundations of free private property capitalism.

Friedman continued to participate in national public policy issues through the 1950s, and his involvement skyrocketed in the 1960s. He appeared on many University of Chicago Round Table national radio discussion programs, increasingly wrote for popular audiences, and spoke to public and student audiences around the nation as a visiting lecturer and speaker. He continued to testify before Congress as a private citizen. After presenting the quantity theory of money to a Joint Economic Committee of Congress in 1959, he had this exchange with the chairman:

> *The Chairman:* Mr. Friedman, the Federal Reserve Board loves to brief Senators and Congressmen on economic affairs. . . . I wonder if we could arrange a seminar in which you could brief these gentlemen on these equations. . . . I think an advanced course for the Federal

Reserve and possibly even the Council of Economic Advisers would be very good. Could you possibly do that?
Mr. Friedman: A professor is always willing to profess.[1]

Friedman recalls that Senator Paul Douglas, the chairman of the committee who previously had taught at Chicago, called him whenever he wished to have someone testify against Federal Reserve Board policies.

Starting in the 1950s, the popular media began to take notice of Friedman's intellectual abilities and engaging personality, and he began to be identified as a leading economist. Since he was both a renowned academic and politically conservative (or, in his terminology, a classical liberal or libertarian), he was an excellent counterpoint guest to representatives from the dominant liberal view. He was adamant that an overwhelmingly liberal (in a twentieth-century sense) opinion pervaded and prevailed in academia, journalism, and much of government from the 1940s to 1970s and in many respects to the present. He commented in 1995, to an interviewer in his thirties:

You're a young man, and you have no idea of the climate of opinion in 1945 to 1960 or '70. I really have a hard time knowing how to tell you about that, because it really is unbelievable.... I published *Capitalism and Freedom* in 1962.... It's a book that's now sold close to a million copies. It was not reviewed by any American publications, other than the *American Economic Review*.... I was a full professor at the University of Chicago; I was very well known in the academic world—it is inconceivable that a book on the other side by someone in that same position would not have been reviewed in every publication—the *New York Times,* the *Chicago Tribune* . . .

The evidence is overwhelming about the kind of intellectual atmosphere. I had a letter two or three years ago from . . . [someone who] had been a student at Duke University in the 1950s. He was taking economics, and he was finding himself always at odds with his teachers. Finally, he went to one of his teachers and said, isn't there any economist who agrees with what I'm . . . saying? And they said, well, when we have . . . discussions among ourselves, we always say you sound like a crazy fellow out in Chicago by the name of Milton Friedman.[2]

The intellectual atmosphere was so confining at many colleges and universities, according to Friedman, that their libraries did not contain copies of his books.

Others provide testimony that when he began to enunciate his views, Friedman was largely considered a heretic, a Rasputin, or a numskull, or some combination of all three. According to John Turner, even in the early 1970s Friedman was "viewed outside of the department as on the fringe, so conservative."[3] Robert Lucas notes that Paul Samuelson in his *Foundations of Economic Analysis* (1947) went out of his way to downplay Friedman by "disagreeing with a point in Friedman's 1935 article on elasticities, and this after dismissing the whole idea of elasticities as unimportant 'except possibly as mental exercises for beginning students'!"[4]

According to Gary Becker: "Friedman's rise to the top was not smooth and was filled with controversy. The obstacles were personally painful, but they renewed his dedication to research and accustomed him to being unpopular. The obstacles also made all the sweeter the adoption of many of his ideas . . . and the introduction by governments the world over of many of his programs—such as flexible exchange rates, flatter tax schedules, and privatization of many government activities."[5]

Capitalism and Freedom is Friedman's popular work most likely to enter the pantheon of great works in political philosophy. In retrospect, it has taken on somewhat more importance in his thought than it did at the time of publication. The work is something of a departure from his main work in academic economics. In fact, it is the beginning of his career as an advocate of less government and freer and more competitive markets as the principle by which to order societies.

The book developed over a number of years. Apparently his first sustained writing in political philosophy is a 1951 piece, "Neo-Liberalism and Its Prospects," written for a Norwegian journal. In this little-known article, he first develops the idea, following the British historian A. V. Dicey, that there is a difference between trends of opinion and courses of action, and that the latter often follow the former at the remove of a generation or more in public policy. There is a lag in politics as well as in economics.

An article he wrote in 1955, "Liberalism, Old Style," for *Collier's Year Book* is the more proximate predecessor of *Capitalism and Freedom*. "Liberalism, Old Style" was written in response to an article by Russell Kirk, who in 1953 published *The Conservative Mind*—the work from which the contemporary conservative (as distinct from libertarian) movement dates. In 1954 Kirk wrote an article on conservatism for *Collier's*. A reader wrote suggesting an entry on liberalism. Friedman's essay the next year was one result, together with an article by Seymour Harris titled "Liberalism Today." In the 1940s and 1950s, what is today called libertarianism, classical liberalism, or nineteenth-century liberalism was often termed "true liberalism" by proponents to distinguish it from the variant that emerged in America in the 1930s, which was the subject of Harris's article.

Friedman's move from technical academic economics to popular writing in public policy coincided with his switch over time from economics to political philosophy, or at least to works more concerned with social organization than with immediate economic practice. He became less a social scientist and more a public figure, less an economist and more a political philosopher. In addition, later in this second stage of his career, he wrote a number of essays (often in the form of introductions or forewords) that contributed to an understanding of the historical development of libertarian and classical liberal thought in the twentieth century.

From 1956 to 1961, he participated in a series of conferences sponsored by the William Volker Fund, which played a leading, though often unheralded, role in propagating libertarian ideas from the 1940s to the early 1960s. As well as sponsoring the conferences in which Friedman and others participated, the fund paid for Ludwig von Mises's position at New York University and Hayek's and Director's positions at the University of Chicago. It published a series of books as well and provided initial support for the Institute for Humane Studies and the Foundation for Economic Education.

The Volker conferences in which Friedman participated were held each year in June and lasted a week to ten days. He attended those held at Wabash College in Indiana, the University of North Carolina, Claremont Men's College in California, and Oklahoma State University. Friedman was on the faculty for the conferences, each of which gathered about thirty or so primarily young academics from around the nation.

Rose subsequently organized Friedman's Volker lectures into the form in which they appear in *Capitalism and Freedom*. The title page lists the work as "with the assistance of Rose D. Friedman."[6] Milton said that Rose should more appropriately be considered its coauthor.

In the political philosophy that he presents in *Capitalism and Freedom*, Friedman is highly influenced by John Stuart Mill, Hayek, and the American founding fathers. With respect to Mill and his utilitarian predecessors, Friedman writes that to the "free man, the country is the collection of the individuals who compose it, not something over and above them."[7] This is a very similar sentiment to what Mill's intellectual godfather and the founder of utilitarianism, Jeremy Bentham, expressed: "The interest of the community is one of the most general expressions that can occur in the phraseology of morals. . . . The community is a fictitious body, composed of the individual persons who are considered as constituting as it were its members. The interest of the community then is, what?—the sum of the interests of the . . . members who compose it."[8]

Friedman's philosophy, following the utilitarians, is individualism. "The heart of the liberal philosophy is a belief in the dignity of the individual,"[9] he writes. Friedman passionately believes that each individual has value. This is why he so emphasizes human freedom. Only in a condition of freedom can each individual develop himself or herself to the fullest. There is no good of society not found in the good of individuals, just as there is no society apart from the individuals who compose it. Friedman's, the libertarian, the classical liberal, and the utilitarian philosophies all place the individual at the center of the universe and place the individual's greatest good, happiness, and freedom as the *summum bonum,* or ultimate good. It says much about Friedman that his two major popular works have "free" in their titles: *Capitalism and Freedom* and *Free to Choose.*

Many passages in *Capitalism and Freedom* contain echoes of Mill, especially from *On Liberty,* Mill's great classical liberal and libertarian work. *Capitalism and Freedom* is a linear descendent of the freedom philosophy enunciated in *On Liberty.* Together with *On Liberty* and *The Road to Serfdom, Capitalism and Freedom* is one of the great brief works in libertarian thought and policy. Animating all these works is their emphasis on the individual—on the importance of each individual and on the moral necessity to treat each human being as someone of utmost worth. Friedman's focus is individual human freedom.

Like Mill, Friedman emphasizes the importance of genius and writes that the great accomplishments in history "were the product of individual genius."[10] Mill's parallel statement in *On Liberty* was: "There are but few persons, in comparison with the whole of mankind, whose experiments, if adopted by others, would be likely to be any improvement on established practice. But these few are the salt of the earth; without them, human life would become a stagnant pool."[11] Friedman wrote in *Capitalism and Freedom* of "the exceptional few," saying that "they . . . are the hope of the future" and that "the specially talented are always few."[12]

Like Mill, Friedman emphasizes a "social climate permitting variety and diversity."[13] Mill wrote in *On Liberty* that "free scope should be given to varieties of character."[14] Friedman wrote in *Capitalism and Freedom* that "[g]overnment can never duplicate the variety and diversity of individual action."[15] Mill concluded *On Liberty:* "A State which dwarfs its men . . . will find that with small men no great thing can really be accomplished."[16] Friedman holds that "freedom has nothing to say about what an individual does with his freedom. . . . Indeed, a major aim of the liberal is to leave the ethical problem for the individual to wrestle with."[17] According to Mill: "The human faculties of perception, judgment, discriminative feeling, and even moral preference, are exercised only in making a choice.... The mental and moral, like the muscular powers, are improved only by being used."[18] Friedman writes: "Freedom is a tenable objective only for responsible individuals. We do not believe in freedom for madmen or children."[19] Mill held that the libertarian doctrine is "meant to apply only to human beings in the maturity of their faculties. We are not speaking of children."[20]

Even Friedman's metaphors and phraseology appear not infrequently to resemble some of Mill's. Friedman writes: "Freedom is a rare and delicate plant."[21] Mill wrote that "[c]apacity for the nobler feelings is in most natures a very tender plant."[22] Given Friedman's exceptional verbal recall, he may have been more influenced by Mill than he recognizes.

Friedman's philosophical debt to Hayek is more explicit. Hayek was a colleague at the University of Chicago when Friedman wrote *Capitalism and Freedom*. Friedman regularly participated in his seminar, which mostly concerned political philosophy, including sessions on "The Liberal Tradition" and "Social and Political Thought." Also, Hayek's major work of his Chicago period, *The Constitution of Liberty*, appeared in 1960. Friedman was among those who read chapter drafts of the manuscript.

Many passages in *Capitalism and Freedom* reflect Hayek's influence. When Friedman writes that "[e]ven though the men who wield this [state] power initially be of good will and even though they be not corrupted by the power they exercise, the power will both attract and form men of a different stamp,"[23] he could practically be paraphrasing Hayek, who held that in a collectivist society, "the worst get on top."[24] Like Hayek, Friedman terms his own position liberal (in a nineteenth-century sense), not conservative. Friedman refers to Hayek in the text of *Capitalism and Freedom:* "Recognizing the implicit threat to individualism, the intellectual descendants of the Philosophical Radicals—Dicey, Mises, Hayek, and Simons, to mention only a few—feared that a continued movement toward central-ized control of economic activity would prove *The Road to Serfdom*, as Hayek entitled his penetrating analysis of the process." When Friedman says that "the great threat to freedom is the concentration of power,"[25] he expresses an idea similar to that of Hayek, who said: "It is not the source but the limitation of power which prevents it from being arbitrary."[26]

From America's founding fathers, Friedman was impressed, like so many others, by the idea of limited government. When he writes, "Government is necessary to preserve our freedom, it is an instru-ment through which we can exercise our freedom; yet by concentrat-ing power in political hands, it is also a threat to freedom. . . . [T]he scope of government must be limited,"[27] he makes almost the same argument that James Madison did in *The Federalist*: "What is govern-ment itself, but the greatest of all reflections on human nature? If men were angels, no government would be necessary. If angels were to govern men, neither external nor internal controls on government would be necessary. In framing a government which is to be admin-istered by men over men, the great difficulty lies in this: you must first enable the government to control the governed; and in the next place oblige it to control itself."[28] Limited government means cir-cumscribed, nonarbitrary, delineated government.

Capitalism and Freedom is mostly made up of chapters that dis-cuss important contemporary public policy issues. The essential spirit of the work is given by the titles of the first two chapters, "The Relation Between Economic Freedom and Political Freedom" and "The Role of Government in a Free Society." Among the great twen-tieth-century contributions to the classical liberal tradition was to emphasize the importance of economic liberty to political liberty, a relationship that was not well understood prior to that time. The goal of most liberal reformers in the seventeenth through nineteenth centuries was to extend voting rights. The key issues were political rather than economic. If voting was extended to all adult members of society, earlier liberal reformers often believed, all would be well.

Those reformers frequently viewed political democracy as the panacea of societal issues.

Friedman, following in the footsteps of Hayek and others, argues that without *economic* liberty, political liberty is impossible:

> There is an intimate connection between economics and politics. . . . [O]nly certain combinations of political and economic arrangements are possible. . . . [A] society which is socialist cannot also be democratic . . . .. Historical evidence speaks with a single voice on the relation between political freedom and a free market. I know of no example in time or place of a society that has been marked by a large measure of political freedom, and that has not also used something comparable to a free market to organize the bulk of economic activity.[29]

Economic democracy, in the form of state control of productive enterprise, is a false concept, according to Friedman; it is not democratic. It merely substitutes one overpowering business owner—government—for many competing ones. In addition, state control of economic production is inefficient. Again, following predecessors such as Hayek and Mises, Friedman argues that free private property capitalism is the most productive form of economic order and that socialism—or greater government intervention in the economy generally—is inefficient. Today these beliefs may seem truisms; in the late 1950s and early 1960s, however, they were anything but. When Friedman, Hayek, and others put forward the ideas that capitalism is consistent with—indeed, is the economic embodiment of—freedom and that it is the most productive economic order yet discovered, only a small minority held these beliefs.

At a 1962 testimonial dinner for Hayek as he prepared to move from Chicago to Freiburg, West Germany, Friedman made the following comments on differences between scientific and popular influence. Since these remarks are on the cusp of his own move from mostly scientific work to mostly attempting to influence public opinion, they are of particular interest:

> The thing that is interesting about Fritz Hayek . . . is the extent to which he has succeeded in straddling two kinds of worlds. The membership of

this room consists of people who are here because of their interest in Fritz Hayek's work in science and also those who are here because of their interest in the enormous role he has played in spreading ideas among the public at large. . . . This attempt to influence opinion is something that is very seldom combined with thorough, deep, and profound scholarly work that can influence the course of science . . . . And I think it is probably true that the people of each of the two groups here do not recognize how costly and difficult it is to bridge these two worlds. . . .

I think . . . there is a very big cost that is not easy to recognize in terms of the effect on the attitude of the rest of the scholarly world that derives from . . . influencing opinion. Of course, we have to recognize that the effect depends on what kind of an opinion you are trying to influence. There is no cost in terms of the attitudes of the rest of the scholarly world if one is simply expressing the majority opinion. . . .

I've always thought, incidentally, that many of us should welcome the fact [that] . . . a particular policy idea we hold does have this adverse effect on the opinions of other people . . . because it means that those of us who hold our views have to be better to get recognized than people who hold the other views. And in the long run, what matters is the quality of people who propose the ideas and not their number and not their position.[30]

Friedman considered *Capitalism and Freedom* to be his best work for a popular audience. Comparing it to the later *Free to Choose,* he said that "*Capitalism and Freedom* is a better book."[31] He also wrote that the "earlier book is the more philosophical and abstract, and hence more fundamental."[32]

16

TRAVEL AND GOLDWATER

he Friedmans were great travelers. Interspersed throughout Milton's academic career were many trips abroad and in the United States. *Capitalism and Freedom* appeared in 1962, as did *Price Theory: A Provisional Text,* based on students' notes from his price theory course. *A Monetary History of the United States* was published in 1963. In part as a reward for all this work, Milton and Rose decided to travel around the world in 1962 and 1963. By this time, their children were in college—Jan at the University of California at Berkeley and David at Harvard. Milton and Rose were freer than they had been for years.

The practical purpose for the year-long sojourn was to allow Milton to observe monetary arrangements in countries other than the United States, which had been his focus for a decade and a half on the *Monetary History* project, and Great Britain, where the family had spent the 1953–1954 academic year. The nonprofessional reason was to allow the couple to have a great experience and to celebrate their twenty-fifth wedding anniversary abroad.

They spent two months or more each in Yugoslavia, Israel, Greece, India, and Japan, and visited sixteen other countries for shorter periods. They started their *Wanderjahr* ("wandering year"), as they refer to it, in Paris, sailing from New York on the SS *Queen Elizabeth.* They then proceeded to Belgium for a meeting of the

Mont Pelerin Society. Thereafter they went to Poland and the Soviet Union.

The trip to the Soviet Union began inauspiciously. Milton and Rose decided to travel by bus in order to see more of the country. Their bus broke down and, as a result of Soviet regulations, they and their fellow passengers literally had to push the bus across the Polish-Soviet border because the Polish tow truck was not permitted to cross the border. The bus was then towed by cattle truck to Brest in the Soviet Union. Rose says that the hotel there was "by all odds the worst . . . we have ever stayed in—and in the course of a long life of extensive travel, we have stayed at some bad ones." She also notes that the rural areas they passed "showed little change from descriptions of . . . fifty or a hundred years ago. The same village well and horse-drawn carts, a preponderance of women bent double working in the fields, and an almost complete absence of mechanized equipment."[1] The trip provided Milton a valuable opportunity to see communism firsthand.

From the Soviet Union they traveled to Yugoslavia. Although communist, Yugoslavia was independent of Soviet control and evolved a more open system of communism than existed elsewhere in eastern Europe and the Soviet Union. Friedman worked at the Yugoslav national bank with a student of a former student. Here, he quickly determined that "the key relations . . . we had established for capitalist United States held in communist Yugoslavia. Monetary theory per se is strictly nonideological."[2]

The next stop was Israel. As elsewhere, there many former students were delighted to host the couple. That the Friedmans have had so many friends around the world who were always glad to see them says much about their character. In Israel, he gave seminars at Hebrew University and various talks. As elsewhere, he and Rose did much sightseeing.

They spent the week before Christmas in Austria with Jan and David, where Milton engaged in one of his favorite sports, skiing, an activity he continued into his eighties. Then the couple went to

Greece, where Milton worked at the central bank in Athens. At this time he recognized that the legal status of checks greatly influences their use. In Greece, because writing a bad check is merely a civil offense, checks are not used much; the penalty for their improper use—suing someone—is cumbersome. Where, however, writing a bad check is a criminal offense, as in the United States, the use of checks is common because the police and the criminal court system will enforce the laws. Accordingly, the "legal structure has a substantial effect on monetary figures,"[3] Friedman recognized. Currency is a larger proportion of the quantity of money in countries where checks are uncommon than in countries where they are used frequently.

The third major stop in the *Wanderjahr* was India, where Milton had spent a few weeks in 1955. As with so many visitors, he and Rose were impressed by both the country's beauty and its abysmal poverty. He studied monetary practices, gave lectures and talks, and had informal discussions with business and government leaders. As always, former students were available to meet, greet, and escort the couple. Milton was especially struck by the wastefulness of central planning, exchange controls, and restrictions on foreign trade in India, believing them to contribute greatly to the country's poverty. In addition, he observed the wastefulness and even counterproductiveness of much foreign aid, particularly when it strengthened the central government.

In two lectures in India (reprinted in his 1968 *Dollars and Deficits*), he makes the following comments:

(1) Inflation is always and everywhere a monetary phenomenon.
(2) Inflation is not inevitable in the course of development.
(3) Inflation is not likely . . . to promote development, unless it accelerates, in which case it can be only a temporary panacea.[4]

Let anybody buy and sell foreign exchange at any price mutually agreeable to buyer and seller. Remove import controls, remove subsidies on exports, and let there be a free market.[5]

Q: Do you approve of planned economic development?

> *A:* I am not sure I know what planned economic development is. . . .
> [T]his expression is . . . a contradiction in terms. If you . . . have
> extensive central planning . . . , you won't have much economic
> development.[6]

Throughout his career Friedman has made a number of predictions that subsequently proved correct, despite the fact that most other economists held opposing views. For example, in these lectures in India (together with an introductory note that he appended to them), Friedman predicted that the rupee would be devalued (he thought, in 1963, to about 7 rupees to the dollar; it was devalued to 7.5 rupees to the dollar in 1966); that inflation would increase in the United States and that some system of wage and price guidelines would be unsuccessfully attempted there; and that a fixed exchange rate in India not in line with the rate that would prevail in free international exchange would not endure. He was also prescient in his lecture "Why the American Economy Is Depression-Proof," reprinted in *Dollars and Deficits* as well, in maintaining before a Swedish audience that a major depression was unlikely to beset the American economy again, notwithstanding that many, perhaps most American economists thought otherwise at the end of World War II.

On the way to Japan, their last major stop, Milton and Rose visited Hong Kong, where he later played a leading role as a philosophical inspirer of and occasional technical adviser on the colony's highly successful free enterprise system. Jan and David joined their parents for the summer in Japan. Here as elsewhere, Milton found that essential monetary relationships hold—monetary relationships do not vary on the basis of country or culture. While in Japan, he received an honorary degree.

Milton and Rose visited twenty-one countries in their year of traveling. He wrote of the experience: "The trip was worthwhile and highly productive scientifically. Aside from my own writing, I did stimulate a good deal of work on monetary issues by other scholars. . . . More important for me personally, it gave me an insight into the politics as well as economics of monetary matters that I . . . could

[not] have gained in any other way."[7] Theoretical insight benefits from all sorts of empirical research and observation.

Friedman thought that the United States was headed in a libertarian direction in the early 1960s. He believed that American college students would have been receptive to libertarianism before the Vietnam War and especially before the draft, but those two events channeled change in a different direction. He writes: "In the early 1960s there was . . . a rising tide of support among the young for the party of liberty, for the principles of free, private enterprise, and a strictly limited government. I believe that tide would have continued to rise if the passions of the young had not been diverted by the Vietnam War and above all by conscription."[8]

Friedman's was not the only voice calling for a more libertarian society in the late 1950s and early 1960s. At the time, perhaps the best-known popular voices were Senator Barry Goldwater and novelist Ayn Rand. In his *The Conscience of a Conservative* (1960), Goldwater looked forward to politicians of the future who would see it as their duty to have "little interest in streamlining government or mak[ing] it more efficient," for they would mean "to reduce its size," whose aim would be not "to pass laws, but to repeal them."[9] An allied source of libertarian thought was William F. Buckley's *National Review,* which became the leading conservative news and opinion magazine in the United States at that time.

Among intellectual sources for the libertarian movement in the immediate postwar decades, Milton and Rose mention "Hayek's *Road to Serfdom,* Ayn Rand's *Fountainhead* and *Atlas Shrugged,* our own *Capitalism and Freedom,* and numerous others."[10] In a 2000 interview, he remarks that over the course of his career, when he has asked people about who changed their views from support for government to a more free market view, "two names have come up over and over again: Hayek . . . and Ayn Rand."[11]

On returning to the United States, refreshed and ready for new challenges, Friedman resumed teaching at the University of Chicago. Before the publication of *A Monetary History of the United States* in

1963, no one questioned his technical virtuosity; after its publication, he was one of the very few undisputed leaders of the economics profession, whether individuals agreed with his views or not. His teaching load at the University of Chicago decreased in the later 1960s. He taught two quarters a year, winter and spring, rather than the three he had taught previously, and spent the other two quarters in New Hampshire, where Milton and Rose enjoyed watching the leaves turn color in the fall.

Friedman became involved in the Goldwater for president campaign soon after returning to Chicago. He had met the senator in the early 1960s and occasionally corresponded with him. Impressed by Goldwater's personality and agreeing with him politically, Friedman's involvement in this campaign marked his emergence on the national scene as a significant actor.

Friedman was becoming known as the leading conservative economist in the United States. A January 1964 *Newsweek* article remarked: "Friedman may . . . do for Barry Goldwater what Galbraith once did for John F. Kennedy. For the past three years, the 51-year-old economist has been an unofficial adviser to . . . the Arizona senator."[12] Two months before, on publication of *A Monetary History of the United States, Business Week* ran an article "Theorizing for Goldwater?" which was subtitled "University of Chicago economist Milton Friedman is regarded as the logical man to become the senator's adviser; his new book gives conservatives a wealth of economic ammunition."[13]

Friedman in fact did become Goldwater's chief economic adviser during the 1964 campaign, although he did not actively campaign. He mostly wrote memos and drafts of possible speeches for the candidate. In an October 1964 essay in the *New York Times Magazine,* "The Goldwater View of Economics," he wrote: "What is the economic philosophy of Barry Goldwater? . . . Freedom and opportunity are Senator Goldwater's basic goals for mankind: freedom of the individual to pursue his own interests so long as he does not interfere with the freedom of others to do likewise; opportunity for the ordinary man to use his resources as effectively as possible to advance the well-being of himself and his family."[14] This was, of course, also Friedman's own economic philosophy.

Friedman received an unexpected offer to teach at Stanford University in 1964. Though Rose had long wished to return to the West Coast, he ultimately decided not to accept this opportunity, because he could not "face deserting the intellectual climate at Chicago in which I felt something of a proprietary interest and that I found so stimulating."[15] Instead, he spent the 1964–65 academic year at Columbia University as a visiting professor, holding the Wesley Clair Mitchell Research Professorship in Economics, appropriately enough. This provided a chance for the couple to see old friends and make new ones, and for Milton to teach graduate students at an institution other than Chicago. His mother had by this time passed away, but his sister Toots continued to live in Rahway, and he occasionally saw her and her family.

Friedman was impressed during his year at Columbia by the degree of intellectual insularity there, which he believes to be endemic in academia, the media, and much of government. He has frequently been out of the mainstream during his careers in academia and advocacy. With respect to his views on Goldwater, he found, to "exaggerate only slightly," that his interlocutors had

> never talked to anyone who really believed, and had thought deeply about, views drastically different from their own. As a result, when they heard real arguments instead of caricatures, they had no answers, only amazement that such views could be expressed by someone who had the external characteristics of being a member of the intellectual community. . . . Never have I been more impressed with the advice I once received: "You cannot be sure that you are right unless you understand the arguments against your views better than your opponents do."[16]

Martin Anderson, who served as a leading domestic and economic policy adviser in the Reagan administration, recalls interacting with Friedman as a young faculty member at Columbia. Anderson and his wife were invited to a small party at the Friedmans' apartment on the Upper West Side in New York City:

All the guests were professors and their spouses . . . Around 11:00 P.M. I got into an argument with Friedman over some point of political or economic theory, the substance of which I cannot recall. What I do remember is the zest and exhilaration of that discussion. Arguing with Milton Friedman was the intellectual equivalent of attempting to climb Mount Everest. We went on until close to 2:00 A.M. . . . I finally admitted that I was tired and sleepy and had to go home. Friedman smiled, his eyes twinkling, and said, "All right, I win."[17]

17

COLLEAGUES

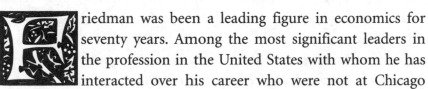riedman was been a leading figure in economics for seventy years. Among the most significant leaders in the profession in the United States with whom he has interacted over his career who were not at Chicago (though even some have Chicago connections) are Franco Modigliani, Paul Samuelson, John Kenneth Galbraith, and James Tobin. None of these men share his ideological perspective and all are considered modern liberals. Modigliani, who won the Nobel Prize in Economics in 1985, remembered Friedman from the perspective "never of friendship, but of real professional respect." Modigliani recalled an early interaction with Friedman when the former was a young scholar at Chicago in 1948–49. He wrote a letter to the editor suggesting increased government taxation to replace price controls and rationing. Friedman was "indignant": "Your suggestion . . . is immoral, shame on you! It's a trick to make fun of the rules of the market. The rules of price formation must be allowed to work freely without any manipulation."[1]

Paul Samuelson no doubt views himself in the same way that Friedman viewed himself (though neither, of course, expresses it): as the leading economist of his generation. Samuelson's *Foundations of Economic Analysis* (1948) and extremely successful *Economics* textbook (seventeen editions between 1948 and 2001, the last eight with William Nordhaus) have greatly influenced the economics profession.

Samuelson received the first John Bates Clark Medal presented by the American Economic Association in 1947, and he received the Nobel Prize in Economics the second year it was awarded, in 1970, becoming the first American to receive the prize. In conversation, Rose Friedman says that she considers Samuelson to be Milton's chief contemporary rival as an economist and that the two men have often been paired. Likely Sameulson is held in higher esteem within the economics profession than Friedman, with respect both to technique and to political outlook. Samuelson has received more honorary degrees, particularly from the most prestigious institutions, and has served as an officer in more professional societies than Friedman has.

In the 1976 tenth edition of *Economics*, Samuelson discusses Friedman, often in footnotes and focusing on his work on the consumption function. He presents Friedman as a libertarian: "People of all political persuasions should read Friedman's *Capitalism and Freedom*. It is a rigorously logical, careful, often persuasive elucidation of an important point of view. . . . Although one may, on reflection, agree with many or few of the positions advocated, it has been well said: 'If Milton Friedman had never existed, it would have been necessary to invent him.'"[2]

Through the editions of his textbook *Economics*, Samuelson's views on monetary and fiscal policies have moved substantially in Friedman's direction, without recognition or attribution. As Mark Skousen notes, in the 1955 edition Samuelson wrote: "Today few economists regard federal reserve monetary policy as a panacea for controlling the business cycle."[3] By 1973 Samuelson's view was that "both fiscal and monetary policies matter much."[4] In 1995 Samuelson and Nordhaus wrote: "Fiscal policy is no longer a major tool of stabilization policy in the United States. Over the foreseeable future, stabilization policy will be performed by Federal Reserve monetary policy."[5] Todd Buchholz comments that in the 1985 edition of *Eco-*

nomics, Samuelson and Nordhaus "conceded that 'early Keynesianism has benefited from "the rediscovery of money." Money definitely matters. In their early enthusiasm about the role of fiscal policy, many Keynesians unjustifiably downgraded the role of money.' Samuelson and Nordhaus did not mention the names of any perpetrators"![6]

Samuelson, Modigliani, and Robert Solow have all spent much of their careers at the Massachusetts Institute of Technology (MIT), one of the leading centers in academic economics for much of the postwar era. Friedman has criticized MIT's mathematical methodological approach. Commenting in 1988 on differences between his own methodology and that at MIT, he says that at MIT economics is viewed as a "branch of mathematics . . . as an intellectual game and exercise."[7] By way of contrast, his own approach, using Marshall's phrase, is to look at economics as "an engine of analysis."[8]

John Kenneth Galbraith was, with Keynes and Friedman, one of the three best-known economists in the twentieth century. A tall, urbane, good-looking man, Galbraith, who taught at Harvard, did not receive recognition from the economics profession commensurate with his popular standing. He never received the Nobel Prize in Economics.

Friedman discussed Galbraith in a 1970s talk at London's Institute of Economic Affairs, whose advocacy of freer markets, deregulation, and a generally lesser government role established it as the leading think tank in Britain, and perhaps in the world, from the 1960s to the 1980s. Friedman said: "I want to start out by explaining that I have no prejudice against John Kenneth Galbraith. Indeed some of my best friends are Galbraithians, including John Kenneth." Nonetheless, Friedman subjected Galbraith to severe professional criticism:

> The statistics on government spending made Galbraith's theme of private affluence [in *The Affluent Society*] versus public squalor an absurd claim. . . . [H]ow difficult it is to get testable hypotheses out of the Galbraithian canon. Galbraith speaks in broad general terms; he makes as-

sertions about the world at large. But they are very seldom put in a form in which they yield testable hypotheses. . . . Instead of regarding him as a scientist seeking explanations, I think we shall get more understanding if we look at him as a missionary seeking converts.[9]

Galbraith wrote in his autobiography that his nomination as president of the American Economic Association in 1970 was initially opposed by Friedman in committee. Friedman scholar Robert Leeson quotes committee member Mark Perlman, who was present when Friedman chaired the nominating committee: "Friedman can be a perfect gentleman, and he presented [Galbraith's] nomination in good grace. All present knew what pain it cost him, but we all admired his composure."[10] Friedman and Galbraith occasionally visited each other in the summers in New England and also saw one another in India. In his 1967 book, *The New Industrial State,* Galbraith footnoted that "Professors Stigler and Friedman are, by wide agreement, the two ablest exponents of conservative economic attitudes in the United States."[11] Both Friedman and Galbraith have to some extent been outcasts from much of the academic economic mainstream for much of their careers.

James Tobin received the Nobel Prize in Economics in 1981. At Yale for his entire career, he became chair of the Cowles Foundation (formerly the Cowles Commission) in 1955 when it moved to that institution. Initially he may have been somewhat unsympathetic toward Friedman personally because there were hard feelings when the Cowles Commission left Chicago, although Tobin was not with Cowles there. Tobin engaged in considerable controversy with Friedman, particularly in the area of monetary theory and policy. In 1970 and 1971, together with other economists, they had an exchange on Friedman's monetary views where Tobin strongly criticized Friedman: "I have been very surprised to learn what Professor Friedman regards as his crucial theoretical differences from the neo-Keynesians. . . . Friedman's 'theoretical framework' does not provide monetarism, either its short-run or its long-run propositions, with strong theoretical support."[12]

In his 1965 review of *A Monetary History of the United States,* Tobin wrote, criticizing Friedman's theory: "We don't know what money is, but whatever it is, its stock should grow at 3 to 4 percent per year."[13] Friedman wrote in his 1971 response to Tobin that much of his "criticism . . . leaves me utterly baffled. We seem to be talking at cross-purposes. I disagree far less with the substance of what he says than with the views he attributes to me,"[14] and noted that Tobin did not provide empirical evidence for some of his views.

Friedman says many times that his ideas, like those of pioneers in thought generally, are not infrequently misunderstood and mischaracterized. He describes the process:

> There is a standard pattern. When anybody threatens an orthodox position, the first reaction is to ignore the interloper. The less said about him the better. But if he begins to win a hearing and gets annoying, the second reaction is to ridicule him, make fun of him as an extremist, a foolish fellow who has these silly ideas. After that stage passes the next, and the most important, stage is to put on his clothes. You adopt for your own his views, and then attribute to him a caricature of those views saying, "He's an extremist, one of those fellows who says only money matters . . . Of course money does matter, but . . ."[15]

Interestingly, Mohandas Gandhi has had a somewhat similar course of the development of action attributed to him: "First they ignore you. Then they laugh at you. Then they fight you. Then you win."[16]

Friedman has been widely discussed professionally since the 1950s, and this is the greatest compliment that can be paid to a scholar, whether others agree with him or not. Robert Solow, a fierce Friedman critic, commented in 1964 that although "only a small minority of the profession is persuaded by his opinions, around any academic lunch table on any given day, the talk is more likely to be about Milton Friedman than about any other economist."[17] Numerous similar statements could be proffered on the extent of Friedman's influence.

Friedman's 1967 presidential address to the American Economic Association (AEA), "The Role of Monetary Policy," is judged one of the most influential speeches ever given before that body. The address builds on his earlier work in monetary history and theory. In it he rebuts the notion of a "Phillips curve"—that there is a long-run trade-off between inflation and unemployment. In 1958 A. W. Phillips argued that the higher inflation is, the lower unemployment will be and that the lower inflation is, the higher unemployment will be. Keynesians seized on this purported trade-off to argue for interventionist and expansive monetary and fiscal policies. Inflation, from Phillips's perspective, stimulates employment. Samuelson, for example, said in 1967 of the Phillips curve that it is "one of the most important concepts of our times."[18]

Friedman argues against the existence of a long-run Phillips curve. He agrees that, in the short run, unanticipated inflation can temporarily boost employment and output, but eventually the short run becomes the long run. If an economy has become used to inflation, then inflation will have all of its bad effects in distorting price signals (the relative change of prices in guiding production is lost in the cacophony of generally rising prices) and in discouraging saving. The only way to maintain the temporarily beneficial effects of inflation is for inflation to rise at increasing, unanticipated rates, which is unsustainable. According to Friedman: "Keynes's key theoretical proposition . . . [is] that even in a world of flexible prices, a position of equilibrium at full employment might not exist."[19] Friedman's view, on the other hand, is that in a world of flexible prices, equilibrium at full employment *will* exist.

Friedman's view in the middle 1960s was that a regime of generally stable prices is the best public policy. To accomplish this goal, he recommends a fixed annual increase in the money supply, variously estimated (in part based on the money aggregates used) at 2 to 5 percent, about equal to long-term growth in the economy. He opposes discretionary manipulation of the money supply—a view that, in his call for inflation targeting, the new Federal Reserve chairman Ben

Bernanke endorses more than his predecessor, Alan Greenspan, did. Friedman emphasizes the long-range benefits of a consistent monetary policy and stable aggregate prices.

The quantity theory of money is, in Friedman's view, a theory of the demand for money. If demand for money as an asset and for transactions were not relatively constant, then changes in the quantity of money would not have the effect on prices that they do have. Moreover, Friedman notes that, contrary to what Keynes thought, changes in the money supply are typically correlated positively with monetary velocity—that is, an increase in money supply generally leads to higher velocity and a decrease in money supply leads to lower velocity.

Friedman used his 1967 AEA presidential address to bring the concept of a natural rate of unemployment to the attention of the economics profession. By a "natural rate of unemployment," he means the "level of unemployment which . . . is consistent with equilibrium in the structure of *real* wage rates. At that level of unemployment, real wage rates are tending on the average to rise at a 'normal' secular rate, i.e., at a rate that can be indefinitely maintained so long as capital formation, technological improvements, etc., remain on their long-run trends." Many factors influence the natural rate of unemployment, including "market imperfections, stochastic variability in demands and supplies, the cost of gathering information about job vacancies and labor availabilities, the costs of mobility."[20]

There will always be some unemployment as a result of individuals who are between jobs, technological improvement, seasonal variations in employment, and so on. "The existence of a natural rate of employment" means that "the goal of zero unemployment is not realizable."[21] Friedman observes that the natural rate of unemployment subsequently became "part of conventional wisdom in the profession except that the Keynesians . . . introduced the term NAIRU [nonaccelerating inflation rate of unemployment] . . . to describe the same concept."[22] From a policy perspective, if the monetary authorities attempt to hold the real rate of unemployment below the natural rate, inflation will result and any decline in unemployment will be only temporary.

Of Friedman's colleagues at Chicago, Lloyd Mints typically does not receive as much attention as others do, but he was a significant figure in the emerging Chicago school of economics. Friedman acknowledges him, along with Knight, Simons, Director, Hayek, and Stigler, in the original preface of *Capitalism and Freedom* as among the "distinguished group" of "teachers, colleagues, and friends" at the university to whom "I owe the philosophy expressed in this book and much of its detail."[23] Leeson emphasizes the influence of Mints's graduate course in money and banking in the formation of Friedman's monetary views.

Mints helped to shed light on a criticism that irks Friedman: that there was no quantity theory of money tradition at Chicago before Friedman began to teach there. In a 1969 article, "The Chicago Tradition, the Quantity Theory, and Friedman," Don Patinkin had argued that Friedman's belief that Chicago had a quantity theory tradition dating from the 1930s was in error. In a 1972 letter to Patinkin, Mints wrote:

> As I recollect the situation during the 1930's it was as follows. The primary interest of several of us at Chicago, in such public statements as were made, was in monetary policy and its relation to economic activity. We tacitly assumed that monetary behavior had an important influence on economic activity. It was the era of the great depression and we believed that the actions of the Federal Reserve System and of the government were woefully wrong.[24]

Friedman was especially irritated by Patinkin's suggestion because it was used by Harry Johnson, in his 1970 Richard T. Ely lecture before the AEA, to charge Friedman with the

> invention of a University of Chicago oral tradition that was alleged to have preserved understanding of the fundamental truth among a small band of the initiated through the dark years of the Keynesian despotism. . . . Don Patinkin has very recently—and over-belatedly . . . —exploded these efforts to provide bridges between the pre-Keynesian

orthodoxy and the monetarist counter-revolution. . . . There was no lonely light constantly burning in a secret shrine on the Midway, encouraging the faithful to assemble in waiting for the day when the truth could safely be revealed to the masses. . . . Nevertheless, one should not be too fastidious in condemnation of the techniques of scholarly chicanery used to promote a revolution or a counter-revolution in economic theory.[25]

Friedman was understandably incensed by Johnson's lecture. Leeson recapitulates the situation: "Tobin used his presidential prerogative to invite [Johnson] to deliver the 1970 Ely lecture. Tobin chaired this eagerly anticipated session and remembers that Johnson's lecture 'created quite a stir.' It appeared to be a *deliberate* attempt to shoot Friedman down in flames."[26] In 1972 Friedman participated in a symposium on his monetary theory with several critics, including Patinkin. In a preliminary draft of his article, Friedman wrote that Patinkin was a "heartstruck swain" and that "libels [were] erected on that shaky foundation by Harry Johnson."[27] On the advice of a referee, Friedman deleted these references from the published version.

In 2001, Friedman said with respect to this question of intellectual history that he is "baffled . . . at what all the fuss was about. . . . [V]ery little was at stake."[28] Leeson helps to provide the answer: "This controversy has all the ingredients of a fascinating dispute involving evidence, egos, and jealousy among colleagues . . . The disputants were playing for higher stakes than the subject matter. . . . From the late 1960s . . . both [Patinkin and Johnson] were highly agitated: this can only adequately be explained by Friedman's increasing influence . . . , the competition for Nobel Prizes, and their sense of being oppressed by the shadow of Friedman." From the late 1960s, Patinkin and Johnson "rarely missed an opportunity to ridicule Friedman's account."[29]

There was, or became, no love lost professionally between Johnson and Friedman. Johnson wrote Patinkin in 1969, after the latter's article: "I just read your . . . hatchet job on Milton. . . . You have shown him to be a crook."[30] Friedman retained better relations with Patinkin and now considers himself to have "always got along very well" with Johnson personally: "We regarded Harry and his wife Liz as good friends. . . . Our house was on Harry's way home from his office . . . and he very often would stop in and have a drink in the late afternoon." Friedman played a considerable role in recruiting Johnson to work at the University of Chicago: "I had gotten to know him . . . the year we were in Britain. . . . I thought then that we needed to have a Keynesian at Chicago, and of those I met in Britain, he seemed to me far and away the brightest."[31] A colleague recalls Friedman describing Johnson, who was a very heavy drinker, as a "writing machine powered by whiskey."[32] Friedman's standing joke about Johnson was that he was a monetarist in England and a Keynesian in Chicago. Johnson was an excellent editor of the *Journal of Political Economy* and was a prolific author before dying at fifty-four in 1977.

During his term as president of the American Economic Association, Friedman shepherded through the conversion of the AEA's *Journal of Economic Abstracts* to the *Journal of Economic Literature* and oversaw appointment of Mark Perlman as its first editor. After his term as president, he chaired the committee that selected the *American Economic Review*'s new editor, George Borts, a former student.

In addition to the AEA, Friedman was involved in many other organizations, professional and otherwise. Between 1970 and 1972, he served as president of the Mont Pelerin Society, a term that coincided with the society's twenty-fifth anniversary. He took advantage of this occasion to write on the society's future:

> Our basic problems arise out of our success. Attendance at our meetings by members and guests has become so large the organization of each general meeting is a major enterprise. In order to have enough space, we are driven to large cities, to using a number of hotels, and to holding sessions at a separate location from the hotels. This dispersion inhibits those informal contacts, free-wheeling discussion sessions, and inten-

sive arguments that have for many of us been the major product of the meetings . . . . . [The] meetings are such pleasant occasions at which we can meet many old friends . . . that, to an increasing number of participants, I fear they have become tourist attractions.[33]

His recommended solution was for the society to consider disbanding; this did not, however, receive support. Rose writes of the situation:

If the need for them [organizations] still exists after some twenty or thirty years, then new people will form a new society. New blood and new ideas would make the organization more alert and more effective. Needless to say, . . . not many members agreed with this idea. The old rule, "once organized, never disbanded" is as true in the Mont Pelerin Society as it is in other societies and especially in government bureaucracies.[34]

Other organizations in which Friedman has been involved include the Intercollegiate Society of Individualists (now the Intercollegiate Studies Institute), the Philadelphia Society, and the American Enterprise Institute. The Intercollegiate Society of Individualists (ISI) was founded by Frank Chodorov in 1953. One of its key chapters was at the University of Chicago, and Friedman and Hayek were two of three advisers to the chapter's publication, the *New Individualist Review.*

Friedman was enthusiastic about the influence of the Mont Pelerin Society, the ISI, and the *New Individualist Review.* In a 1981 introduction to a republication of the journal, he writes that "two organizations . . . served to channel and direct"[35] the resurgence of classical liberal and libertarian thought stirring in the early 1960s, before the Vietnam War tracked popular discussion, especially among the young, in a leftward direction—the Mont Pelerin Society and ISI. In a January 1964 article, published shortly before the leftward political dam broke around the globe, Friedman said that a classical liberal or libertarian movement might be in the offing: "I'm much more optimistic than I was fifteen years ago. . . . There is no doubt whatsoever in the change of atmosphere—even in Chicago, this hotbed of liberalism. I find undergraduates I speak to coming around to the view: Friedman's probably wrong, but I'd like to find out what his position is."[36] Then, as a result of the Vietnam War, reform went in another direction.

The Philadelphia Society grew out of the work of Don Lipsett, who in the early 1960s was a director of ISI. The Philadelphia Society is, in the words of historian of conservatism George Nash, a "kind of American equivalent of the Mont Pelerin Society."[37] The members (now several hundred strong) meet in conferences to give and discuss papers, to network, and to socialize in an atmosphere of those who support free market, conservative, and libertarian ideas. Friedman was on the organizing committee for the Philadelphia Society and served several terms on its board of directors. The first meeting of the society was held in Chicago in 1965. Among others involved in this society from the start are Ed Feulner, now longtime president of the Heritage Foundation, and William Buckley.

The AEI was begun in 1943 and reached prominence under William Baroody, president from 1954 to 1980. It has been a leading right-of-center think tank in Washington for more than half a century and is sometimes considered a home for out-of-office Republican worthies, nonreligious conservatives, and neoconservatives. In the current ideological spectrum of libertarian-conservative think tanks in Washington, it is to the right of Cato and to the left of the Heritage Foundation. The AEI has emphasized a somewhat less partisan and more neutral presentation than either of those organizations, but has moved to the right, along with much of the rest of the larger society, in recent years.

Friedman served as an active member of the AEI's Academic Advisory Board from 1956 to 1979. The board met several times a year, reviewed all manuscripts, and considered proposed studies. The standard of quality during Friedman's tenure was excellent. He resigned from the board in 1979 because (following his and Rose's move to California) he could no longer serve as easily on its board.

His participation in the AEI reintroduced him to the Washington scene, following his youthful service on the National Resources Committee and in the Treasury Department. He participated in meetings with such Republican notables as Melvin Laird, Donald Rumsfeld, and Gerald Ford (before he became president). The AEI published a pamphlet by Rose, "Poverty: Definition and Perspective," in 1965.

George Shultz succeeded Allen Wallis as the dean of the business school when Wallis left Chicago for the University of Rochester in 1962. Friedman and Shultz are not as close personally or professionally as Milton is (or was) with those colleagues from his youth, but they have now been affiliated at Chicago, on the larger political stage, and at the Hoover Institution for more than forty years. Shultz says that Milton's "brilliance as an economist is well known but perhaps as important and less exalted is his capacity as an expositor. He has a gift of clarity. . . . [I]f he winds up talking with someone he thinks is worthwhile he has immense patience, and a willingness to engage and argue. Milton is a great arguer, and we used to say that everyone loved to argue with Milton—when he wasn't there!"[38]

Ronald Coase was among the leading economists of the twentieth century, and his influence continues to grow. His best-known contribution is the Coase theorem, essentially the idea that freedom of exchange is the ultimate requirement to reach Pareto optimality, whereby no exchange will increase any party's welfare. In particular, the initial allocation of legal rights will not affect ultimate economic outcome as long as freedom of exchange is uninhibited. Friedman and Coase have had good relations over the years, although they have never been especially close personally or professionally. Coase went to Chicago in 1964 and received the Nobel Prize in Economics in 1991. He is a greater admirer of Frank Knight and Aaron Director.

Director was a significant figure in his own right. Melvin Reder emphasizes Director's role among Chicago economists, writing in 1982 that in conducting his own work on the history of economics at the University of Chicago, he was "struck by the many strong expressions of intellectual indebtedness both of Chicago economists and legal scholars (such as Edward Levi and Robert Bork) to Aaron Director. . . . Director appears to have exercised a great deal of influence upon the principal figures in Chicago economics from the 1930s to the present."[39] According to Coase: "Director was extremely effective as a teacher, and he had a profound influence on the views of some of his students and also on those of some of his colleagues . . . both in law and economics."[40] Stigler wrote in 1974 that in "forming most present day policy views of Chicago economists, Director and Friedman have been the main intellectual forces."[41]

Milton and Rose's friends at Chicago outside economics were the university's elite, including Ed and Laura Banfield in political science, Daniel and Ruth Boorstin in history, and Edward and Kate Levi in the law school, among many others. Levi later became president of the University of Chicago and attorney general of the United States; Boorstin became Librarian of Congress.

Freidman's involvement in professional and other organizations has strengthened and broadened his influence. His major contribution remains intellectual. He believes that the rule of a fixed expansion of the money supply each year might not be the ideal monetary policy, but it would be a good one. He concluded "The Role of Monetary Policy," his 1967 presidential address to the AEA, by saying: "Steady monetary growth would provide a monetary climate favorable to the effective operation of those basic forces of enterprise, ingenuity, invention, hard work, and thrift, that are the true springs of economic growth. That is the most that we can ask from monetary policy at our present stage of knowledge. But that much—and it is a great deal—is clearly within our reach."[42]

18

PUBLIC INTELLECTUAL
AND POLICY PROPOSALS

riedman's participation in the 1964 Goldwater campaign was his first major step in becoming a national public figure. While before this he was occasionally identified in the national media as a prominent conservative economist, his renown did not extend much beyond academia. His campaign participation paved the way for the tri-weekly opinion column that he wrote from 1966 to 1984 for *Newsweek*, the major forum in which he became known to a national audience. The column followed other popular writing, including in the *National Review*. In the August 24, 1965, edition of the *National Review*, his article "Social Responsibility: A Subversive Doctrine" was featured most prominently on the cover. In this article he put forward his view, repeated elsewhere, that businesses have no responsibility other than to their stockholders; the best course for businesses to follow is to maximize profits and leave it to stockholders to spend their share of returns as they desire.

His *Newsweek* columns make interesting reading, particularly juxtaposed to those of fellow columnist Paul Samuelson. When Friedman began the column he was perhaps not as well known as Samuelson, and was on the edge of academic opinion rather than in the middle. Though a blurb in the 1965 *National Review* edition that included the

169

article on social responsibility described Friedman as "among the two or three outstanding economists in the world,"[1] it is an open question whether this was the general opinion, either inside or outside academia, at the time. In the mid-1960s and beyond, many looked on Barry Goldwater as a right-wing nut. To be associated with the senator did not enhance Friedman's reputation—certainly not in academia—though it brought him initial public prominence.

Friedman's first *Newsweek* column appeared in the September 26, 1966, edition. This column opposed the recent rise in the minimum wage from $1.25 to $1.60 per hour: "Women, teen-agers, Negroes and particularly Negro teen-agers will be especially hard hit. I am convinced that the minimum-wage law is the most anti-Negro law on our statute books."[2] He correctly predicted that unemployment of African American youth would increase in the years ahead.

His second column for *Newsweek* was prescient with respect to trends in the economy, although he was a bit ahead of himself as to timing: "Our record economic expansion will probably end sometime in the next year. If it does, prices will continue to rise while unemployment mounts. *There will be an inflationary recession* [emphasis in original]." Although "[m]any will regard this prediction as a contradiction in terms,"[3] it proved correct in the stagflationary 1970s.

He wrote about 300 columns for *Newsweek* between 1966 and 1984. These were the writings that most people, regularly, over the longest period of time, would have been familiar with. Specimen column comments include:

A free and orderly society is a complex structure. We understand but dimly its many sources of strength and weakness.[4]

Draft or no draft, this country would be now engaged in a searching debate over Vietnam. But the virulence and the divisiveness of the debate have been greatly increased by the draft, with its threat to civil liberties and with its closing of all alternatives except open revolt to young men who disagree strongly with our policy. Must we continue to add to the strain on our society by using a method of manning our armed forces that is inequitable, wasteful and basically inconsistent with a free society?[5]

Few U.S. industries sing the praises of free enterprise more loudly than the oil industry. Yet few industries rely so heavily on special government favors.[6]

Changes in monetary growth affect the economy only slowly—it may be six or twelve or eighteen months or even more before their effects are manifest.[7]

Inflation is always and everywhere a monetary phenomenon.[8]

From the 1940s to 2006, Friedman put forward a bevy of public policy proposals, many of which have at least to some extent been implemented or considered—this can be said of very few individuals. Daniel Patrick Moynihan remarked in 1971: "If you were to ask me to name the most creative social-political thinker of our age I would not hesitate to say Milton Friedman."[9]

Starting in the 1940s, Friedman put forward the idea of floating exchange rates, which were implemented in the United States in the early 1970s. In the 1950s, he developed his idea of a fixed expansion of the money supply each year. Although this policy proposal had only mixed success, his general emphasis that the way to limit inflation is to limit increases in the supply of money became the accepted opinion in the late 1970s to early 1980s.

In *Capitalism and Freedom*, he identifies fourteen "activities currently undertaken by government" in the United States that cannot, in his mind, "validly be justified":

1. Parity price support programs for agriculture
2. Tariffs on imports or restrictions on exports
3. Government control of output
4. Rent control . . . or more general price and wage controls
5. Legal minimum wage rates, or legal maximum prices
6. Detailed regulation of industries
7. Control of radio and television by the Federal Communications Commission
8. Present social security programs

9. Licensure provisions
10. Public housing
11. Conscription to man the military services in peacetime
12. National parks
13. Legal prohibition on the carrying of mail for profit
14. Publicly owned and operated toll roads[10]

Although he says that the list is "far from comprehensive,"[11] at least two aspects of it deserve attention. First, notwithstanding what he thinks, a considerable portion of it has been implemented to some extent. Second, and perhaps even more interesting, the list is, in fact, relatively modest in scope.

With respect to the first two inappropriate government activities, expenditures for all federal agricultural programs now total about one-quarter of 1 percent of gross domestic product in the United States, and many tariffs on imports and restrictions on exports have been reduced since 1962 and continue to be reduced. Regarding items 3 and 4, government control of output and rent control and more general government control of prices and wages have diminished since *Capitalism and Freedom* was first published.

Item 5, a legal minimum wage, remains, but it has declined as a proportion of average income. Item 6, detailed regulation of industries, remains and has grown more extensive—with environmental, health and safety, disability, and labor laws becoming increasingly complex—but there was considerable deregulation of targeted industries in the United States in the late 1970s and 1980s.

Item 7, control of radio and television by the Federal Communications Commission, remains, but the explosion of television channels and the Internet render it less relevant. Item 8, social security, remains, has grown, and has become an increasing proportion of payroll taxes, but some market-based reforms were included in 2004 changes in Medicare. Item 9, licensure provisions, remain but do not seem to be expanding. Item 10, new government-built housing, is not the issue that it was.

The draft (item 11) has been eliminated, and national parks (item 12) remain and are expanding.

Item 13, the legal prohibition on carrying mail for profit, remains, but expansion of businesses like Federal Express and the Internet makes it less meaningful. Publicly owned and operated toll roads (item 14) remain but are not increasing. In all, progress (from Friedman's perspective) has been made on about ten or so of his list of fourteen inappropriate government activities, though only one, conscription to man the military, has been completely eliminated.

Major public policy proposals on which he has worked over his career include flexible international exchange rates, a fixed rate of monetary growth each year, a negative income tax, an all-volunteer army, indexation of taxation to accommodate inflation, limitations on taxation and government spending and requirement of a balanced federal budget, countenance of government budget deficits to stem increased government spending (if spending restraint is not otherwise possible), reductions in high marginal income tax rates, school vouchers, legalization of drugs, and health saving accounts. Overarching all these proposals are his support for a generally lesser role of government and preeminently his view that inflation is always and everywhere a monetary phenomenon that national governments should work to eliminate.

Friedman proposed flexible international exchange rates as early as 1948. During the 1950s, as he and Anna Jacobson Schwartz worked on *A Monetary History of the United States,* he developed the proposal for a fixed rate of monetary growth each year.

Among his most significant contributions to economic policy discussions from the 1960s to the present are the ideas of a negative income tax, indexation for inflation, limitations on taxes and government spending, countenancing government budget deficits to restrain the growth of government, and reduction of marginal income tax rates, all the while—particularly from the mid-1960s to early 1980s—preaching and advising against inflation. Another focus of his in discussions of economic public policy not applicable to the

United States, but which he has advocated abroad, is denationalization of state-owned industries. It is hard to think of anyone who has
contributed so much intellectually in so many areas of public policy
so effectively around the world in the last four decades.

Friedman proposed a negative income tax in the 1950s. The idea
of this tax is to replace the myriad social programs financed by government with a single program: Every individual or family would be
guaranteed a certain minimum income that would vary on the basis
of family size and other characteristics. Advantages of a negative income tax are efficiency and simplicity. It would replace with a single
program social security, welfare, food stamps, housing support, and
in principle every other government program directly affecting personal living standard.

The negative income tax idea garnered substantial support. 1,200
economists from 150 different colleges and universities—though not
including Friedman—signed a petition in 1968 in support of a version
of a negative income tax. When Richard Nixon became president in
1969, he proposed a version of a negative income tax in which individuals who worked would always be better off as a result of working. As
the bill, termed the Family Assistance Program, emerged from the
House of Representatives in 1970, this provision had been eliminated
and individuals with incomes between (at that time) $3,600 and
$5,000 per year would actually have been worse off by working than
not working.

Friedman testified before the House Ways and Means Committee
against the House version of the Family Assistance Program. The negative income tax dominated welfare reform discussion for about a year,
before failing in the Senate Finance Committee in the spring of 1970.

Friedman largely abandoned discussion of a negative income tax
since the early 1970s, although the earned income tax credit in 1975
was similar in many ways to the failed 1970 version. Nixon called the
Family Assistance Program an "idea ahead of its time."[12]

With respect to price indexation to accommodate inflation, in
the 1960s and 1970s as inflation increased, Friedman's idea here be-

came to counter some of its negative effects rather than to eliminate it altogether (or at least he felt that countering the negative effects of inflation might be more politically feasible than eliminating it altogether). In principle, all contracts and other agreements for the payment of money would be indexed for inflation. If prices went up by 10 percent, for example, so would wages. In addition, interest rates would be variable to account for inflation.

He was never really comfortable with the indexation idea, in large part because it merely treats the symptoms of inflation rather than addressing inflation itself, a much preferred course. A significant outcome stemming in part from the indexation idea, though, was the indexation of tax brackets to account for inflation. Previously, as a result of inflation, individuals' tax rates effectively rose with higher average prices (taxpayers were pushed into higher brackets of income taxation). When, during Ronald Reagan's presidency, indexation of tax brackets was implemented as part of the Tax Reduction Act of 1981, a major systemic demand for inflation by politicians was removed. Since then inflation has markedly declined and stayed low, though there is no direct cause-and-effect relationship between indexed tax rates and inflation.

Friedman's views on taxes, spending, balanced government budgets, and government deficit spending have evolved over the decades. In the 1930s and 1940s, he was, if not a Henry Simons liberal, much closer to this position than he became. Friedman advocated progressive income taxation and egalitarian outcomes early in his career. He supported government budget deficits in economic downturns and budget surpluses in expansions. At least in the early 1940s, he thought that fiscal policy plays a large role in determining inflation. Although he departed from this last position by the 1950s, some echoes of it can be found in later work.

As his thinking developed, he began to look at fiscal policy less from the perspective of macroeconomic stabilization (and destabilization) and more from the perspective of microeconomic incentives and the general government role that different fiscal policies foster. Essentially, he has become opposed to government taxation and spending on at least the margin in virtually every area, particularly (with respect to spending) in areas in which government became involved in the twentieth century. He favors less taxation and less government spending irrespective of macroeconomic influence, which he does not consider significant.

Consider these representative comments from the 1960s:

> I oppose a tax increase because I believe that the Federal government is already absorbing too much of the community's resources. We need lower taxes, not higher taxes.[13]

> True fiscal responsibility requires resisting every tax increase and promoting tax decreases at every opportunity.[14]

> The first step toward true fiscal responsibility is to let the surtax expire ... and to cut the cost of Federal spending to the revenues that other taxes will yield. That step taken, it will be easier to take the next—and equally urgent—step: to start a program of moderate but steady reduction in the level of Federal taxes.[15]

One of the most interesting aspects of his arguments with respect to taxation is that he countenances a federal government budget deficit to the extent that this restrains government spending. He has repeatedly said that he would rather have a larger deficit and less government spending than more government spending and a balanced budget. In other words, his support for a balanced budget is strictly secondary to his support for less government spending. This is to a large extent the policy that the Reagan and George W. Bush administrations have followed.

Friedman wrote as early as 1967:

> If taxes are raised in order to keep down the deficit, the result is likely to be a higher norm for government spending. Deficits will again mount and the process will be repeated. . . .
>
> Those of us who believe that government has reached a size where it threatens to become our master should therefore (1) oppose any tax increase; (2) press for expenditure cuts; (3) accept large deficits as the lesser of evils. . . . [16]

He says later:

> By concentrating on the wrong thing, the deficit, instead of the right thing, total government spending, fiscal conservatives have been the un-witting handmaidens of the big spenders. The typical historical process is that the spenders put through laws which increase government spending and say, "My God, that's terrible; we have got to do something about that deficit." So they [fiscal conservatives] cooperate with the big spenders in getting taxes imposed. As soon as the new taxes are imposed and passed, the big spenders are off again, and then there is another burst in government spending and another deficit.[17]

In a 1988 retrospective of the Reagan administration, its author notes, of Friedman's view: "Budget deficits may count. But they are of a second order—a very distinct second order—of importance. . . . Meanwhile, Friedman argues, borrowing has some advantages. Politicians are less likely to spend the government's money if they know a large part of it is borrowed."[18]

Friedman has favored limitations on government spending more than a balanced budget. He writes in his memoirs of his participation on the National Tax Limitation Committee starting in 1975 that the U.S. constitutional amendment initially proposed by the committee did "not require a balanced budget. It was our view that what was important was cutting government spending. . . . As I have said repeatedly, I would rather have government spend one trillion dollars with a deficit of half a trillion than have government spend two trillion dollars with no deficit." In "trying to promote the proposed amendment with members of Congress it quickly became apparent that political support would be greatly enhanced by including provision for a balanced budget."[19]

In part on the basis of his monetary reinterpretation of the Great Depression, Friedman does not think that fiscal policy has much influence on the economy. The target of his opposition is government spending, not government budget deficits.

In addition to his views with respect to aggregate government spending and taxation, he advocates a flat-rate tax and a reduction in top marginal income tax rates. He proposed a flat-rate tax in 1962 in *Capitalism and Freedom,* and he wrote in 1968 in support of a flat tax that if "every deduction were eliminated except occupational expenses strictly interpreted, and if income of all kinds in excess of personal exemptions were subject to a single low flat rate, we could double our personal exemptions . . . and still raise as much revenue. That would be more equitable, vastly simpler, and far more efficient" than the current system. A flat tax is essentially a nonprogressive, proportional tax. According to Friedman, an advantage of a flat tax is that it would "release all of us from the unpaid bookkeeping we are forced to engage in . . . and make available for productive use the highly skilled accountants and lawyers who now devote their . . . talents to advising their clients how to avoid taxes."[20]

As a second best alternative to a flat-rate tax, which he believes would be politically difficult to achieve, he supports a reduction in top tax rates. He remarked during Jimmy Carter's presidency that "reducing oppressively high marginal rates would do far more to promote effective use of resources" than Carter's economic plans. He also said at that time, in response to a question about what to do to increase productivity: "Reduce the top rate of the personal income tax (from 70 percent) to 25 percent."[21] During Ronald Reagan's presidency, the top income tax rate was reduced to 28 percent.

Friedman writes of the "disastrous effects on incentives"[22] of high tax rates. He has always been a "supply-sider"—a term that came in vogue in the late 1970s to contrast with the Keynesian emphasis on demand—as he favors reduction in tax rates to increase productivity and advocates a stable monetary environment. He has never adopted the idea of the Laffer curve, however, whereby tax cuts pay for themselves. Nor is he a proponent of a gold standard, as many supply-siders are. Friedman says that "supply-side fiscal policy . . . consists of cutting high marginal tax rates in order to stimulate innovation and entrepreneurship. . . . Experience suggests that it is very effective in stimulating economic growth. It is a policy for the long run."[23]

Overarching his efforts in the 1960s and 1970s to reduce government spending and taxation and in opposition to fixed international currency exchange rates were his attempts to persuade the public and policy makers around the world that inflation is always and everywhere a monetary phenomenon—and that the way to reduce inflation is to decrease the rate of monetary growth. Friedman and events were largely successful in conveying this last message. As Friedman predicted, inflation did go down around the world in the 1980s and 1990s in response to more restrictive monetary policies.

With respect to an all-volunteer army, Friedman considers his involvement in this area to have been as rewarding as any in which he participated. Long before he was appointed by President Nixon in early 1969 to the Advisory Commission on an All-Volunteer Armed Force, he had advocated the elimination of the draft. Friedman probably overstates the role that the commission played in ending the draft. Candidate Nixon declared as early as 1967 that the draft should be eliminated. As president, he established the commission to enable him to accomplish this goal. The commission submitted its final report in February 1970, after more than 100 hours of meetings and much outside work. In accordance with the commission's recommendations, the draft ended in January 1973.

Others on the commission included Alan Greenspan and Allen Wallis. Friedman's sometimes acerbic manner reduced his effectiveness with some commission members. According to Stephen Herbits, the commission's youth representative, Friedman was "so cutting, so concise, that people could really get their backs up."[24] According to Greenspan, however: "I later spoke to Tom Gates, who chaired the commission, who said that he . . . opposed eliminating the draft but Milton turned him around."[25] The all-volunteer armed force commission marked the first but not the last time that Friedman and Greenspan would work together. Like Friedman, Greenspan is a student (though a post–World War II one, at Columbia) of Arthur Burns.

Friedman remembers the most "dramatic episode" in the course of the commission's deliberations as when General William Westmoreland, commander of American troops in Vietnam, "testified against a volunteer armed force. In the course of his testimony, he made the statement that he did not want to command an army of mercenaries. I stopped him and said, 'General, would you rather command an army of slaves?' He drew himself up and said, 'I don't like to hear our patriotic draftees referred to as slaves.' I replied, 'I don't like to hear our patriotic volunteers referred to as mercenaries.'"[26]

In 1968 Friedman and Samuelson engaged in an exchange in their *Newsweek* columns on the "New Economics" that dominated economic policy making during the Kennedy and Johnson administrations. Samuelson wrote of "the solid accomplishments of the New Economics, of which certainly the most important has been our unprecedented pace of sustained growth. . . . I can predict with confidence that Richard Nixon will be using the New Economics if only for the reason that new times make it inescapable."[27] For Friedman, on the other hand: "The Nixon Administration will confront major economic problems in three areas: inflation, balance of payments, and government budget. . . . In each area, the New Economics has managed in eight years to turn a comfortable, easy situation into a near crisis. . . . What a mess to have to straighten out! What a legacy to leave the opposition!"[28]

Starting in the late 1960s, Friedman began to be featured regularly and frequently in the national media to present a view of economics and society different from that of John Maynard Keynes, John Kenneth Galbraith, Paul Samuelson, Walter Heller, and others. Friedman, appearing on the cover of *Time* magazine on December 19, 1969, was described in the accompanying article as "a man totally devoted to ideas."[29]

The same month, *Fortune* magazine ran an article on him, "The Intellectual Provocateur," in which it stated that he is the "rare theorist whose influence is best measured not by the devotion of his followers—which can be extreme—but by the extent to which his ideas have altered the thinking of his opponents. The mixture of supreme self-confidence and good-humored needling expresses the personality that makes some of Friedman's sharpest critics consider themselves close personal friends." In the article, Labor Secretary George Schultz quotes a former colleague: "I wish I were as sure of anything as Milton is about everything." Friedman's son David is quoted: "I was brought up with the feeling that the normal way of conversation was to argue with people." Milton Friedman had just been to Harvard, where he said: "I believe that fiscal policy is *very* important"—long pause—"but not in its effect on inflation."[30] The audience loved it.

A month later, in January 1970, he appeared on the cover of the *New York Times Magazine*—the third major feature on him in two months. He was now a media superstar. This profile's tongue-in-cheek title was: "Friedmanism, n. Doctrine of most audacious U.S. economist; esp., theory 'only money matters.'"[31]

By the end of the 1960s, Friedman was the most prominent conservative public intellectual at least in the United States and probably in the world. His rise to popular fame in that decade stemmed from a number of sources:

- *Capitalism and Freedom*
- *A Monetary History of the United States*
- Participation in the Goldwater campaign
- His *Newsweek* column
- His tireless lecturing and appearances around the nation and popular writing in addition to his *Newsweek* column
- His appearances on television programs such as *Meet the Press*

He regularly turned down lucrative opportunities to address business groups in order to speak to student audiences.

Through the 1960s and first half of the 1970s, Milton and Rose continued to spend summer and fall in New England. In 1965 they bought 120 acres of land on a rural hilltop in Vermont. Here they built a hexagonal, modern home with large picture windows. It is a beautiful spot, particularly to watch the leaves turn color in the fall. They named the residence "Capitaf," after *Capitalism and Freedom.*

In his popular writings, Friedman engages in a conversation with the reader, trying to persuade the reader that his conception of the world is accurate, the way the world is and should be. He does not use much emotion in attempting to influence the reader's point of view. He is fair in the sense that he is no rigid ideologue and attempts to judge issues on their merits, sometimes with surprising results. His critics not infrequently consider his work to be unrealistic or utopian (his supporters would say visionary). He is no doctrinaire conservative—indeed, he regularly heaps abuse on conservative positions.

His summary of the differences between writing for academic and for popular audiences is apposite: "The circumlocutions that may be appropriate for a scientific audience will lose . . . your popular audience. . . . For a scientific audience, you are really part of an ongoing process of cumulative knowledge. . . . In respect to popular writing . . . you're trying to convey certain ideas to people, and you don't want excessive qualifications to get in the way."[32] He also says: "It is perfectly understandable that there should be considerable reluctance in releasing figures for general public consumption that have a very large margin of error attached to them. . . . Unfortunately, good public relations may be poor science. For the *analysis* of data, the fundamental point is that it is always better to have some data than none"; the "real problem of statistical analysis is to squeeze information from whatever data are available."[33] Thus Friedman believes that it is better to present data than not to present it, even if it is incomplete and possibly inaccurate.

He says further:

> Of course, selection in publication is inevitable; no one can or should present every last figure he has collected. . . . But at least in publications intended primarily for a scientific audience, it seems to me highly inappropriate for authors to suppress information. . . . The fundamental premise of scientific work must be that knowledge is better than ignorance. . . . The responsibility of scientific workers is to present their data accurately and precisely, and as fully as time, space, and resources will permit. . . . No one can predict in advance what uses . . . will be made of any particular information. The history of science is studded with examples of the unexpected fruitfulness of material originally supposed of little or no value.[34]

Truth has great utilitarian value, even if it is not always recognized at the time. Throughout his career as a public intellectual, he has continued to write for an academic audience.

Friedman considers his popular works to have been beneficial in his development as a writer and thinker. As he says in a preface to a collection of his *Newsweek* columns: "The task has been challenging and highly rewarding. . . . I have learned . . . how easy it is to be misunderstood or—to say the same thing—how hard it is to be crystal clear. I have learned . . . how numerous are the perspectives from which any issue can be viewed."[35]

19

NIXON AND THE NOBEL PRIZE

riedman has advised two presidents of the United States in particular, Richard Nixon and Ronald Reagan. Friedman first met Nixon in the last years of the Eisenhower administration. Allen Wallis, a special assistant to the president working with a cabinet committee that Vice President Nixon chaired, arranged for Friedman to have a long meeting with Nixon. Friedman recalls this session: "I was very favorably impressed. . . . He was highly intelligent, an intellectual in the sense that he was interested in discussing abstract ideas, extremely knowledgeable, and enjoyed engaging in discussion with someone who had different ideas. . . . He was also personally pleasant."[1]

Friedman played no role in the 1960 Kennedy-Nixon race, but, as discussed, he was one of Goldwater's key economic advisers in 1964. In the 1968 election, Arthur Burns, at Nixon's request, put together an advisory committee on the economy to provide recommendations to Nixon in the event that he was elected. Friedman was one of the committee members.

After the 1968 election but before Nixon was inaugurated, Friedman met with him in New York, giving the president-elect a memorandum recommending flexible exchange rates, which Friedman had long advocated. He wrote in *Newsweek* the year before: "We should set the dollar free and let its price in terms of other currencies be determined by private dealings. Such a system of floating exchange rates would eliminate the balance of payments problem . . . and informal exchange controls, and [would allow the ability] to move unilaterally toward freer trade."[2] A negative balance of payments, or trade deficit, was much more of a problem in a system of fixed exchange rates than in one of market-determined exchange rates, because under the latter system, there is no loss of national government financial reserves when there is a trade deficit in order to maintain a currency's value. The system of flexible international exchange rates has accompanied the greatest expansion of world trade and greatest period of prosperity in the world's history.

This is not how it appeared to all at the time. Burns, whom Nixon appointed to head the Federal Reserve System, opposed flexible international exchange rates. Friedman laments that in "many long discussions with Arthur about floating versus fixed exchange rates, I had failed to persuade him of my view."[3] In his memoirs, Friedman makes no real mention of his policy disagreements with Burns fraying their personal relationship. According to Anna Jacobson Schwartz, however, after Burns came out for wage and price controls in 1971, the men's personal relationship became less close.

Friedman met with Nixon four times when Nixon was president, in 1970 and 1971. On one occasion Nixon asked Friedman to use his connection with Burns to encourage the Federal Reserve Board to pursue a more expansionary monetary policy, but Friedman declined. After Nixon imposed wage and price controls in August 1971, he and Friedman had one final meeting in the Oval Office in September. As the meeting ended, Nixon commented, "Don't blame George [Shultz, then administering price controls] for this monstrosity." Friedman replied: "I don't blame George. I blame you."[4]

Nixon thought highly of Friedman's intellectual ability, remarking once in an interview: "I have great respect . . . for Milton Friedman."[5] In 1969 the president received a synopsis of a column including a suggestion by Friedman of how to diminish protests on college campuses. The column, by Willam Buckley, called for a "cut-off date after which the president would send no more draftees to Vietnam, and fight the war with volunteers. This, Friedman thinks, could take the wind out of much of the anti-war rhetoric." On the margin, Nixon wrote: "Get [Defense Secretary Melvin] Laird's comment on this intriguing idea."[6] Another early idea Friedman proposed to Nixon about the draft that Nixon liked was to reduce the years of a young man's draft eligibility from seven to one.

Friedman served the Nixon administration in several official capacities. In addition to the 1968 economic advisory committee—with respect to which he was prominently identified in the media as a Nixon economic adviser—the president appointed him to the Advisory Commission on an All-Volunteer Armed Force, adopted his negative income tax idea, and appointed him to the Commission on White House Fellows, a group that selects fifteen to twenty young people each year to serve as assistants to the president and cabinet-level officials.

Friedman had not served in a full-time government capacity since the New Deal and World War II. More than once he had the opportunity to serve on the Council of Economic Advisers, but he declined. The only position that he has said that he would have been interested in is chairman of the Federal Reserve Board.

His temperament is more professorial than political. He is perhaps too intelligent for politics; it would have bored him. He prefers to follow his own agenda, schedule, and interests. In his mature career, he would have found it difficult to have parroted the views of an incumbent administration. How could his lifestyle have been much better than it was during the 1960s and 1970s? He preferred the University of Chicago, Vermont, and then California to Washington, D.C. Besides, over the long run, his influence may be greater for not having accepted a permanent government position. His reputation for nonpartisanship was enhanced, and he did not spend time on the mundane. Adam Smith made a great mistake in serving as a minor government official the last dozen years of his life rather than spending this time on scholarship.

Friedman's views of Nixon evolved from strong support to, at best, tepid net indifference. He strongly supported Nixon in 1968, less so in 1972, and since then had come to the conclusion that Nixon had a very mixed record, effective in foreign policy and counterproductive in economic policy.

His assessment of Nixon's economic policies is harsher in retrospect than it was at the time. Friedman writes in his memoirs: "In my opinion, Nixon's imposition of wage and price controls . . . did far more harm to the country than any of the later actions that led to his resignation."[7] However, in 1972 he responded to the question "What marks would you give President Nixon for economic performance in 1971?" by saying "Compared with the New Economists' promised land, 0. Compared with my hopes and expectations, 75. Compared with what his 1968 opponent [Hubert Humphrey] would have done, 100."[8]

He also had this exchange in an interview with *Playboy* magazine in 1973:

> *Interviewer:* . . . [I]n the past election, you supported Nixon despite his imposition of controls. . . .
>
> *Friedman:* . . . I regret that he imposed them; yet in doing so, I think he behaved the only way a responsible leader of a democracy could. He resisted controls for nearly three years . . . He tried to make the case against controls . . . [b]ut he failed, and finally gave in to the popular demand for some kind of immediate and extreme measure to halt rising prices, and controls were the measure most people seemed to agree on. As a leader, that was a proper thing for him to do, even though he felt it was the wrong solution. . . .
>
> *Interviewer:* Aren't you saying that there's been a large element of political opportunism in Nixon's reversals?
>
> *Friedman:* One man's opportunism is another's statesmanship. There is a very delicate balance between the two. . . . Good politics is what we should demand from our politicians—to a degree. . . . I think Nixon acted properly. The real problem is educating the public, and there he was unsuccessful.[9]

When Friedman underwent open heart surgery at the Mayo Clinic in 1972, Nixon telephoned his surgeon to express his interest and concern. Similar to the way that Friedman disparages Nixon in his memoirs, Nixon does not consider Friedman in his.

Many have criticized Friedman's involvement in Chile, but this is not how he viewed his role there at all. Between 1957 and 1970, about 100 Chilean students studied economics at the University of Chicago. Friedman had minimal contact with them. Typically the only way that he knew them was if they took one of his courses or participated in his money and banking workshop. On returning to Chile, these students, generally strong advocates of a free market, became known as the "Chicago Boys."

The Chicago Boys had little influence on Chilean society and played little role in the Chilean government before the coup d'état that brought General Augusto Pinochet to power in September 1973 and resulted in the death of the democratically elected Marxist president, Salvador Allende. For the first year or so after the coup, little changed with respect to the Chicago Boys' influence. But as time went on, they increasingly became key economic advisers to the new Chilean government.

In March 1975 Friedman visited Chile for six days together with another member of the economics faculty at Chicago, Arnold Harberger, who directed the Chicago-Chilean studies program. As in similar trips abroad, Friedman had a busy schedule of seminars and public talks. He, Harberger, and several others had a forty-five-minute meeting with Pinochet.

Friedman discussed the fragility of freedom in two talks in Chile, characterizing the existing regime there as unfree. He turned down two offers of honorary degrees from Chilean universities because he thought that accepting them could be interpreted as political support for the Pinochet government. He believes that by advancing the cause of economic freedom in Chile, he advanced prosperity and the prospects for political reform there. In remarks honoring Friedman in 2002, among the areas that President George W. Bush singled out was his influence on Chile: "We have seen Milton Friedman's ideas at work in Chile, where a group of economists called the 'Chicago Boys' brought inflation under control and laid the groundwork for economic success."[10]

In September 1975 the *New York Times* reported that Friedman was the "guiding light of the junta's economic policy."[11] An Anthony Lewis column appeared the next month that claimed that the Chilean "junta's economic policy is based on the ideas of Milton Friedman."[12] In response, there were student protests at the University of Chicago. The student paper, the *Chicago Maroon,* carried a front-page story under the headline "Radicals Plan Friedman Protest; Harberger Also Accused of Role." The *Maroon* reported:

> Left-wing campus and area organizations . . . have formed a united front to protest the involvement of University professors Milton Friedman and Arnold Harberger in policy making for the ruling military junta in Chile.
> The united front, officially titled the "Committee against Friedman/Harberger Collaboration with the Chilean Junta," has called for a protest demonstration . . . in front of the Administration Building.[13]

Posters were printed for this event: "Drive Friedman Off Campus through Protest and Exposure."

There is a cost in expressing views not in sync with the majority. Over the next decade, there were frequent protests against Friedman as a result of his purported role as the intellectual economic mainstay of the Chilean government. For years he entered speaking engagements via side entrances in order to avoid protestors. Angry letters to the editor denounced him, particularly after he received the Nobel Prize in Economics.

He has always considered the protests against him for his visit to Chile to be hypocritical and baseless. He wrote the following letter to the Stanford student newspaper some years after his trip to Chile:

> I have just returned from a 12-day stay in Communist China. . . . I gave a series of talks. . . . In addition, I had a two-hour private meeting with Zhao Ziyang, the General Secretary of the Chinese Communist Party. . . .
> Under the circumstances, should I prepare myself for an avalanche of protests for having been willing to give advice to so evil a government? If not, why not?[14]

Friedman did not consider receiving the 1976 Nobel Memorial Prize in Economic Sciences to be the pinnacle of his career. He says, rather, that he is more interested in what economists will think of his work fifty years hence. He received notice that he had won the Nobel Prize on October 14, 1976, as he campaigned in Michigan for a state ballot measure to limit taxes. Only when one of many reporters at the event asked what his reaction was to winning the Nobel Prize did Friedman learn that he had received it.

Friedman was the twelfth recipient of the Nobel Prize in Economics, in the seventh year that it was awarded (there was more than one recipient some years). The Nobel Prize in Economics is a latecomer to the Nobel list, added in 1969, sixty-eight years after the prizes in Physics, Chemistry, Medicine, Literature, and Peace were initiated.

There is some indication that Friedman was passed over for the prize before 1976 for political reasons. According to Robert Skole, a foreign correspondent in Sweden, even when the prize was finally awarded: "We journalists waited two hours past the original time set for the Academy of Sciences to announce its Economics Prize. . . . [T]he Friedman announcement was delayed, and it was pretty obvious that some members of the Academy were arguing against him."[15] In their memoirs, Rose writes that opposition to Milton's receiving the prize was "not among the professional economists who made the recommendation . . . but among the broader committee of the Swedish Academy of Science."[16]

The response—both negative and positive—to Friedman's receiving the Nobel Prize was perhaps greater than to that of any other laureate, at least in economics. Many on the political left were incensed, as a result both of his economic views and his trip to Chile. On October 24, 1976, the *New York Times* published two letters condemning Friedman, each signed by two Nobel laureates. George Wald and Linus Pauling wrote: "In a deplorable exhibition of insensitivity, the Nobel Memorial Committee on economics has awarded the prize this year to Milton Friedman."[17] And David Baltimore and

S. E. Luria wrote: "At this time, when the issue of the responsibility of scientists to be concerned with the social consequences of their work is being raised forcibly and effectively, it is very disturbing that a Nobel prize for economics should be awarded to Prof. Milton Friedman."[18]

Of Friedman's "record as a consultant and adviser to repressive regimes around the world," *Nation* magazine said that among "his clients has been the military junta in Chile which . . . has become one of the most repressive and murderous governments in the world."[19] Melville Ulmer wrote in the *New Republic* that Friedman's receipt of the Nobel Prize "seemed as incongruous as a peace prize for Idi Amin, or a literature prize for Spiro Agnew. . . . [Friedman] is a hyperactive extremist of the right. . . . Is a modern restatement of the 1776 thesis of Adam Smith worthy of a Nobel Prize in economics?"[20]

It would be a mistaken impression, however, that most of the response to Friedman's receiving the Nobel Prize was negative. The vast majority of even the media response was positive. *Newsweek* wrote that he "loves a good fight, and he is jaunty in the fray: flashing a grin, relishing a fine point or a slip by his opponent, demolishing a whole line of argument with a blunt fact or a pointed lesson in logic, Milton Friedman will follow a fact no matter where it leads."[21] The *Wall Street Journal* editorialized: "The academy's selection is a credit to its members."[22] According to the London *Financial Times,* "Friedman is unquestionably the most influential economist of our day."[23]

His friends were of course even more favorable. He received literally hundreds of congratulatory messages from around the world, both from people he knew and from those he did not. Many were signed by both husband and wife and addressed to Milton and Rose. He received dozens of telegrams, some signed by whole departments of economics.

His standard reply letter began: "I appreciate very much your letter. . . . The nicest thing about the award has been the warm outpouring of congratulations from so many friends and colleagues around the world."[24] He would then often personalize the response with a brief anecdote.

In its press release announcing the award of the 1976 Nobel Prize in Economics, the Royal Swedish Academy of Sciences said that it was for Friedman's "achievements in the fields of consumption analysis, monetary history and theory, and for his demonstration of the complexity of stabilization policy." The release also noted that the "widespread debate on Friedman's theories . . . led to a review of monetary policies pursued by central banks. . . . It is very rare for an economist to wield such influence . . . not only on the direction of scientific research but also on actual policies."[25]

Friedman's Nobel lecture was on the subject "Inflation and Unemployment." He used the occasion to reaffirm his view that the methods and criteria for success that are used in the physical sciences should also be used in the social sciences. In both the social and physical sciences, "there is no 'certain' . . . knowledge; only tentative hypotheses." Repeating his argument from "The Methodology of Positive Economics," he said: "Positive scientific knowledge that enables us to predict the consequences of a possible course of action is clearly a prerequisite for the normative judgment whether that course of action is desirable."[26]

Several thousand people protested in Stockholm the day of the Nobel ceremony. During the presentation of the Nobel medal to him, one protester stood up and yelled, "Down with capitalism, freedom for Chile."[27] This was the first time that a Nobel ceremony had been interrupted by an outburst. Rose notes that as a result, after presentation of his medal and certificate, "Milton stood for a longer ovation than had been received by any of the preceding six laureates."[28]

Among Friedman's favorite letters after receiving the Nobel Prize was one from a class of elementary students, who wrote him that they were "studying economics, too." Their teacher had said that Friedman was an admirer of Adam Smith. Friedman wrote back that he was

> delighted to hear that you are studying his great book, *The Wealth of Nations*. It has much to tell us today. In many ways we have come full circle since that book was written.

At the time Adam Smith wrote there were many government regulations and restrictions. His book was a blow for freedom. It succeeded. However, it took some seventy years before it did. Since then we have been drifting back, and today we again have a situation in which we have extensive controls and restrictions on human freedom. We need a new Adam Smith to strike a new blow for freedom.[29]

A great source of Friedman's success is his sense of humor. Examples over the years include:

There's no such thing as a free lunch.

Hell hath no fury like a bureaucrat scorned.

There is nothing so permanent as a temporary government program.

Not during my first eighty-seven years, but I make no guarantees as to the future [in response to the charge that because he favors legalization of marijuana, he must smoke it].

This is like burning down the barn to roast the pig.

When you stand before a civil servant, is there any real doubt who is the servant and who is the master?

Another good aspect of his work are the obiter dicta he expresses, which frequently give broader insight than the particular subject under consideration. He writes, for example, in *Capitalism and Freedom:*

So great is the capacity for self-justification.[30]

There is seldom anything truly new under the sun in economic policy.[31]

He offers these pearls, among others, in *A Monetary History:*

Here is a striking example of the deceptiveness of appearances, of the frequently dominant importance of forces operating beneath the surface.[32]

The changes in men's ideas were no less important than the changes in institutions.[33]

This entire silver episode is a fascinating example of how important what people think about money can sometimes be.[34]

Other things being the same . . . But, of course, other things are seldom the same.[35]

In lectures:

A common human characteristic is that if anything bad happens it is somebody else's fault.[36]

He would write in *Two Lucky People:*

As so often is the case, what "everyone knows" is not so.[37]

Nothing is harder than for anyone, whatever his character, to admit that his plans for a major project were defective.[38]

Over a long life, I have learned repeatedly how large a gap separates the giving of advice from the taking of advice.[39]

Anyone who is converted in an evening isn't worth converting. The next person of opposite views . . . will unconvert him.[40]

In correspondence:

I have always felt that understatement is more effective than over-statement.[41]

Milton and Rose enjoyed their thirty years in Chicago very much. When they left, shortly after he received the Nobel Prize, they had no way of knowing that the best was yet to come with respect to public influence. Milton writes, "It was our great good fortune to enjoy a more stimulating intellectual environment at Chicago than any we have ever encountered elsewhere."[42]

Part Three

1977–2006

20

FREE TO CHOOSE

ilton and Rose moved to San Francisco in January 1977, a few weeks after he received the Nobel Prize. Rose had long wished to live on the West Coast, and in the Bay Area in particular, where the climate is warmer than in Chicago. Milton, retired from teaching, could now live anywhere. There were better and more profitable uses of his time than continuing to teach and supervise graduate students and interact in department and university affairs. He would turn sixty-five that year, formerly the mandatory retirement age at the University of Chicago. He had already lived sixteen years longer than his father had lived. Both Jan and David, and their families, now live in northern California. Friedman's last class at Chicago was in the fall of 1976, his workshop in money and banking.

The Friedmans also moved to California because Milton was invited to be a senior research fellow at the Hoover Institution by Glenn Campbell, who had previously been affiliated with the American Enterprise Institute. The Hoover Institution on War, Revolution and Peace was founded in 1919 by Herbert Hoover at his alma mater, Stanford University, before he became president of the United States. The Hoover Institution is a public policy research center whose purpose is advanced study of politics and economics in the United States and around the world. It has excellent archival collections and top-notch scholars. Friedman enjoyed his opportunities at Hoover—to do research, meet individuals, and participate in seminars and such—where he remained active until his death.

Both Milton and Rose had offices at Hoover. In the Hoover archive, there are only a few busts; one is of him. Other fellows at Hoover include Martin Anderson, George Shultz, and Thomas Sowell. A number from Chicago, including Gary Becker and Richard Epstein, hold joint appointments at Hoover.

Friedman has written for a number of Hoover publications, including essays by he and Rose in two major Hoover works: *The United States in the 1980s* (1980) and *Thinking About America: The United States in the 1990s* (1988). In the former, the Friedmans' essay, "The Tide Is Turning," appears first. In *Thinking About America*, which begins with an essay by Richard Nixon and concludes with one by Ronald Reagan, the Friedmans contribute "The Tide in the Affairs of Men."

Another of Milton's publications for Hoover is "Why Government Is the Problem" (1993), in the Hoover series *Essays in Public Policy*. He here inveighs against the government role in area after area: education, crime, homelessness, family values, housing, medical care, the financial system, highway congestion, and air traffic control, among others. He makes a wrong prediction in this work in describing the ills of government, noting that he has "not even mentioned the botched economic policies: the reverse Reaganomics that the Bush administration practiced contributed to the recession of 1990–1991, condemned us to a very slow and erratic recovery from a mild recession, and, very probably, promises a relatively slow 1990s, almost regardless of what the Clinton administration does."[1] He here ascribes more potency to fiscal and regulatory policies (the practices that he criticized in the first Bush administration) than he does elsewhere. In any event, the main macroeconomic practices that the Clinton administration followed with respect to fiscal policy were raising taxes (which Friedman opposed), reducing the budget deficit and then bringing it into surplus, decreasing military spending, and slightly decreasing total government spending as a percentage of gross national product. These practices were coincident with great economic growth, not a slow 1990s. He also has incorrectly predicted for two decades that there will be another period of inflation, and he has foreseen periods of economic downturn and slowdown that did not emerge. He is not always prescient.

Friedman's secretary from Chicago, Gloria Valentine, followed him to California. Since she lives in San Francisco and commutes to Stanford each day, she brought Friedman his mail in the evening that he received at Hoover. He taped responses that she transcribed and he then approved.

Rose became his primary collaborator and colleague since they left Chicago. Their three best-known books from this period are *Free to Choose* (1980), *The Tyranny of the Status Quo* (1984), and *Two Lucky People: Memoirs* (1998).

They lived in California for more than twenty-nine years, from early 1977 to the present, almost as long as their three decades in Chicago. Indeed, since the family spent considerable time away from Chicago during Friedman's academic years there and was in New England almost every summer, and then summer and fall, he has now spent more time in California than anywhere else.

They originally moved into an apartment in San Francisco, then ten years later bought a larger apartment in the same building. Theirs is a beautiful home, high up a multistory complex, overlooking the San Francisco Bay and Alcatraz Island. Their living room is on a corner overlooking the city and bay; the floor plan and furniture placement create an open feeling. His office, messy as ever, has a great tall window view of the city. There are papers spread everywhere in stacks and a personal library of perhaps 1,200 to 1,500 volumes and bound magazines and separate magazine articles. The apartment is decorated somewhat sparsely, with a few knickknacks of Milton's, but mostly art collected and arranged by Rose. A table bearing their periodical reading includes twenty or so magazines and journals, ranging from popular to academic. These include, on the popular side, *Newsweek*, *Commentary*, *Liberty*, and formerly *The*

Public Interest. The guest restroom is decorated with framed editorial cartoons of Milton.

The couple originally thought that they would continue to vacation in Vermont. But a couple of years after moving to California, they purchased a retreat at Sea Ranch, a small planned development coastal community about two and a half hours north of San Francisco. Their getaway was located on a bluff, with a beautiful view of the Pacific. Until they recently sold Sea Ranch, they spent about half their time there each year. Milton observes in their memoirs: "All in all, while I sometimes still miss Vermont in the summer time, Sea Ranch has proved a splendid substitute for Capitaf, and on a year-round basis."[2]

After moving to California, Milton first spent three months as a visiting scholar in the Federal Reserve Bank of San Francisco. He and Rose anticipated that he would continue primarily to pursue academic studies, at a more leisurely pace than before retirement. A few days after arriving on the West Coast, however, they received a phone call that redirected them to, in Rose's words, "the most exciting venture of our lives"[3]—what became the *Free to Choose* television series and book. Milton's old friend Allen Wallis was chairman of the Corporation for Public Broadcasting during the Ford administration, and he recommended Milton to Robert Chitester, head of a Pennsylvania public broadcasting station.

Chitester contacted Friedman with an ambitious project: a $2.5 million television documentary series that would allow him to expound his views to a larger audience than ever. Friedman wrote that he was willing to "devote a large part of my time and energies during the next year to eighteen months to a TV series designed to present my personal social, economic and political philosophy,"[4] though the commitment turned out to be closer to three to four years.

The first step was for Chitester to raise the money to make the idea a reality. Fortuitously, John Kenneth Galbraith had recently starred in a series on the history of economic thought from Adam Smith to the present. Some viewed Friedman's series as an opportunity to achieve ideological balance. Major funders of *Free to Choose* included the Sarah Scaife Foundation, which contributed $500,000, and the Getty Oil Company, which contributed $330,000. The Reader's Digest Association gave $300,000 in cash and promoted the series. The Public Broadcasting System declined to help fund *Free to Choose*.

In its introduction and first chapter, the book version of *Free to Choose* presents some of Friedman's most convincing arguments for capitalism. He begins on the note that the United States was founded on the twin ideas of economic and political freedom. By political freedom, he essentially has in mind the ideas expressed by Thomas Jefferson in the Declaration of Independence: "We hold these truths to be self-evident, that all men are created equal, that they are endowed by their Creator with certain unalienable Rights; that among these are Life, Liberty, and the pursuit of Happiness."

Friedman's conception of the optimal polity is individualistic. Democracy is not paramount in his hierarchy of political values; individual human rights are. He believes the individualist ideas of the Declaration were also expressed by John Stuart Mill, who held in *On Liberty:* "The sole end for which mankind are warranted, individually or collectively, in interfering with the liberty of action of any of their number, is self-protection. . . . [T]he only purpose for which power can be rightfully exercised over any member of a civilized community, against his will, is to prevent harm to other persons. . . . Over himself, over his own body and mind, the individual is sovereign."[5]

By economic freedom, Friedman has in mind the ideas of Adam Smith—one of Friedman's unheralded accomplishments is to have contributed to the popular rehabilitation of Smith. Through the 1970s, Smith had been more likely to be looked on as a historical curiosity who had put forward ideas that were antiquated and obsolete even in his lifetime (1723–1790). For decades his idea of an "invisible hand" was routinely ridiculed. But according to Friedman in *Free to Choose:* "Smith's key insight was that both parties to an exchange can benefit and that, *so long as cooperation is strictly voluntary,* no exchange will take place unless both parties do benefit."[6] The great merit of free exchange, whether at home or abroad, is that both parties believe that they benefit. Exchange is not a "zero-sum" game, as some would have it. Rather, trade is win-win, and therefore should be encouraged to the greatest extent possible.

This is why, Friedman believes, an individual who, in Smith's words, "intends only his own gain" is led to promote the benefit of others: "Man has almost constant occasion for the help of his brethren," Smith wrote, "and it is vain for him to expect it from their benevolence only. He will be more likely to prevail if he can interest their self-love in his favour. . . . Give me that which I want, and you shall have this which you want, is the meaning of every such offer"[7] of exchange.

Following Friedrich Hayek, Friedman emphasizes the information-transmitting nature of prices. Prices transmit information instantaneously at no (or little) cost of worldwide demand for and supply of all goods and services. Prices are, furthermore, based on exclusive use of goods and services; prices require, therefore, private property. Private property of both goods and services is necessary for the price system to operate.

The *Free to Choose* television series consisted of ten programs. As one of the "four essential requirements for the series" before its initial production, Friedman stated: "I am going to speak my own words and no one else's." He notes in his memoirs that this "requirement reflected my own judgment about my capacities."[8]

Each televised segment of *Free to Choose* consists of a half-hour presentation by Friedman on a particular topic filmed on location around the world, followed by a half-hour discussion with Friedman and politically diverse guests on subjects raised in the program. Among the guests were Donald Rumsfeld, William McChesney Martin, Michael Harrington, Thomas Sowell, Frances Fox Piven, Robert Lekachman, Nicholas von Hoffman, and Albert Shanker.

The *Free to Choose* television series was a popular success around the globe, and the book was the best-selling nonfiction title in the United States in 1980. The original hardback sold about 400,000 copies, and paperback and foreign editions total a million more. It has been translated into at least seventeen languages; it was translated into underground versions in the Soviet Union, Poland, and several other eastern European countries before the collapse of Communism. The book was a best-seller in Japan, selling 200,000 copies.

Milton and Rose traveled around the world to film the series—from America, to Britain, to Hong Kong, to India. He had no written script for each program, though he had written and lectured on a topic previously in preparation. He would go on location and speak extemporaneously.

Dozens of stories appeared about the series, and the accompanying book was widely reviewed. The *Christian Science Monitor* wrote: "He and his wife have finally brought their most important arguments together, condensed them, organized them into a powerful whole, expressed them for the reader who has no formal schooling in economics, and illustrated them with present-day examples."[9] According to *Reader's Digest:* "Milton Friedman brings verities back into focus and puts us in touch with how a free and abundant society can work—if we will let it."[10] The *New York Times Book Review* opined: "Noteworthy for its clarity, logic, candor, and unequivocal stand on political implications."[11]

Free to Choose is dedicated to Milton and Rose's grandchildren at the time, Ricky and Patri, Jan's and David's respective sons from their first marriages. Both Janet and David have since remarried. David has two more children, Rebecca and William, from his second marriage. Janet is an attorney, and David, like his father, is a professor of economics.

Milton and Rose were not rich before he received the Nobel Prize and they wrote *Free to Choose*. The royalties from *Free to Choose* exceed by a magnitude of several times the royalties from all his other works combined. After the book's success, the Friedmans' financial status was higher than it had ever been.

Friedman introduced many of his basic themes to television audiences around the world through *Free to Choose,* including educational vouchers, the monetary source of inflation, the power of the market, and the counterproductiveness of much government activity. In preparing the series, he offered these thoughts. To change the course of the previous half-century from collectivism to renewed individualism will

> require reinforcing our heritage rather than simply living on it. It will require reining the ambitions of our political authorities. . . . It will require once again widening the field within which the individual, the family, the voluntary organization can exercise initiative and ingenuity. . . . It will require dismantling many of the shackles with which we have bound the economic activities of our citizens. . . . This is how . . . we can achieve a fresh renaissance of culture, humanity, and wealth.[12]

Rose writes of *Free to Choose:* "Who would have dreamed that after retiring from teaching, Milton would be able to preach the doctrine of human freedom to many millions of people in countries around the globe through television, millions more through our book based on the television program, and countless others through videocassettes."[13] Milton comments that Rose's "title as associate producer was far more than a formality. She played an indispensable role: she participated in every planning session and every editing session; she was on every shoot and involved in every discussion about the content of my statements to the camera; she was the best critic of my performance, . . . the only one willing to be blunt in criticizing me, and the most helpful in setting me on the right track."[14]

21

REAGAN AND

INTERNATIONAL INFLUENCE

t is not too much to say that *Free to Choose* provided much of the domestic blueprint for Ronald Reagan's presidency, which started in 1980 with Reagan's election as president, the same year that *Free to Choose* appeared. Friedman first met Reagan in 1967, when Reagan had recently been elected governor of California and Friedman was a visiting professor at the University of California at Los Angeles. Reagan impressed Friedman with his opposition to the financing for higher education in California at that time, whereby, in Friedman's words, "the people in Watts were paying the college expenses of the people from Beverly Hills." He recalls of this first meeting with Reagan that he was "delighted to find that he was not only a warm, attractive human being, but his views on educational issues were very much in line with my own."[1]

Friedman and Reagan's next major interaction was six years later, in 1973, when Reagan was pushing a ballot proposition in California that would have limited state spending. The men barnstormed the state for a day, flying from one campaign site to another. At the end of the day, a reporter asked Friedman whether he would support Reagan for president in 1976. Friedman said that he would.

According to Martin Anderson, a key Nixon and Reagan adviser, Reagan read "some of the best economists in the world, including the giants of the free market economy—Ludwig von Mises, Friedrich Hayek and Milton Friedman."[2] Friedman tells the story about a friend coming across Reagan reading a copy of *Capitalism and Freedom* when he first ran for governor of California.

Reagan sometimes referred to Friedman in his regular radio addresses after he left the governorship in 1975 and before he was elected president in 1980. He remarked in a 1977 address: "The unemployment figure in America is distorted by the availability of unemployment benefits. Milton Friedman has said, 'a large fraction of our unemployment figure does not constitute a human problem—it constitutes people taking advantage of very good arrangements.'"[3] After becoming president, Reagan spoke in 1981 to the Conservative Political Action Conference, some of his most fervent supporters. He here identified Friedman as one of the six "intellectual leaders" who "shaped so much of our thoughts."[4] The others were Russell Kirk, Henry Hazlitt, James Burnham, Hayek, and Mises.

Unusual for him, Friedman became increasingly pessimistic in the later 1970s about the survival prospects of capitalism and democracy. His writings from this period convey the view that America faced a genuine choice: to continue on its historical path of political and economic freedom or to descend into some form of collectivism. He expressed similar concerns about the West generally and, in particular, Great Britain.

In a series of essays and addresses, he questioned whether the status quo was tolerable, whether it would endure, whether it could be replaced by a more free market direction, and whether America and the rest of the West could and would change course. He remarked in 1975: "Those of us fortunate enough to have been born in the United States in the twentieth century take freedom for granted: it seems to us the natural state of mankind. But that is a misconception. Freedom is an extraordinarily unusual situation. If one looks back through history, one finds that the natural state of mankind in most periods has been tyranny and misery."[5]

He continued this theme in essays written for the *Saturday Evening Post* over the next several years, some of which were early material for *Free to Choose:*

> What I have to say has to do with the question of whether America is what it was—whether America is the land of opportunity which produced over the past 200 years the greatest freedom and prosperity for the widest range of people that the world has ever seen . . . ?
>
> Or is America what it has seemed to be becoming these past few decades? . . . Is it instead a land of growing bureaucracy and diminishing freedom? . . .
>
> I believe very deeply that we are nearing the point of no return.[6]

He wrote in a 1979 symposium that the "key issue of the 1980s is whether we shall . . . reinvigorate the human freedom and economic freedom that together have made the U.S. a magnet . . . or whether we shall succumb to creeping collectivism and become a totalitarian state."[7]

In September 1980 Reagan gave the following speech while running for president, making these Friedmanian points:

> We must move boldly, decisively and quickly to control the runaway growth of federal spending . . . and to reform the regulatory web . . .
>
> We must reduce personal income tax rates . . .
>
> We must establish a stable, sound, and predictable monetary policy.[8]

As with Nixon, Friedman served on a committee prior to Reagan's election that prepared policy papers for implementation if Reagan were elected. "Once in office," Friedman remarks, "Reagan acted very much along the lines that we recommended."[9] George Shultz, secretary of Labor and the Treasury under Nixon and Reagan's secretary of state from 1982 to 1989, chaired the Reagan preelection economic policy committee. The Friedmans and Shultzes watched the 1980 election returns together, when Reagan won a landslide victory, unexpectedly taking with him a Republican majority in the Senate for the first time in a quarter of a century.

Allen Wallis was undersecretary of state for economic affairs while Shultz was secretary. Martin Anderson, affiliated with the Hoover Institution at this time, was perhaps Reagan's key domestic adviser while he was running for president and during the administration's first years. Beryl Sprinkel, one of Friedman's students, was a chairman of the Council of Economic Advisers during Reagan's presidency. According to Edwin Meese—perhaps Reagan's closest personal adviser and attorney general—Friedman was the "guru"[10] of the Reagan administration. Many others who knew, were influenced by, or were students of Friedman participated in the Reagan administration as well as elsewhere in government, academia, and business.

Friedman, Alan Greenspan, Shultz, Arthur Burns, Paul McCracken, Herb Stein, William Simon, Martin Anderson, and others served on the President's Economic Policy Advisory Board during Reagan's White House years. This group of outside economists met with the president regularly, particularly during his first term—as many as half a dozen times a year or so. Anderson provides these observations of Friedman and his influence in the context of discussing Reagan's economic advisers:

> Perhaps those with the most influence were Milton Friedman, Alan Greenspan, and William Simon. . . . Reagan was especially taken with Milton Friedman. He just could not resist Friedman's infectious enthusiasm and Reagan's eyes sparkled with delight every time he engaged in a dialogue with him.
>
> Of the thousands of people who have helped shape the new intellectual forces sweeping around the world, Milton Friedman probably has had the greatest influence. By his articles, lectures, books co-authored with his brilliant wife, Rose, and television series, Friedman has had an enormous impact on the . . . changing view of the nature of a free society. The breadth and depth of this influence cannot be explained by just the words he wrote and spoke. A lot of it can only be explained by his extraordinary personality.[11]

Meese writes: "Of special importance among the academic advisors was Professor Milton Friedman . . . [who] was a particular favorite of the President. His staunch advocacy of private enterprise, the free market, and tax limitation (dating back to California), and his extensive knowledge of monetary matters were invaluable to the administration."[12] According to Donald Regan, after becoming Reagan's Secretary of the Treasury, he "reviewed the economic theories on which the President's remarks were . . . based. . . . It was clear, first of all, that he was influenced by the economic theories of Milton Friedman."[13]

William Simon, whom George Shultz recruited into government service, remembered dinners with Friedman in the early 1970s. Shultz frequently had Simon over for dinner, along with "guests like Milton Friedman and George Stigler. . . . They would engage in the highest level of debate I had ever encountered, arguing points and counterpoints, . . . playing devil's advocate, but always in a tenor of intellectual inquiry rather than mental combat. For me, it was fun and exciting and inspiring and exhilarating, but also exhausting and, at times, intimidating."[14]

Rich Thomas, *Newsweek*'s chief economic correspondent, summarized Reagan's economic program in 1988, upon his departure from office:

> Before there was Reagonomics, there was Milton Friedman. . . . Friedman became Reagan's tutor on economics. . . . Friedman's gospel stresses the paramount importance of money—the absolute necessity of stable growth in the supply of cash and credit circulating in the economy at any one time. But Friedman also has a little-known theory about budget policy that Reagan absorbed and practiced from Day One in the White House.
>
> In Friedman's view, the most important thing about budgets is the level and direction of spending—not the size of the deficit. . . . Guided by Friedman's theory, Reagan set aside the deficit problem when he came to Washington.

The largest photo accompanying the article is of Friedman. Below it is the caption: "Tutor: Economist Friedman taught Reagan the importance of tight money and low taxes."[15]

In January 1981, the month of his inauguration, Reagan was quoted first in the paperback edition of *Free to Choose* endorsing the work: "Superb."[16] Friedman writes in his memoirs, "No other president in my lifetime comes close to Reagan in adherence to clearly specified principles dedicated to promoting and maintaining a free society."[17] In 1988, as he was preparing to leave the White House, Reagan contributed the final essay to the Hoover Institution collection *Thinking About America: The United States in the 1990s,* in which he made these remarks: "In the mid-1960s, Nobel-Laureate-to-be Milton Friedman wrote *Capitalism and Freedom,* which traced the critical link between capitalism and economic prosperity on the one side and democracy and political freedom on the other. Given this link, it is not surprising that the trend to economic freedom in the 1980s has proceeded in parallel with an equally strong resurgence of democracy."[18] Friedman wrote in a 2004 obituary: "Few people in human history have contributed more to the achievement of human freedom than Ronald Wilson Reagan."[19]

Friedman's influence extends beyond the United States. It is particularly strong in the English-speaking world. One of the avid watchers of *Free to Choose* in Great Britain was the new prime minister, Margaret Thatcher, who came to office in 1979. In February 1980, just before the series was to run in England and while Reagan was running for president in the United States, Thatcher met with Friedman in England. *Punch* magazine ran a cartoon of her bowing reverently before a television set playing Friedman when the series aired.

Friedman's intellectual role in Britain is largely unknown to Americans, but it is broadly similar to the one that he has played in the United States. Both countries are bound together by the tie of language in a way that transcends America's relationship with non–English-speaking countries. From music, to science, to culture, English-speaking contributors dominate the world. During the twentieth century, the United States, Great Britain, and other English-speaking nations received about half or more of the Nobel Prizes in physics, chemistry, and medicine, and about three-quarters of those in economics.

Friedman became known in England a few years after coming to prominence in the United States. The primary institution with which he was affiliated in Great Britain is the London-based think tank the Institute of Economic Affairs (IEA). Friedman says that "without the IEA, I doubt very much whether there would have been a Thatcherite revolution."[20]

He was a major force in the IEA in the 1970s. According to Richard Cockett, foremost historian of libertarian think tanks in Great Britain: "Friedman became the Institute's most celebrated exponent of monetary stability. . . . [H]e was a frequent contributor to IEA forums and debates, and published numerous papers for the IEA. . . . Friedman became the most famous exponent of the free-market economy during the 1970s." The IEA helped to prepare *Free to Choose* for British television; according to Cockett, the series had an "enormous impact on British public opinion."[21] Among those who played a particular role in promoting monetarism in England was Alan Walters, who first heard Friedman lecture at Cambridge in 1953–1954, and who later became a top Thatcher adviser. Arthur Seldon, longtime editorial director of the IEA, refers to the "Friedmanite counter-revolution against Keynes 'sponsored' at the IEA."[22]

Cockett writes that "probably" the "most famous publication"[23] by the IEA is Friedman's 1970 Wincott Lecture sponsored by the Institute, "The Counter-Revolution in Monetary Theory." As discussed in chapter 12 on Keynes, Friedman used the lecture to explore the inadequacies of Keynesianism. Essentially, Friedman's view is that fiscal policy—aggregate government spending and taxing, and running budget deficits or surpluses—has little effect on national macroeconomic outcomes in the short run. Tax policies are important with respect to forming long-term rewards and expectations, thereby influencing effort and direction in employment and occupation. His key macroeconomic views include the belief that nations should expand their money supply at a fixed rate of about 2 to 5 percent a year and practice free international trade. If a nation adopted these policies, it would do well. The policies might not be perfect or all-encompassing, but they are very good ones. His other ideas of optimal government economic macropolicy include keeping government spending, marginal tax rates, and regulation low.

In his Wincott Lecture, Friedman discussed, among other things, the importance of monetary policy as opposed to fiscal policy in determining short-run macroeconomic fluctuations. In the second half of the 1960s, there were several occasions when monetary and fiscal policies diverged with respect to their intended consequences. In each case, monetary policy proved more potent. He made this point with respect to Japan and the United States in 1999:

> Repeated fiscal stimuli [by Japan] since 1992 have been accompanied by restrictive monetary policy. . . . During the past six years, growth in the monetary total . . . has averaged 2.8% a year. . . . So this is a clear case where monetary, not fiscal, policy determined the course of the economy.
>
> The U.S. is currently another such case. Fiscal policy has been highly restrictive for some years, with a shift from large deficits to surpluses in a few years. Monetary policy has been expansive. . . . The economy has been in an expansion. As in Japan, monetary policy has clearly determined the course of the economy.
>
> Some years back, I tried to collect all the episodes I could find in which monetary policy and fiscal policy went in opposite directions. As in these two episodes, monetary policy uniformly dominated fiscal policies.[24]

Friedman's influence is not restricted to the English-speaking world. His work has been translated into more than twenty foreign languages. He is among the few American intellectuals to enter the international lexicon both academically and popularly.

He was in frequent demand around the world for close to sixty years, the length of time that he advised foreign governments on economic policy. He traveled outside of the United States scores of times to give lectures and to advise foreign governments, including officials at the very highest levels of power. He frequently visited students in many countries and participated in international intellectual gatherings.

His message was the same wherever he went. He preached the virtues of free markets, stable prices, denationalization, privatization, free trade, less regulation, reducing the size and scope of government, lower taxes, flexible international exchange rates, and noninflationary monetary policies. It is a message that many national and political leaders, as well as economists, have sought and seek to hear.

Countries that he has visited in part to advise on economic issues include Australia, Brazil, Chile, China, Greece, India, Iran, Israel, Japan, the United Kingdom, and the former Yugoslavia. Milton and Rose happened to travel to Israel shortly after Menachem Begin was elected prime minister in 1977, and Begin consulted with him.

Friedman has had considerable influence in the People's Republic of China. As have many others around the world, the Chinese have followed his admonition that inflation is a monetary phenomenon. Friedman thinks that monetarism and the quantity theory of money are nonideological. The quantity theory simply describes a relationship between the amount of money in an economy, the rate at which it changes hands, goods and services sold, and prices. In a properly working monetary order, prices are simply relative values. Friedman notes that Karl Marx was a quantity of money theorist, in the sense that Marx tied average prices to the money supply. At the same time, to the extent that there were less consistent relationships between money and prices than Friedman postulates, a larger discretionary role for government might be required. Empirical Keynesianism is inherently more interventionist than empirical monetarism.

Friedman had a significant 1988 meeting with Zhao Ziyang, the reforming general secretary of the Communist Party and the heir-apparent to Deng Xiaoping, about eight months before the Tiananmen Square crackdown and Zhao's fall from power. Friedman and Zhao spoke (through a translator) at the meeting of about two hours, much longer than Zhao's typical meetings with visitors, particularly foreign ones. In addition, a reporter from the *People's Daily*, China's leading paper, was present, and—almost unheard of—Zhao accompanied Milton and Rose to the driveway, where photos were taken that were printed in Chinese newspapers. After the Tiananmen Square crackdown, Friedman's influence on Zhao was mentioned frequently in the media.

Hong Kong is (or was) sometimes described as practicing the policies that are most consistent with Friedman's vision. When, in 1998, he spoke out against changes there in response to the ascension of the People's Republic of China, the Hong Kong stock market tumbled. A *Wall Street Journal* article in 1998 says that he is "idolized" in Hong Kong. "During his frequent visits . . . , the economist has been mobbed like a rock star . . . and kissed by a television journalist."[25]

Friedman stood in very high standing among dissidents in the former Soviet Union and Communist eastern Europe. Vaclav Klaus, who served as prime minister of the Czech Republic, is influenced by Friedman. Margaret Thatcher writes that when she visited the Soviet Union in June 1990 and met the mayor of Moscow, she found him a "devotee of Milton Friedman and the Chicago School of Economics."[26] Yegor Gaidar, one of former Russian president Boris Yeltsin's key advisers on denationalization and liberalization of the Russian economy, read Friedman. Leszek Balcerowicz, Poland's finance minister, is a strong supporter. Many of Friedman's works have been translated into languages of countries that formerly were Communist; as mentioned, before the fall of Communism, they appeared in underground versions.

Friedman is fascinated by the collapse of Communism. He says that it is not a result of intellectuals like himself, but of other forces—primarily economic productivity in different societies: "People are not influential in arguing for different courses in the economy. . . . The role of people is to keep ideas alive until a crisis occurs. It wasn't my talking that caused people to embrace these ideas. . . . Collectivism was an impossible way to run an economy. What has brought about the change is reality, fact—and what Marx called the inevitable forces of history."[27]

22

HAYEK AND THE ROLE OF IDEAS

he name that Friedman is perhaps most associated with in libertarian circles is that of Friedrich Hayek. They are often considered the two leading libertarian thinkers of the twentieth century. The two met in 1946 in Chicago, when Hayek was visiting the University of Chicago for several weeks from the London School of Economics. They became even better acquainted the following year at the first meeting of the Mont Pelerin Society.

Friedman's first extant letter to Hayek is dated January 2, 1947, accepting an invitation to the Mont Pelerin gathering:

> It is hard for us here to judge the importance to Europeans of such a conference. Some indication of its possible value . . . is provided by the number of names on your list that are unfamiliar to us. It is unfortunate, to say the least, that we should know so little about the work of Europeans in the same tradition.
>
> Our faith requires that we be skeptical of the efficacy, at least in the short run, of organized effort to promulgate it. But it also requires a belief in the long-run efficacy of the kind of discussion this conference is intended to promote. So I sincerely hope that your plans succeed, and that the conference is held.[1]

He sent Hayek this letter following the meeting:

> It was certainly wonderful to have the stay in England after the conference. All of it was very much worthwhile and we are deeply indebted to you for having made it possible.

The final dinner at your house just before we [Friedman and Aaron Director] left put the final pleasant touch on our visit.[2]

Hayek and Director were especially close—Director had been at the London School of Economics for a year just before World War II.

Friedman and Hayek were good friends, though not departmental colleagues, when Hayek was on the Committee on Social Thought at Chicago from 1950 to 1962. Friedman considers it a strength of the University of Chicago that although Hayek was not able to become a member of the economics department, there was another and better way for him to get on the faculty. While Hayek was at Chicago, Friedman participated regularly in his seminar. They became particularly close in the late 1950s, when Friedman became more active in the Mont Pelerin Society (he did not attend a conference, after the first one, until 1957), and when he and Hayek served as advisers to the Intercollegiate Society of Individualists' student publication, the *New Individualist Review*.

Friedman is more plentiful in praise of Hayek than the latter was of him, a fact that in part reflects their temperaments. Hayek's letters of recommendation were relatively sparse in praise; Friedman's are more generous.

Hayek discussed Friedman most with respect to monetary issues in the 1970s. For example, Hayek wrote in 1978 that the "chief defect" in Friedman's monetarism was that by its "stress on the effects of changes in the quantity of money on the general level of prices, it directs all-too exclusive attention to the harmful effects of inflation and deflation on the creditor-debtor relationship, but disregards the even more important and harmful effects of the injections and withdrawals of . . . money . . . on the structure of relative prices and the consequent misallocation of resources and particularly the misdirection of investments which it causes." Hayek also criticized Friedman for not being able to say what money is; James Tobin and Paul Samuelson agreed with Hayek on this point. "It seems to me," Hayek wrote, that Friedman draws a "sharp distinction between what is to be regarded as money and what is not, [a distinction] which in fact does not exist."[3]

In addition, Hayek criticized Friedman for using statistical data and for being a logical positivist. Hayek said in 1977:

> Friedman is an arch-positivist who believes nothing must enter scientific argument except what is empirically proven. My argument is that we know so much detail about economics, our task is to put our knowledge in order. We hardly need any new information. Our great difficulty is digesting what we already know. We don't get much wiser by statistical information except in gaining information about the specific situation at the moment. But theoretically I don't think statistical studies get us anywhere.[4]

Hayek and Friedman share a common commitment to freer markets and less government. Their general philosophical positions are similar in this respect. Nonetheless, in his more technical criticism of Friedman, Hayek's comments did not hit the target. Contrary to Hayek's view that what is important about monetary activity is where money is injected into or withdrawn from the economic system, this seems to be quite secondary in importance. Friedman's view—that the most important aspect of monetary stimulus or contraction is its degree both with respect to economic activity and average prices—is, in any event, much more common among economists at this time.

On the idea that Friedman is a logical positivist, Hayek said: "Milton Friedman . . . preached positive economics . . . on the *assumption of complete knowledge of all relevant facts* [emphasis added]"[5]—the logical positivist criterion for scientific status; here Hayek was not correct. Although Friedman calls his philosophy "positivism," its criterion for scientific acceptability is more tentative than the Viennese circle of logical positivists required. Moreover, much of Friedman's use of the word "positive" is simply to distinguish economic facts from economic values (the fact/value distinction) and has nothing to do with the Viennese logical positivists with whom Hayek was familiar.

With respect to the proposition that it is hard to describe money for policy purposes, Friedman acknowledges that this is a real problem. He thinks, however, that by concentrating on one measure of money over time—preferably some variant of M2 (currency plus demand and time deposits)—a reasonable enough approximation of the money supply can be attained for policy purposes. Regarding Hayek's argument that not much information can be gained from statistical data, Friedman thinks that this view is very inaccurate, and it is hard not to agree with him here.

Friedman is typically more optimistic than Hayek was. In a March 1981 "Report on Mrs. Thatcher's Progress by Hayek and Friedman," in the British *Listener,* the author quoted both men on British prospects two years into Thatcher's prime ministership:

> *Hayek:* Things have gone much more slowly than I both hoped and thought was necessary to give Mrs. Thatcher a chance to succeed, certainly within one term of government and possibly even if we count in terms of an eight-year period. . . . The attempt has to be made, and if it fails this time it just means that the decline will go on and people will still have to learn the lesson and be prepared to do what they are not prepared to do now. . . .
>
> *Friedman:* The story isn't over. We have only seen the first stages of the battle. I think the battle goes on and I have considerable confidence that you have much better prospects in the next couple of years. . . . Inflation is falling, and as inflation falls, and as people come to recognize and take into account the falling of inflation, you will have the groundwork laid for a very strong boom in the British economy.[6]

Sometimes, in his later years, Hayek said that Friedman seemed to have taken his place with respect to public prominence in the libertarian or free market movement. In Britain, Hayek was more identified as a philosophical inspirer of Thatcher than Friedman was.

As Communism in eastern Europe and then the Soviet Union crumbled and then collapsed, Hayek's star rose higher. Hayek and Ludwig von Mises had been right all along about the economic nonproductiveness of collectivism, contrary to what the vast majority of their contemporaries, particularly those who were most esteemed professionally and most recognized publicly, thought.

Friedman praised Hayek highly. He wrote in a 1976 foreword to a collection of essays on Hayek by members of the Mont Pelerin Society: "From the time I first read some of his works, and even more from the time . . . I first met Friedrich Hayek, his powerful mind, his moral courage, his lucid and always principled exposition have helped to broaden and deepen my understanding of the meaning and the requisites of a free society."[7] His most superlative praise is included in a 1992 obituary, where he stated that Hayek was "unquestionably . . . the most important intellectual leader of the movement that has produced a major change in the climate of opinion," and "his ideas will live on and influence the course of events long after the rest of us are gone."[8]

Larry Sjaastaad, a colleague of Friedman's and Hayek's at Chicago, makes the interesting comment, in response to a question about whether there was any jealousy between them, that their "egos are sufficiently large that they are not jealous of anyone else."[9] Hayek's philosophical approach did not mirror Friedman's empirical method, especially the latter's emphasis on prediction.

Both Hayek and Friedman are concerned with the role of ideas in societal change. Friedman best explained his conception in a 1988 publication, "The Tide in the Affairs of Men," coauthored by his wife, Rose. They preface the piece with the words of Shakespeare:

> There is a tide in the affairs of men
> Which, taken at the flood, leads on to fortune;
> Omitted, all the voyage of their life
> Is bound in shallows and in miseries.

Milton and Rose hypothesize that a

> major change in social and economic policy is preceded by a shift in the climate of intellectual opinion, itself generated, at least in part, by contemporary social, political, and economic circumstances. . . . At first it will have little effect on social and economic policy. After a lag, sometimes of decades, an intellectual tide "taken at its flood" will spread at first gradually, then more rapidly, to the public at large and through the

public's pressure on government will affect the course of economic, social, and political policy.[10]

The concept of lags runs through Friedman's work.

Milton and Rose think that the past two and a quarter centuries have been typified by three different intellectual tides in society and government: "The Rise of Laissez-Faire (the Adam Smith Tide)," "The Rise of the Welfare State (the Fabian Tide)," and "The Resurgence of Free Markets (the Hayek Tide)."[11] They consider the Adam Smith tide, which advocates free trade and limited government, to have washed ashore in the realm of ideas from about 1776—with the publication of Smith's *Wealth of Nations* and start of the American War of Independence—to 1883 and to have reached its primary public policy influence from about 1820 to 1900 in Britain and slightly later in the United States.

Friedman emphasizes there is a difference between the tide in the realm of opinion and the tide in the field of events. Like other social commentators, including Keynes, Hayek, and A. V. Dicey, Friedman believes most individuals form their essential political views (the tide in opinion) by about their middle or late twenties and that the tide in events follows by about twenty to thirty years.

Friedman thinks that the Fabian tide started to replace the Adam Smith tide in the realm of ideas in 1883, the date of the founding of the Fabian Society in Great Britain, and that it lasted intellectually in Britain until about 1950 and in the United States until about 1970. The intellectual tides against collectivism surfaced with Hayek's *Road to Serfdom* in 1944 and gathered strength in the realm of practice starting in the late 1970s and 1980s in both Britain and the United States, when Thatcher became prime minister and Reagan became president. According to Friedman, the Hayek tide, the resurgence of free markets, has far to go. "If the completed tides are any guide," he wrote in 1988, "the current wave in opinion is approaching middle age and in public policy is still in its infancy. Both are therefore still rising and the flood stage, certainly in affairs, is yet to come."[12]

Friedman's views of another Austrian libertarian economist, Ludwig von Mises, are interesting. He thinks highly of much of Mises's work but considers the man to have been personally intolerant. He said in 1995: "The other person [besides Hayek] in that whole [Austrian] group, who really needs a book on him, is von Mises. . . . He's always fascinated me . . . I agree with so much of what he says, and yet I disagree absolutely with his methodology and his intolerance."[13] In 1996 Friedman wrote that Mises was "certainly of a quality that would have made him an entirely appropriate recipient of a Nobel Prize."[14]

Friedman writes that ideas are important "less by persuading the public than by keeping options open, providing alternative policies to adopt when changes ha[ve] to be made."[15] He expressed similar thoughts in a 1991 question-and-answer session: "Ideas are important, but they take a long time and are not important in and of themselves. Something else has to come along that provides fertile ground for those ideas."[16]

23

SCHOOL VOUCHERS
AND SOCIAL ISSUES

The primary issue on which Friedman had worked in recent years is school vouchers. He traced evolution of the vouchers idea in 2005: "Little did I know when I published an article in 1955 on 'The Role of Government in Education' that it would lead to my becoming an activist for a major reform in the organization of schooling." His primary reason for supporting educational vouchers—whereby parents would receive financial credits that would be reimbursed or redeemed for their children's educational costs—was not because he thought that the United States had poor elementary and secondary public schools in 1955. Rather, his "interest was in the philosophy of a free society. Education was the area that I happened to write on early. I then went on to consider other areas as well. The end result was *Capitalism and Freedom* . . . with the education article as one chapter."[1] It is noteworthy that his larger interest in liberty springs largely from the vouchers idea.

Though Friedman says he was not influenced by him in this respect, John Stuart Mill put forward the essential idea of school vouchers in *On Liberty* almost a century before. Mill wrote that government might "leave to parents to obtain . . . education where and how they pleased, and content itself with helping to pay the school fees of the poorer classes of children."[2] Both Friedman and Mill oppose state schools for the same reason: They see them as inconsistent with a regime of liberty. Liberty and freedom flourish in an environment of diversity. State schools, by enforcing common modes of thought and action, lead to homogeneity of outlook and attitude, not the heterogeneity Friedman seeks.

He argues that government involvement in schooling can be justified on two grounds. The first is "neighborhood effects"[3]: circumstances in which actions by one person impose costs or confer benefits on others for which it is not easily possible to compensate or to charge them. Where neighborhood effects are strong, the market breaks down, for market cost is less than social cost or market gain is less than social gain.

In the case of education, the entire community benefits from an educated citizenry, but parents may not be able to afford or be able to provide an education for their children. Accordingly, state assurance that all children are educated may be justified on the ground that the social benefits that accrue from an educated citizenry are greater than the costs of providing the education. Similarly, the significant costs imposed on a community by an uneducated citizenry make it in the interests of others than just children's parents to ensure that all children are educated.

The second argument that Friedman advances for state provision of education is the paternalistic one that, because children are unable to provide for themselves, it is up to others to provide for them. Although the classical liberal or libertarian believes that this is generally best done through the family, nonetheless, if a family is unable or unwilling to provide its children with an education, doing so becomes the responsibility of the entire community.

Friedman notes that government could merely require parents to provide their children an education—just as it often imposes requirements on individuals in cases of neighborhood effects—and not make any general provision of education. State subsidies for education could, in this case, be limited to the needy. He does not, at least in *Capitalism and Freedom,* think that such a policy would be possible: "Differences among families in resources and in number of children, plus the imposition of a standard of schooling involving very sizable costs, make such a policy hardly feasible."[4] He here accepts that state provision of children's education is an appropriate government function. His argument is not with this function but with how it is performed.

He believes that a system of voucher schools would lead to an educational renaissance, particularly for students from lower socioeconomic backgrounds. Friedman writes passionately of the benefits that he believes students would receive from the voucher system—of the increased opportunities that they would experience through diversity, choice, and competition, and of the improved performance that all schools, including existing public ones, would experience. School vouchers would primarily benefit lower socioeconomic students in large, urban school districts and Friedman thinks that a system of voucher schools would especially benefit African American students. He does not understand why more African American leaders do not embrace school choice through vouchers. He believes that the main opponent of vouchers is the educational establishment, particularly teachers' unions.

His essential formula for improving inner cities and reducing racial tension is to implement vouchers in education, legalize drugs, cut welfare, and eliminate affirmative action. Friedman endorses the argument of Thomas Sowell that among the negative consequences of affirmative action is that it mismatches participants' fields of endeavor with their abilities, to their detriment (an individual who would be a success at a state university is instead, for example, admitted to an Ivy League university, where he or she is more likely to fail). Friedman also opposes affirmative action because it brings the wrong sentiment or ethos to a society—that people should be evaluated by group membership rather than by individual merit.

Friedman believes that the current illegal status of drugs does much harm. This is perhaps the issue on which he is farthest from the conservative mainstream, although many of the other leading proponents of drug legalization, including William F. Buckley and George Shultz, are Republicans. Friedman's argument against current drug policy is both ethical and practical. He believes that adults should have the legal right to do as they wish as long as they are not harming anyone else, and he believes that the illegal status of drugs creates a huge black market and causes much unnecessary violence, chaos, criminal activity, and imprisonment. He is scornful of the havoc that illegal drugs in America cause in many places outside of the United States.

Friedman does not really consider the argument that the use of drugs, especially of hard drugs and by young people, might increase if drugs were legalized. Nor does he really put forward a plan for how drugs would be distributed if they were legalized, although he appears to favor the public sale of currently illegal drugs—presumably including heroin, cocaine, and methamphetamines—under regulations similar to those applied to alcohol and cigarettes. He commented in a 1991 interview: "I would legalize drugs by subjecting them to exactly the same rules that alcohol and cigarettes are subjected to now."[5] He acknowledges that "drugs are a scourge that is devastating our society"[6] but thinks that the costs of the current illegal status of drugs outweigh its benefits and that the benefits of drug legalization would outweigh its costs. In a 1991 op-ed for the *Wall Street Journal*, he presented a graph showing a large, sharp decline in all criminal activity in the United States after the prohibition of alcohol ended in the 1930s.

Of all illegal drugs, Friedman felt the strongest argument for legalization can be made for marijuana. He wrote in 2006: "As for the legalization of marijuana, I agree that it is the currently illegal drug for which there is the strongest case for legalization."[7] In 2005, he headed a list of more than 500 economists endorsing a report on cost associated with marijuana prohibition. He thinks that the experience of the Netherlands—where small amounts of marijuana are legal, and the proportion of the population who uses marijuana is less than in the United States—indicates marijuana use might not increase much if it were legalized.

His comments on possible outcomes of drug legalization sometimes appear utopian; at least, most others do not share his ideas (as they have not shared his utopian views in the past with respect, for example, to flexible international exchange rates). When asked how he saw America "changing for the better" under a system in which drugs were legal, he made these comments on a public affairs talk show: "I see America with half the number of prisons, half the number of prisoners, ten thousand fewer homicides a year, inner cities in which there's a chance for these poor people to live without being afraid for their lives, citizens who might be respectable who are now addicts not being subject to becoming criminals in order to get their drug, being able to get drugs for which they're sure of the quality."[8] The Reverend Billy Sunday famously proclaimed—in a spirit not completely dissimilar from Friedman's, though completely different in policy intent—on the benefits of alcohol prohibition: "The reign of tears is over. The slums will soon be a memory. We will turn our prisons into factories and our jails into storehouses. . . . Men will walk upright now, women will smile and children will laugh. Hell will be forever for rent."[9] Whether Friedman is empirically right with respect to what the consequences of drug legalization would be is an open question; most on both the political left and the right disagree with his empirical conclusions.

Regarding welfare, his believes that the government should not provide for the indigent, unemployed, elderly, sick, and disabled. Although he wrote in 2005 that "I remain persuaded that repeal of all of the specific welfare measures and their replacement by a very low level negative income tax would be an improvement"[10] over current government measures, his ultimate position is complete government withdrawal from these functions. He wrote in a 1972 *Newsweek* column that "voluntary action on the part of the rest of us to assist our less fortunate brethren" would be the best way to provide for "people who, through no fault of their own, . . . were unable to earn what the rest of us would regard as an acceptable minimum income."[11]

He also wrote recently: "If people are born into a world in which there are very few welfare supports, in which the culture is one that requires people to be responsible for themselves, there will be many fewer such people than if they are born into a society in which it is taken for granted that the government will come in and help them out." Contemporary welfare and social service programs have the "negative effect of creating a different kind of culture and a different kind of human being."[12]

Vouchers and a negative income tax are philosophically and practically related. In each case, Friedman's preferred policy is for government to give individuals money or credits rather than for government to provide services directly.

With respect to stem cell research and gay marriage, Friedman writes in 2005 correspondence that on "stem cell research, I believe that it should be freely open but that the government should not be financing it. It does seem to me wrong for the government to be spending its citizens' tax money on programs which a significant fraction of the population find morally abhorrent." Regarding gay marriage, "I do not believe there should be any discrimination against gays. . . . The only question is whether th[e] laws should have a special category for a family unit whose primary objective is child-rearing."[13] On abortion, he believes that it should be legal, but, similar to his position on stem cell research, that government should not pay for abortions.

Friedman believes that the current public school system operates largely like a monopoly, with the inefficiency and lack of innovation that monopoly invariably entails. Universal vouchers would revolutionize education for the better, he believes; many new schools of all sorts would emerge. He does not believe that vouchers would lead to increased socioeconomic or racial separation in or of schools—he believes, in fact, the opposite.

In recent years Milton and Rose chose to direct their personal efforts and fortune most to the issue of school vouchers. They established the Milton and Rose D. Friedman Foundation to promote educational choice. Their children, Janet and David, serve on the board of directors along with the elder Friedmans.

The school voucher idea has had much influence in the United States and elsewhere. Not only has the school voucher idea been considered outside of this country, but here and abroad the concept of vouchers—providing funding through government but leaving provision of services in competitive, private hands—has proved capable of extension to many other areas, resulting in privatization of government activities.

Moreover, within education, notwithstanding the lack of political success that vouchers have had up to this point, the idea of expanding school choice has had many ramifications, from open student transfer policies to, in part, charter schools and home schooling. Although he rejects any comparison with John Dewey, Friedman is not just, with Keynes, one of the two leading economists of the twentieth century; he is arguably, with Dewey, one of the two leading educational reformers.

Notwithstanding that he is the great champion of school vouchers, Friedman would ultimately support the complete withdrawal of government from education, including even vouchers. He writes in a footnote in his memoirs: "I hasten to add that while a case can be made for both compulsory schooling and financing, it is by no means a conclusive case. Indeed, we have . . . been persuaded by the empirical evidence on the extensiveness of schooling in the absence of government involvement that neither is justified."[14] He says that vouchers are a "means, not an end." They would be a "way of possibly making incremental progress in schooling. The ideal would be government completely out of education. . . . Such a drastic change is not in the realm of possibility right now. Vouchers would be a sizable step in the right direction."[15]

He believes that implementation of school vouchers is only a matter of time. Friedman wrote in 1995, in words that appear on the return envelope with solicitation letters from the Milton and Rose D. Friedman Foundation: "I sense that we are on the verge of a breakthrough in one state or another, which will then sweep like wildfire through the rest of the country as it demonstrates its effectiveness."[16]

24

FRIEDMAN PRIZE

riedman's pace had of course slowed in recent years. He turned ninety-four on July 31, 2006. Were it not for advances in medical technology, he might well not have lived past his fifties. Heart and back difficulties slowed him for a time in the mid-1990s, but Rose enforced a regimen of less activity on him. He played tennis and skied into his eighties and even occasionally rode his grandson's skateboard. He and Rose had been as active as any nonagenarians can be.

He remarked in the 1982 preface of *Capitalism and Freedom* that there is "enormous inertia—a tyranny of the status quo—in private and especially governmental arrangements."[1] Then, in his and Rose's 1984 *Tyranny of the Status Quo*, while reaffirming this view, they also expressed a somewhat different sentiment: "We have ourselves always regarded the American structure as a virtue, not a vice. While it is certainly harder to make good changes in our system than in a parliamentary system, it is also harder to make bad changes."[2]

Friedman's views on foreign policy are interesting, though he considers his opinions in this area to be especially avocational, and not of the weight that he intends for his work in economics to be accorded. He was conventionally interventionist in World War II. He early and strongly supported American involvement in the war. After the war, Friedman appears to have been, through the early 1960s, at least a moderate interventionist with respect to the battle against worldwide Communism. Although he made few references to noneconomic international events, they were typically in a strongly anticommunist direction. For example, he wrote in an April 3, 1961, letter to Arthur Seldon of the Institute of Economic Affairs, regarding events in Laos (where a Communist takeover seemed imminent): "I am very much distressed at the moment by the situation in foreign affairs. Britain and the U.S. seem to be prepared to sell yet another country down the road."[3]

Partially under the influence of the Vietnam War, Friedman seems to have become if not radicalized, then, in a post-1960s sense, liberalized in foreign policy. Although his comments on the Vietnam War per se (as opposed to the draft) are few, as a result of his involvement in the antidraft movement, he associated with many leaders of the anti–Vietnam War movement. David Friedman thinks that he may have influenced his father in an antidraft direction. In recent years Milton Friedman had become more isolationist or, at least, less supportive of U.S. military action around the world. He had always emphasized waste in defense spending and the danger to political freedom posed by militarism. He opposed the Gulf war in 1991. He thought that, although the United States should not have militarily intervened in Iraq in 2003, having done so it should see this involvement through to satisfactory completion.

He outlived all of his birth family by decades and outlived almost all his fellow students and early colleagues. Most of his instructors died years ago. Many of the political leaders he advised, including Nixon, Goldwater, and Reagan, are gone now. Of fellow graduate students at the University of Chicago, Rose is among the few left. Anna Jacobson Schwartz remains active at the National Bureau of Economic Research. His two best lifetime friends, George Stigler and Allen Wallis, died in 1991 and 1998 respectively.

Friedman's final position with respect to monetary policy was that it should seek stable aggregate prices. He favored neither inflation nor deflation. He became more optimistic with respect to the possibility of central banks as currently constituted to achieve price stability than he was in the past, believing that will is very important to control inflation. He feared that some decades hence, the world will forget what causes inflation and that all of the old, inaccurate purported causes of inflation (greedy employers, grasping employees, etc.) will return to the fore. If an epitaph were inscribed on his tombstone, he said it should read: "Inflation is always and everywhere a monetary phenomenon."[4]

His final policy recommendation with respect to money is contained in a Hoover Institution publication, where he proposes that the "quantity of high-powered money—non-interest-bearing obligations of the U.S. Government—be frozen at a fixed amount."[5] This would be, in effect, a "monetary rule of zero growth in high-powered money." Such a policy, he wrote in 2004, would be a "simple but very powerful"[6] one.

With respect to public policy generally, he is popularly perceived as the leading intellectual champion of libertarianism—the idea that less government, in all ways and at all levels, should be the wave of the twenty-first century. The time has come again, he argues, as at the end of the mercantilist era and the start of the capitalist era in the late 1700s and early 1800s, to sweep away the panoply of government regulations, preferences, and restrictions that benefit some at the expense of others and result in less economic production than would be the case in a social system of less government.

It is appropriate that his last major work in economics, *Money Mischief: Episodes in Monetary History* (1992), is on monetary history and practice. Here he traces the myriad influences of monetary policy through a variety of historical situations, mostly in the United States. He notes, as he does previously with respect to monetary phenomena, "how misleading surface appearances can be." He maintains: "I trust that my readers have been impressed, as I have been after nearly half a century of close study of monetary phenomena, with the universal role that money plays, the wide applicability of a few relatively simple propositions about money, and the difficulty that the public at large and even the monetary authorities have in understanding and applying those propositions." He closes this work with the quotation he also used to conclude his Nobel lecture: "Bad logicians have committed more involuntary crimes than bad men have done intentionally."[7] Once again, his emphasis is on positive economics.

In the winter 2001 edition of *The Public Interest*, he has the lead article, a twenty-eight-page contribution (including eight pages of figures and tables) titled "How to Cure Health Care." Here he advocated medical savings accounts as the best method to improve the quality and efficiency of medical care in the United States. He believes that if medical savings accounts and high-deductible catastrophic insurance replaced existing employer, Medicare, and Medicaid health coverage, "health care costs would be more than cut in half as a fraction of GNP."[8]

In this article, Friedman explains the importance of utopian proposals: "While so radical a reform is almost surely not politically feasible . . . , it may become so. . . . [I]t gives a standard . . . against which to judge incremental changes."[9] He is not completely disappointed by the 2003 Medicare reform, incorporating as it did personal health care accounts, competition from private providers, and high deductibles.

Articles continue to be written about Friedman, and he continues to write for various scholarly and, now, mostly popular journals, magazines, and newspapers. A favorite outlet is the *Wall Street Journal*. In October 2005 he had an article on business's social responsibility in *Reason* magazine, and the next month he had one on vouchers in the *American Spectator*. He writes in the *Reason* article:

> A system based on private property and free markets is a sophisticated means of enabling people to cooperate in their economic activities without compulsion; it enables separated knowledge to assure that each resource is used for its most valued use, and is combined with other resources in the most efficient way.
>
> Of course, this is abstract and idealized. The world is not ideal. There are all sorts of deviations from the perfect market—many . . . due to government interventions.[10]

Friedman participated in several recent seminars or conferences on his work, or had the opportunity to review others' recent work. He commented in the preface to the 2002 edition of *Capitalism and Freedom:* "It is a rare privilege for an author to be able to evaluate his own work forty years after it first appeared."[11] He continued to appear on television and to be interviewed. A major television project on his life and ideas, "The Power of Choice," sponsored by the Pacific Research Institute, is to be presented on the Public Broadcasting System in the fall of 2006.

Milton and Rose's memoirs, *Two Lucky People,* appeared in 1998. He individually concludes the preface:

> My vocation has been professional economics. Except for one book (*A Theory of the Consumption Function*), Rose played a secondary role in that part of my work, reading and critiquing everything that I wrote but not being a major participant.
>
> My avocation has been public policy, and in that area Rose has been an equal partner, even with those publications, such as my *Newsweek* columns, that have been published under my own name.[12]

Milton dedicated 1992's *Money Mischief* "To RDF and more than half a century of loving collaboration."[13] He and Rose continued to travel, particularly on cruises. Unlike many retired couples, they actually travelled less in retirement than they did earlier in life, when they often made two trips abroad each year. They sold their home at Sea Ranch in 2002 and resided mainly in San Francisco, where their children and grandchildren visit often.

On the other side of the continent from California, the Washington think tank with which Friedman is most affiliated is the Cato Institute, the leading libertarian (as distinct from conservative) foundation in the United States. Begun in 1977 by Edward Crane and oil magnate Charles Koch, Cato has flourished under the leadership of Crane, David Boaz, and William Niskanen. Niskanen was a member of Reagan's Council of Economic Advisers and is a longtime friend of Friedman's.

Friedman spoke at the dedication of Cato's new building in Washington in 1993, saying:

I have sometimes been associated with the aphorism "There's no such thing as a free lunch," which I did not invent. I wish more attention were paid to one that I did ... and that I think is particularly appropriate in this city, "Nobody spends somebody else's money as carefully as he spends his own." But all aphorisms are half-truths. One of our favorite family pursuits on long drives is to try to find the opposites of aphorisms. For example, "History never repeats itself," but "There's nothing new under the sun." Or "Look before you leap," but "He who hesitates is lost." The opposite of "There's no such thing as a free lunch" is clearly "The best things in life are free."

And in the real economic world, there *is* a free lunch, an extraordinary free lunch, and that free lunch is free markets and private property.[14]

The first Milton Friedman Prize for Advancing Liberty was given on May 9, 2002, at the Cato Institute's twenty-fifth anniversary dinner in Washington. The prize, which includes a $500,000 cash award, is given every other year to an individual who has made a major contribution to advancing liberty. Its first three recipients have been, in 2002, British economist Peter Bauer, who unfortunately died before it was presented; in 2004, Hernando de Soto, the South American advocate of libertarian ideas; and, in 2006, former Estonian prime minister Mart Laar, who implemented free market reforms in his country. Friedman demonstrated his attachment to exact expression in his extemporaneous talk on Bauer at the 2002 dinner: It was a "shame"—no, he corrected himself—"tragedy"[15] that Bauer died before the award could be presented to him.

While in Washington for the dinner, Milton and Rose had lunch at the White House. President George W. Bush said, "It's an honor for me ... to pay tribute to a hero of freedom, Milton Friedman. He has used a brilliant mind to advance a moral vision: the vision of a society where men and women are free, free to choose. ... That vision has changed America and it is changing the world. All of us owe a tremendous debt to this man's towering intellect and his devotion to liberty."[16] Defense Secretary Donald Rumsfeld, a longtime admirer and friend, was on hand and said that Friedman has "changed the course of history."[17] Columnist George Will remarked of the occasion that Friedman is "America's most consequential public intellectual of the twentieth century."[18] George Shultz appraises Friedman as highly as anyone. Shultz believes that Friedman has had as much influence on the world as anyone in the past fifty years—presidents, prime ministers, and premiers included. Among others at the lunch with President Bush and Milton and Rose were Vice President Richard Cheney and Federal Reserve Board chairman Alan Greenspan.

At the dinner that night, Friedman, a few weeks short of his ninetieth birthday, appeared with Rose on the stage. As he rose to speak, the crowd of almost 2,000 political, business, and intellectual leaders stood to applaud him for his lifetime of contributions to the causes of human freedom and economic, political, and civil liberty.

He celebrated his birthday at the University of Chicago a few weeks later, where the Department of Economics hosted him. Gary Becker writes that "no less an authority than . . . Alan Greenspan has indicated that Friedman's emphasis on a stable monetary framework was instrumental in guiding central banks in Europe and the U.S. toward low inflation during the past two decades," and that Friedman is "increasingly recognized as the most influential economist"[19] of the twentieth century. Friedman celebrated his sixtieth and seventy-fifth birthdays at Chicago. He said in 2002 that he looked forward to being back in another fifteen years.

He supported Arnold Schwarzenegger's candidacy for governor of California in 2003. Schwarzenegger wrote in an op-ed piece in the *Wall Street Journal:* "I have often said that the two people who have most profoundly impacted my thinking on economics are Milton Friedman and Adam Smith."[20]

Friedman, in recent years, moved more into occasional writings on the history of ideas and, to a lesser extent, political theory, at least as a proportion of his writings, than once was the case. Not infrequently these writings take the form of introductions or forewords to works, most recently to *The Cure: How Capitalism Can*

Save American Health Care (October 2006). His interviews continued and tended to provide more personal insight and commentary
on issues other than immediate economic issues of the day or economic theory than they did previously. He continued to write for
popular media and academic journals, but as of the summer of 2005
he said that he had no more major writing projects in store.

Friedman published an article in the fall 2005 edition of the American Economic Association's *Journal of Economic Perspectives.* He wrote
here: "What happens to the quantity of money has a determinative effect on what happens to national income. . . . The results strongly support Anna Schwartz's and my 1963 conjecture about the role of
monetary policy in the Great Contraction. They also support the view
that monetary policy deserves much credit for the mildness of the recession that followed the collapse of the U.S. boom in late 2000."[21]

The extent of Friedman's influence on monetary policy is open
to debate, but the direction of monetary policy around the world is
not. Average annual world consumer price index inflation was 22
percent for the period from 1990 to 1994, 8 percent for the period
from 1995 to 1999, and 4 percent for the period from 2000 to 2004.
The proportional decline was even sharper in developing counties.

Ben Bernanke, appointed chairman of the Federal Reserve Board
in 2005, is a great admirer of Friedman. According to Bernanke,
"One can hardly overstate the influence of Friedman's monetary
framework on contemporary monetary theory and practice. He
identified the key empirical facts and he provided us with broad policy recommendations," and "Friedman's monetary framework has
been so influential that, in its broad outlines . . . , it has nearly become identical with modern monetary theory and practice."[22] According to Alan Greenspan, Bernanke's predecessor, "There are very
few people over the generations who have ideas that are sufficiently
original to materially alter the direction of civilization. Milton is one
of these very few people."[23]

Friedman wrote in 2001: "I have always myself emphasized that it
took three words to describe the kind of capitalism I was in favor of:

free private property." He also says: "Capitalism refers primarily to the economic organization of a society on the basis of private property and free markets."[24]

Positive economics has contributed to free private property capitalism by emphasizing that by better understanding the sources of wealth and prosperity, humanity can achieve them more effectively. This is the link between Friedman's empirical and normative views. It is through knowledge of economic cause-and-effect that humanity can produce the most.

Friedman's vision of a libertarian society is one in which government at all levels (local, state, and national) would be reduced to no more than 10 to 15 percent of the economy for all functions, including defense (other than in time of war). He favors decentralization of government and thinks that what government activity remains in the future should take place more at the local and state than at the national level. He does not believe that most on the right and left oppose such a society but that the "present society is not such a society. Inertia and the tyranny of the status quo assure that there is no ongoing movement to reach such a society, but it is meaningless to ask whether they [those on the right and left] favor it or oppose it when they have no comprehension of what it is."[25]

His essential message is factual, a view of the way that the world is. He believes that by restricting government to the functions of "defending the nation from foreign enemies, protecting each of us from coercion by our fellow citizens, adjudicating our disputes, and enabling us to agree on the rules that we shall follow,"[26] humanity could produce the most and be happiest and freest.

Here, this biography of Milton Friedman closes. He makes passing reference in "The Methodology of Positive Economics" to the value of biography:

> Progress in positive economics will require not only the testing and elaboration of existing hypotheses but also the construction of new hypotheses. On this problem there is little to say on a formal level. The construction of hypotheses is a creative act of inspiration, intuition,

invention; its essence is the vision of something new in familiar material. The process must be discussed in psychological, not logical, categories; studied in autobiographies and biographies, not treatises on scientific method; and promoted by maxim and example, not syllogism or theorem.[27]

EPILOGUE

ilton Friedman died on November 16, 2006, just days after this biography was finished. He had been in somewhat declining health over the past year, but nothing beyond what would be expected for a man of his age. His eyesight was increasingly poor and he suffered from leg problems. Nonetheless, as recently as October 17, he had been well enough to have lunch in a San Francisco restaurant with Mark Skousen, who happened to be in town. Friedman walked with a cane, but other than this was as bright and clear as ever, and he and Skousen enjoyed over an hour together. Friedman went into the hospital with a serious viral infection on about November 1. After a day or two in intensive care, he improved to some extent and went home, but on November 16, his heart gave out.

Tributes to him were expressed around the world. Margaret Thatcher said, "Milton Friedman revived the economics of liberty when it had been all but forgotten."[1] According to Paul Samuelson, "He, more than any other person, has changed the composition and ideology of the economists' profession."[2] Ed Crane commented that "ultimately, what Milton believed in was human liberty and he took great joy in trying to promote that concept."[3] Friedman was a towering intellect, and in the end that is how he was remembered: for the insight he conveyed and his ability to make others think things through anew.

APPENDIX

INTERVIEW

The following interview of Milton Friedman by Nathan Gardels in November 2005 originally appeared in the spring 2006 edition of *New Perspectives Quarterly*.

Interviewer: You've seen a lot in your long life and thought about the big issues. What is on your mind these days?

Friedman: The big issue is whether the United States will succeed in its venture of reshaping the Middle East. It is not clear to me that using military force is the way to do it. We should not have gone into Iraq. But we have. At the moment, the most pressing issue, therefore, is to make sure that effort is completed in a satisfactory way.

There is no doubt that America's stature in the world—in large part due to the attraction and promotion of our liberal freedoms—has been eroded as a result of Iraq. However, if Iraq emerges in the end as a self-governing country that is not a threat to anybody, that will have a favorable effect on the Middle East in general. The end result then would be to increase the prestige of the U.S. But that is not the case now. The effect so far has been the other way.

Interviewer: The so-called "old Europe" of France, Germany and Italy has been stagnating with high levels of unemployment. Germany—one of the last bastions of the Cold War Keynesian welfare state—now has a conservative leader, Angela Merkel. What should be done to get Germany, and by extension old Europe, back on track?

Friedman: They all ought to imitate Margaret Thatcher and Ronald Reagan; free markets in short.

Germany's problem, in part, is that it went into the euro at the wrong exchange rate that overvalued the deutsche mark. So you have a situation in the eurozone where Ireland has inflation and rapid expansion while Germany and France have stalled and had the difficulties of adjusting.

The euro is going to be a big source of problems, not a source of help. The euro has no precedent. To the best of my knowledge, there has never been a monetary union, putting out a fiat currency, composed of independent states.

There have been unions based on gold or silver, but not on fiat money—money tempted to inflation—put out by politically independent entities.

At the moment, of course, Germany cannot get out of the euro. What it has to do, therefore, is make the economy more flexible—to eliminate the restrictions on prices, on wages and on employment; in short, the regulations that keep 10 percent of the German workforce unemployed. This is far more urgent than it would otherwise be if Germany were not in the euro.

This set of policies would open up the German potential. After all, Germany has a very able and productive workforce. It has high-quality products that are valued all over the world. It has every opportunity to be a productive, growing state. It just has to give its entrepreneurs a chance. It has to let them make money, hire and fire, and act like entrepreneurs.

Instead, what you have as a result of past policies is that German entrepreneurs go outside of Germany for many of their activities. They are investing abroad instead of at home because there isn't the openness, fluidity and opportunity they find outside their borders.

Interviewer: British Prime Minister Tony Blair argues there is a "third way"—for example, flexible labor markets without hire-and-fire American-style. This, he argues, is more suitable to the "European social model" with its enduring concern with social justice. Is there an in-between way, or must it be all or nothing?

Friedman: I don't think there is a third way. But it is true that a competitive market is not the whole of society. A great deal depends on the qualities of the population and the nation in how they organize the non-market aspects of society.

Interviewer: Perhaps the Scandinavian countries are a model to look at. They are high-tax but also high-employment societies. And they have freed up their labor markets much more than in Italy, France or Germany.

Friedman: Though it is not as true now as it used to be with the influx of immigration, the Scandinavian countries have a very small, homogeneous population. That enables them to get away with a good deal they couldn't otherwise get away with.

What works for Sweden wouldn't work for France or Germany or Italy. In a small state, you can reach outside [the market] for many of your activities. In a homogeneous culture, they are willing to pay higher taxes in order to achieve commonly held goals. But "common goals" are much harder to come by in larger, more heterogeneous populations.

The great virtue of a free market is that it enables people who hate each other, or who are from vastly different religious or ethnic backgrounds, to cooperate economically. Government intervention can't do that. Politics exacerbates and magnifies differences.

Interviewer: The inflation rate in America as well as globally remains historically low, even as oil prices skyrocket. Why?

Friedman: Inflation is a monetary phenomenon. It is made by or stopped by the central bank. There has been no similar period in history like the last 15 years in which you've had little fluctuation in the price level. No matter what else happens, this will maintain as long as the U.S. Federal Reserve maintains strict monetary policy and control of the money supply.

The same thing is true in Europe. The ECB (European Central Bank) has held down the rate of monetary growth. So there have been stable prices. The pressures in Europe, however, will be much stronger than in the U.S. The main pressure is to print money and be more expansive in order to promote employment.

What the ECB does really depends on whether Germany and France and Italy will back it. Italy may well be the main problem. It has benefited most from the euro by having been able to get the euro interest rate instead of what otherwise would have been its own. That would be much higher because Italy has been accumulating so much debt. In the past, Italy has inflated away its debt. The virtue of the euro is that Italy can't do it alone. A tight ECB policy wouldn't permit that to happen again.

In this sense, the euro is good for Europe. But only if there is flexibility all around. The problem is that, in a world of floating exchange rates, as Italy was before the euro, if one country is subjected to a shock which requires it to cut wages, it cannot do so with a modern kind of control and regulation system. It is much easier to do it by letting the exchange rate change. Only one price has to change, instead of many.

But now, in the euro, that option is taken away. The only alternative if a state has to adjust to a shock is to let internal prices vary. It has to let wages go down, if necessary. It has to let internal interest rates go up, if necessary.

Interviewer: The U.S. Treasury debt is held mainly by China, Japan and South Korea. Is the huge balance of payments deficit a problem for the U.S. and world economy?

Friedman: I don't think so. It may well be a statistical mirage. If you look at the balance sheet, the U.S. is heavily in debt. If you look at the income account—the amount of interest the U.S. pays abroad—it is almost exactly equal to the amount of interest that it receives from abroad. American assets held abroad are earning a higher rate of return than foreign assets held here.

That is understandable because what is most attractive about the U.S. to people and countries with wealth is that it can provide security, insurance really, against political instability. Nobody is afraid that the money they place in the U.S. is at risk of expropriation or of in some other way being taken away. For this safety, the wealth holders of the world are willing to accept a lower rate of return. U.S. assets abroad, in contrast, are riskier and thus yield a higher rate of return.

This explains why there is a rough balance in real terms. It is not clear there really is a debt. It looks like the imbalance concerns are misleading. It doesn't worry me a bit that China and Japan hold so much U.S. debt. In a way, it seems foolish for them to do it because they get lower returns than they might elsewhere. But that is their business.

Interviewer: By pegging their currencies to the dollar, haven't China and Japan de facto established what is in essence "Bretton Woods II"—that is, a stable new currency regime among most of the world's largest trading partners?

Friedman: Yes, for the moment, this is sort of true. But they are not really committed to it. The Chinese currency is starting to appreciate. The Japanese currency has moved quite a lot.

China's productive system draws upon the other East Asian countries to a great extent. It buys from Japan and Korea and others. So, the volume of trade is much larger than the net amount being exported from China. China needs substantial reserves to finance all that.

Interviewer: Does the large U.S. fiscal deficit worry you?

Friedman: Not at all. It is the spending that got us there that worries me. If the U.S. government spends 40 percent of the nation's income, as it does through either borrowing or taxes, that income is not available for people to spend. The deficit is an indirect method of taxation. Of course, politicians prefer to borrow instead of tax because then someone down the road has to deal with the consequences.

If anything, at the moment, the large deficit has a positive effect of holding down further spending. In that sense, it is a good thing. But it is not a good thing if produced by more spending.

Interviewer: China has registered tremendous growth since 1979 through what might be called a "market Leninist" model, or an "authoritarian free-market system" like the Pinochet government you advised in Chile. Can this model last?

Friedman: No. The same thing will happen in China that happened in Chile. Political freedom will ultimately break out of its shackles. Tiananmen Square was only the first episode. It is headed for a series of Tiananmen Squares. It cannot continue to develop privately and at the same time maintain its authoritarian character politically. It is headed for a clash. Sooner or later, one or the other will give.

If they don't free up the political side, its economic growth will come to an end—while it is still at a very low level.

The situation is not all bleak. Personal freedom has grown greatly within China, and that will provoke ever more points of conflict between the individual and state. There is a new generation that is educated and travels abroad. It knows firsthand the alternatives out there. So, the authoritarian character is softening somewhat.

Hong Kong is the bellwether. If the Chinese stick to their agreement to let Hong Kong go its own path, then China will also go that way. If they don't, that is a very bad sign. I'm optimistic.

Interviewer: What impact has the Internet had on freedom and markets?

Friedman: It has had a tremendous effect. Look at what has happened in China. People can talk to each other, and the government, despite its best efforts, can't control it.

The Internet also moves us closer to "perfect information" of markets. Individuals and companies alike can buy and sell across borders and jurisdictions wherever they find the best match of supply and demand. Undoubtedly it has reduced the possibilities of taxation. Why should I buy something here if I can buy it from a company in Japan or England or Brazil with a lower tax?

The Internet is the most effective instrument we have for globalization.

Interviewer: So you see the march of liberty and free markets going forward into the 21st century, not taking a detour backward in China or elsewhere?

Friedman: Yes. The world as a whole has more or less embraced freedom. Socialism, in the traditional sense, meant government ownership and operation of the means of production. Outside of North Korea and a couple of other spots, no one in the world today would define socialism that way. That will never come back. The fall of the Berlin Wall did more for the progress of freedom than all of the books written by myself or Friedrich Hayek or others.

Socialism today has only come to mean government extraction of income from the haves and giving it to the have-nots. It is about the transfer of income, not ownership. That is still around.

Interviewer: Might the state make a comeback, though, because of a new set of realities: demographics, the environment and the combination of inequality and democratization? The rich-country populations are growing old. With the rise of the individual and demise of the family, the state will be called upon to ensure health care and pension security. With the scientific consensus on climate change, there will inevitably be demands for more state regulation on the environment. The spread of global free markets has also meant rising inequality. Inevitably, as democracy also spreads, the majority who are less well off will demand transfers from the wealthy to address social injustice.

Friedman: Sure, the state might come back. The only reason free markets have a ghost of a chance is that they are so much more efficient than any other form of organization.

When you argue for free markets, you are arguing against the trend. When something goes wrong, the natural tendency is to say, "By God, we need to pass a law and do something."

The argument for the free market is a complicated and sophisticated one and depends on demonstration of secondary effects. I have confidence market efficiency will win out. But there is no doubt that the problems you raise are all there. And there is no doubt there will be tremendous pressure to pull in the government as the answer.

At the end of World War II, government spending was 15–20 percent of national income. Then it went up dramatically so that by 1980 it hit 40 percent largely because of programs ranging from Medicare to environmental regulation to Social Security. From 1980 until 2005, it has remained static. We haven't beaten the tendency or rolled it back. We've just stopped the growth. This is an argument that supports your thesis, I'm afraid.

On aging societies, there is no reason why a country that has a lot of old people can't be prosperous if, during their working lives, individuals provide for their retirement. The only reason there is a crisis about Social Security in the U.S. and pensions in Europe and Japan is that you cannot maintain a "Ponzi" scheme indefinitely. We have collected from today's young to pay today's old and counted on tomorrow's young to keep doing so. That was a fine scheme as long as the number of young people was rising faster than old people. When that ratio comes to an end, such a system also has to end. It all would have been much better if individuals saved for their own old age.

Why is it that private insurance companies are not in trouble because people are getting older? Aren't they subject to the same demographics? The difference is that they've accumulated a fund, not a pay-in, pay-out system.

Interviewer: Even in the free market U.S., President Bush, at the height of his power, couldn't convince the American public to move toward privatizing Social Security.

Friedman: There is no doubt this aging issue will test the argument over the efficiency of the market versus political demands for government to step in.

On the question of whether inequality of the market might lead the less-well-off democratic majority to push for state control, I'm not so sure. The important issue is not how much inequality there is but how much opportunity there is for individuals to get out of the bottom classes and into the top. If there is enough movement upward, people will accept the efficiency of the markets. If you have opportunity, there is a great tolerance for inequality. That has been the saving grace of the American system.

In the U.S., the problem now is primary and secondary education. We've had such an increase in inequality because a quarter of American kids don't finish high school! In the current world, with the skills needed, those dropouts are condemned to being members of the underclass. In my view, this is a fault of the American school system, which is a government monopoly.

Interviewer: With globalization, are we seeing the freest world economy we've ever seen?

Friedman: Oh no. We had much freer trade in the 19th century. We have much less globalization now than we did then.

Will we go ahead back to this freedom of the 19th century? I don't know. We have a freer world because of the collapse of the Soviet Union and the changes in China. Those two have been the main contributors to freedom in our time. The countries that have risen and separated out as a result of the collapse of the Soviet

Union are, on the whole, following freer economic policies. Most of these states have freer government and less restrictions on trade.

This free-market base will likely expand from there by example to others not so free. Everyone, everywhere, now understands that the road to success for underdeveloped countries is freer markets and globalization.

Interviewer: In the end, your ideas have triumphed over Marx and Keynes. Is this, then, the end of the road for economic thought? Is there anything more to say than free markets are the most efficient way to organize a society? Is it the "end of history," as Francis Fukuyama put it?

Friedman: Oh no. "Free markets" is a very general term. There are all sorts of problems that will emerge. Free markets work best when the transaction between two individuals affects only those individuals. But that isn't the fact. The fact is that, most often, a transaction between you and me affects a third party. That is the source of all problems for government. That is the source of all pollution problems, of the inequality problem. There are some good economists like Gary Becker and Bob Lucas who are working on these issues. This reality ensures the end of history will never come.

BIBLIOGRAPHICAL ESSAY

Many books and articles have been written on Friedman over the decades. J. Daniel Hammond, *Theory and Measurement: Causality Issues in Milton Friedman's Monetary Economics* (Cambridge University Press, 1996), is a detailed study of Friedman's monetary views from the perspective of causality. Hammond notes that Friedman and Anna Jacobson Schwartz's approach in *A Monetary History of the United States* was "unorthodox and came under attack as the econometrics revolution swept through the profession" (p. 2), and he also calls attention to the extent to which Friedman's method is influenced by the approach of Wesley Clair Mitchell's National Bureau of Economic Research.

Hammond says that Friedman was "considered throughout his career to be working outside standard econometrics" (p. 41). Part of the reason for interest in "The Methodology of Positive Economics" (though Hammond does not emphasize this point) is that it was not in the mainstream of contemporaneous economic methodology in its focus on the accumulation of facts rather than the formulation of hypotheses in its emphasis on induction rather than deduction. Hammond provides an excellent history of *A Monetary History*'s development and a description of reaction to it, including in Great Britain.

Eamonn Butler, *Milton Friedman: A Guide to His Economic Thought* (New York: Universe Books, 1985), is a good introduction to Friedman's work in technical economics. Butler says that Friedman's "views have been gradually, if grudgingly, absorbed into a new economic orthodoxy," and quotes Harry Johnson: "The intellectual revival of the quantity theory . . . has been almost exclusively the work of Milton Friedman" (p. 5).

Although it reflects significant scholarship and erudition, Abraham Hirsch and Neil de Marchi's *Milton Friedman: Economics in Theory and Practice* (New York: Harvester Wheatsheaf, 1990) does not see the whole picture. While Hirsch and de Marchi focus on Friedman's methodology, they do not adequately emphasize (although they consider) his focus on prediction. The first six chapters by Hirsch are the best; de Marchi's listing in chapter 11 of several predictions by Friedman is of interest, as is his presentation of the historical development of Friedman's work.

Hirsh and de Marchi's book explores Friedman's intellectual relation to various figures, including John Dewey, Karl Popper, and John Stuart Mill. The emphasis on some of these figures is not only apposite with respect to influence (always a problematic area, as the authors recognize), but also with respect to intrinsic similarity of ideas. Some of the authors' statements—such as that "[s]ome of Friedman's views about the methodology of political economy are almost diametrically opposed to what he believes about how positive economics should be done" (p. 5)—are not correct. They quote a 1984 letter from Friedman, wherein he writes that "some recent papers I have read [early drafts of Hirsch and de Marchi's work] have persuaded me that my own methodological views are almost identical with those of John Dewey" (p. 6), but this letter should be discounted. Often individuals, swept up in the moment by what a writer or speaker says, unreflectingly or semi-unreflectingly agree with a proposition more than they should.

Hirsch and de Marchi correctly write that "Friedman associates the type of work which concerns itself primarily with formal analysis with the approach of Leon Walras." Their next statement—"and that which concerns itself primarily with substantive hypotheses with that of Alfred Marshall" (p. 19)—is less accurate. Although Friedman sharply distinguishes between Marshallian and Walrasian approaches in economic theory, and although he ascribes a formal approach to Walras, his primary focus with respect to Marshall is practical purpose rather than "substantive hypotheses." Indeed, the latter expression sounds something like the descriptive realism of hypotheses that Friedman abjures.

Hirsch and de Marchi write that "the methodological views which we ascrib[e] to Friedman . . . are very close to those of Wesley Clair Mitchell" (p. 41)—though not in predictive emphasis. They also write that "Mitchell and Friedman are almost unique among major economists in both believing strongly and very explicitly that the logic of the physical sciences *without qualifications* applies to economics" (p. 47). This book contains an excellent bibliography of works on Friedman.

The best collection of essays on Friedman and his work to date is Mark A. Wynne, Harvey Rosenblum, and Robert L. Formaini (eds.), *The Legacy of Milton and Rose Friedman's "Free to Choose": Economic Liberalism at the Turn of the 21st Century* (Dallas: Federal Reserve Bank of Dallas, 2004). New Federal Reserve Board chairman Ben Bernanke notes in his contribution that the fact that many economists thought wage and price controls would tame inflation in the late 1960s and early 1970s is sure evidence that the profession did not always accept the monetary theory of inflation that now dominates thinking in the area of price stabilization.

James Gwartney and Robert Lawson write in *The Legacy* that Friedman is "the godfather of the Economic Freedom of the World . . . project" (p. 217) and make good comments with respect to the value of numerical data. According to contemporary Austrian economist Peter Boettke, on the basis of a citation analysis: "Comparison of the scientific impact of Hayek and Friedman . . . weights strongly in favor of Friedman. . . . Friedman dominates over all the classical liberal economists who have won the Nobel Prize (Buchanan, Coase, and Stigler) and the older generation of Mises and Knight" (p. 148). The Friedmans preface this collection: "A quarter century ago, many people were convinced that capitalism . . . was a deeply flawed system that was not capable of achieving both widely shared prosperity and human freedom. Today it is increasingly recognized that capitalism is the only system that can do so" (p. vii). An earlier collection of papers is Richard T. Selden (ed.), *Capitalism and Freedom: Problems and Prospects* (Charlottesville: University Press of Virginia, 1975).

William Frazer's *Milton Friedman and the Big U-Turn* (Gainesville, Fla.: Gulf/Atlantic Publishing, 1988) is a two-volume work chockful of information about Friedman's life, career, and influence, and his historical and academic background. Frazer well calls attention to ties between British and American policies in the 1980s during the Reagan administration and Thatcher governments. He correctly writes: "Although [Friedman's] reputation extended internationally, his main immediate impact was in the United States and in Britain," and "His remarkable rise to prominence is made more so by its occurrence through the realm of ideas." He quotes Milton Viorst: "Milton Friedman is . . . the quintessence of the intellectual as a Political power. He holds no office and his hands are on none of the levers of influence in Washington. He conquers by the force of his ideas" (vol. 1, p. 21). Frazer emphasizes that for Friedman, freedom is the paramount societal goal, overriding other goals if there is a conflict between freedom and other ends, although Friedman also thinks that the freest society will be the materially most productive society. Frazer examines the relationship between Friedman and Arthur Burns, particularly the extent to which they disagreed on policy in the early 1970s. The references have much to offer.

In *The Legacy of Keynes and Friedman: Economic Analysis, Money, and Ideology* (Westport, Conn.: Praeger, 1994), Frazer writes that he considers "the 1970s as Keynesian dominated, the 1980s as a Thatcher/Reagan decade with a different policy orientation, and the U-Turn as separating the two" (p. 88) and that "Friedman . . . offered monetary ideas that were adopted by governments as a part of what I call a 'U-Turn'" (p. 239). Also see Frazer's *The Friedman System: Economic Analysis of Time Series* (Westport, Conn.: Praeger, 1997), which includes a history of monetarism (chapter 9) with reference, in addition to Friedman, to Karl Brunner, Allan Meltzer, Phillip Cagan, David Meiselman, Richard Selden, Beryl Sprinkel, Anna Schwartz, and Alan Walters.

Thomas J. Sargent's *Some of Milton Friedman's Scientific Contributions to Macroeconomics* (Stanford, Calif.: Stanford University/Hoover Institution, 1987) contains remarks at a 1987 symposium celebrating Friedman's seventy-fifth birthday, focusing on the consumption function, the natural unemployment rate hypothesis, rules for economic stability, optimum quantity of money, and study of monetary history: "Many very good researchers continue to pay Milton Friedman the compliment of thinking hard about issues that he posed, often in terms that he defined, and using methods that he invented" (p. 12). In *Permanent Income, Wealth and Consumption* (University of California Press, 1972), Thomas Mayer counts sixteen types of evidence in support of Friedman's permanent income hypothesis.

Robert Leeson's *The Eclipse of Keynesianism: The Political Economy of the Chicago Counter-Revolution* (New York: Palgrave, 2000) is a provocative work, mostly previously published articles. Some are gems, and this collection will reward those who study it. The work focuses on both Stigler and Friedman. The first pages of the introduction provide an excellent depiction of the political and economic atmosphere of the 1970s. There is a good discussion of the methodological differences between Friedman and econometricians, but similarities between Friedman's and Keynes's methods are overemphasized. The treatment of the historical development of ideas is good.

Chapter 3, which discusses Stigler's sociology of knowledge, is the best in this collection. The summary of Stigler's views of the development of knowledge in academic disciplines is excellent: "Stigler concluded ... that two-thirds of the articles surveyed were virtually worthless. There were commonly only about six really first-class scholars in any field; ... academic consensus (which could be unreliable) was achieved not by a professional 'plebiscite,' but only by an elite group within the profession" (pp. 51–52).

The two-volume work by Robert Leeson, *Keynes, Chicago and Friedman* (London: Pickering & Chatto, 2003), is a collection of materials on whether a quantity theory of money tradition existed at Chicago before Friedman began to teach there. Of the nearly 900 pages, over 150 pages are by Leeson. Friedman contributes the preface. This work provides a history of the quantity theory per se in the twentieth century, as well as of much general historical development in economics.

Leeson's "Patinkin, Johnson, and the Shadow of Friedman," *History of Political Economy* (Winter 2000), included in *Keynes, Chicago and Friedman,* is an easily accessible article on the charge of "scholarly chicanery" leveled against Friedman by Harry Johnson based on the work by Don Patinkin. Leeson notes that Patinkin's essay on Friedman was written on sabbatical at MIT, where "combating Friedman had become an obsession" (p. 743). In the article, Leeson provides a nice example of Friedman's emphasis on words and accurate expression. He reports, in part quoting participant Stanley Fischer, on a 1971 party that Milton and Rose Friedman hosted at which Patinkin's and Johnson's work was discussed. Gary Becker and David Meiselman "supported Friedman's account of the oral tradition, stating that '[Lloyd] Mints of the early 1950s did not believe that velocity was unstable, and Homer Jones said that Mints of the late '20s also emphasized the stability of velocity.'" In his article, Patinkin compiled a list of all theses at Chicago on monetary subjects in the 1930s and 1940s; the list was somewhat sparse for the 1930s. In his three 1956 paragraphs on the Chicago quantity theory oral tradition, Friedman wrote that "students continued to study monetary theory and to write theses on monetary problems" at Chicago in the "1930s and 1940s" (*Essence*, 285). Leeson continues, quoting Fischer: "Milton said that the fact that he had said the 'thirties and forties' in his article covers him for the dearth in the 30s. At which stage, Bob Gordon said 'You always have some qualification which saves you'" (pp. 742–743).

The two-volume *The Legacy of Milton Friedman as Teacher,* edited by J. Daniel Hammond (Cheltenham, U.K.: Edward Elgar, 1999), is a collection of articles by Friedman's students, preceded by descriptions of Friedman as a teacher. Hammond's introduction is excellent. He tells this anecdote from Friedman's first years on the Chicago faculty:

A student ... recalls vividly the day Friedman returned a set of exams. ... The results were terrible. After giving the class a tongue-lashing, Friedman distributed their exam booklets, instructing them to retake the test on an open-book basis. For the next week the students worked diligently, revising their answers, but their revised work prompted a second tongue-lashing. ... To demonstrate how bad their answers were, Friedman selected an exam booklet at random and began reading from it with cutting sarcasm. When the class was over the student from whose booklet Friedman read went to his office to withdraw.... Arriving there he found other classmates with the same intention.... Friedman spent much of the ... day persuading ... [students] they should not withdraw. [pp. xvi–xvii]

Hammond provides a good description of Friedman's role as a teacher at Chicago. He comments that there were "times when Friedman was unable to get to his students' work promptly. In those situations, rather than give it a perfunctory look ... , he would wait until he could give the manuscript his full attention" (p. xxiv). He notes that Friedman sometimes advised students to obtain a copy of H. W. Fowler's *Dictionary of Modern English Usage*. He remarks, as do others, that one of Friedman's admonitions as an instructor is not to let the best be enemy of the good. He also says that Friedman is "himself not known to be quick to admit error" (p. xxv) and observes that Friedman is troubled by neither indolence nor doubt.

Hundreds of academic and popular articles have been written on or consider Friedman and his work over the years. More than 100 of the best academic ones are collected in John Cunningham Wood and Ronald N. Woods (eds.), *Milton Friedman: Critical Assessments*, four volumes (London: Routledge, 1990). These mostly concern Friedman's work in economics as opposed to public policy, with considerable attention to his methodological views.

"The Keynesian Revolution and the Monetarist Counter-Revolution," published in the *American Economic Review* (May 1971), was Harry G. Johnson's Richard T. Ely lecture accusing Milton of "scholarly chicanery" (p. 11). In Elizabeth S. Johnson and Harry G. Johnson, *The Shadow of Keynes: Understanding Keynes, Cambridge and Keynesian Economics* (Oxford: Basil Blackwell, 1978), H. Johnson writes that economics at Chicago after he arrived there in 1959 was "dominated by the memory of the great 1930s days of Frank Knight and Jacob Viner, though in fact Milton Friedman was already clearly in the ascendant, along with George Stigler" (p. 151).

The December 1982 edition of the *Journal of Economic Literature* has three reviews of Friedman and Schwartz's *Monetary Trends in the United States and the United Kingdom: Their Relation to Income, Prices, and Interest Rates, 1867–1975* (1982), by an American, an Englishman, and a non-Chicagoan. The reviews both praise *Monetary Trends* and lament that it is more statistical and less interpretative than the earlier *A Monetary History of the United States*. Thomas Mayer comments: "The handling of the data is meticulous. Such tender loving care of the data is foreign to modern economics with its great emphasis on application of advanced techniques to any set of numbers almost regardless of their meaning. By contrast, F-S eschew the use of elaborate techniques" (p. 1529).

Lawrence H. Summers, "The Scientific Illusion in Empirical Macroeconomics," *Scandinavian Journal of Economics* (June 1991), comments, as part of a broader criticism of formal econometric work: "Surely *A Monetary History of the United States* had a greater impact in highlighting the role of money than any particular econometric study or combination of studies." Summers also says that (in his words) Friedman sees "purely formal theorizing" as "futile" (pp. 130 and 144).

David Laidler's "Hawtrey, Harvard, and the Origins of the Chicago Tradition," *Journal of Political Economy* (December 1993), explores antecedents and the nature of Chicago's monetary economics in the 1930s, focusing on Ralph Hawtrey, Allyn Young, and Lauchlin Currie. Laidler notes the "lack of interest in empirical work of Mints and Simons, which differentiates their contributions so strongly from Friedman's" (p. 1089). A contrasting view to Laidler is provided by George S. Tavlas, "Chicago, Harvard, and the Doctrinal Foundations of Monetary Economics," *Journal of Political Economy* (February 1997). Also see, for development of monetarist ideas, Joong-Koon Lee and Donald C. Wellington, "Angell and the Stable Money Rule," *Journal of Political Economy* (October 1984); Frank G. Steindl, "The 'Oral Tradition' at Chicago in the 1930s," *Journal of Political Economy* (April 1990); and R. Craig McIvor, "A Note on the University of Chicago's 'Academic Scribblers,'" *Journal of Political Economy* (October 1983). McIvor, who was a graduate student at Chicago in the late 1930s, says that Lloyd Mints

explored precisely the same issues, and from the same perspective, as did Friedman at a later date, and he established the validity of essentially the same conclusions that were reaffirmed by Friedman's work. By the later 1930s, Mints's research in this area was providing the basis for lively discussions in his graduate monetary policy course, and there could be no one left in doubt as to his perception of the grave shortcomings of Federal Reserve Board policy in th[e] not very distant past. [p. 889]

In "Milton Friedman and the Emergence of the Permanent Income Hypothesis," *History of Political Economy* (Spring 2003), Hsiang-Ke Chao traces the development of Friedman's work on permanent income from the 1940s to the 1960s. Danny Quah, "Permanent and Transitory Movements in Labor Income . . . ," *Journal of Political Economy* (June 1990), writes: "Friedman's permanent income theory of consumption is one of the outstanding successes of dynamic economic reasoning" (p. 449). Robert Heilbroner, "Analysis and Vision in the History of Modern Economic Thought," *Journal of Economic Literature* (September 1990), writes that Friedman was "by far the most influential economist of the period" (p. 1106) from the mid-1960s to the mid-1980s.

Edmund W. Kitch (ed.), "The Fire of Truth: A Remembrance of Law and Economics at Chicago, 1932–1970," *Journal of Law and Economics* (April 1983), is the transcript of an exceptional gathering of thirty former University of Chicago students and former and current faculty focusing on the contributions of Aaron Director and Ronald Coase to the field of law and economics. Among the participants are Milton and Rose Friedman, Stigler, Wallis, Becker, and Robert Bork, in addition to Director and Coase. There is much history and exploration of the development of ideas.

A number of obituaries were written on Director's death in September 2004. These include Richard M. Ebeling, "Aaron Director on the Market for Goods and Ideas," *Freeman* (November 2004), and Adam Bernstein, "Aaron Director Dies at 102; Helped Fuse Economics, Law," *Washington Post*, September 14, 2004. According to Ebeling, Director's "greatest influence was through his teaching . . . during which he helped change how an entire generation of economists and lawyers thought about government regulation and the impact of antitrust laws on market competition" (p. 2). Also see Coase's biographical entry on Director in the *Palgrave Dictionary of Economics and the Law,* and this writer's obituary of Director in the November 2004 edition of *Liberty:* Director "fought the view that the American economy is best characterized by monopolistic competition. This was a major contribution, for it helped pave the way for the libertarian revival in mainstream academic economics" (p. 42).

Ronald Coase, "Law and Economics at Chicago," *Journal of Law and Economics* (April 1993), includes discussion of Henry Simons, Aaron Director, and Coase's own work. Coase writes that "[b]oth in and out of the classroom, Director was extremely effective as a teacher, and he had a profound influence on the views of some of his students and . . . colleagues" (pp. 246–247). William R. Allen, "Irving Fisher and the 100 Percent Reserve Proposal," *Journal of Law and Economics* (October 1993), includes discussion on the development of this proposal during the 1930s with attention to Simons's role.

The January–February 1972 edition of the *Journal of Political Economy* features memorial articles on Jacob Viner by Fritz Machlup, Paul Samuelson, and William Baumol. Also see Lionel Robbins, *Jacob Viner: A Tribute* (Princeton, N.J.: Princeton University Press, 1970), and Henry W. Spiegel, "Jacob Viner," in *The New Palgrave: A Dictionary of Economics,* vol. 4 (London: Macmillan, 1991). Spiegel comments that "the Chicago of the 1920s . . . was not the Chicago of the later so-called Chicago School" (p. 813). Eugene Rotwein, "Jacob Viner and the Chicago Tradition," *History of Political Economy* (Summer 1983), holds: "There is a significant difference between the early—or principally prewar—and the postwar Chicago School" (p. 205).

The 1973 edition of the *Journal of Political Economy* includes papers delivered by Warner Wick, T. W. Schultz, and George Stigler at a memorial service in Frank Knight's memory. Also see the anonymous "In Memoriam" in the *American Economic Review* (December 1973); James Buchanan, "Frank Knight," in Edward Shils (ed.), *Remembering the University of Chicago* (Chicago: University of Chicago Press, 1991); and Richard S. Howey, "Frank Hyneman Knight and the History of Economic Thought," in Warren J. Samuels (ed.), *Research in the History of Economic Thought and Methodology,* vol. 1 (Greenwich, Conn.: JAI Press, 1983)—the last of which includes significant biographical information.

William S. Kern, "Frank Knight's Three Commandments," *History of Political Economy* (Winter 1987), is a good article on Knight's ethical thought. Stephen F. LeRoy and Larry D. Singell, Jr., "Knight on Risk and Uncertainty," *Journal of Political Economy* (April 1987), explores this central Knightian subject.

W. Allen Wallis, "The Statistical Research Group, 1942–1945," *Journal of the American Statistical Association* (June 1980), is a fond reminiscence. Wallis remarks in a rejoinder: "I am disposed to defend, though not without limit, irrelevance in academic research. In some ways, the most valuable contributions that universities can make . . . is to support research and scholarship that are not subject to tests of relevance" (p. 334). This article is the best history of the Statistical Research Group, in which Friedman participated from 1943 to 1945. Wallis remarked that the group was "in many respects a model that has not been equaled of an effective statistical consulting group" (p. 322).

George J. Stigler, *Memoirs of an Unregulated Economist* (Chicago: University of Chicago Press, 1988), provides background on Chicago and Friedman, and expresses Stigler's own views. Stigler, *The Economist as Preacher and Other Essays* (Chicago: University of Chicago Press, 1982), contains an essay on Henry Simons. In *The Theory of Price* (New York: Macmillan, 1987), Stigler commented that Friedman "established (to my complete satisfaction) his claim as the best debater in a profession that likes to debate" (p. 311).

Other Chicago economists, of an older generation, to write autobiographies were John U. Nef, *Search for Meaning: The Autobiography of a Noncomformist* (Washington, D.C.: 1973), and Paul H. Douglas, *In the Fullness of Time* (New York: 1971). Thomas Sowell's autobiography, *A Personal Odyssey* (New York: Free Press, 2000), includes recollections of his time as a student at the University of Chicago and of Friedman. James M. Buchanan, *Better than Plowing and Other Personal Essays* (Chicago: University of Chicago Press, 1992), includes remembrances of his time studying at Chicago, from 1945 to 1948, emphasizing Knight.

Herbert Stein's chapter "Henry C. Simons," in David L. Sills (ed.), *International Encyclopedia of the Social Sciences*, vol. 14 (New York: Macmillan and Free Press, 1968), is a good introduction: "Simons called his philosophy libertarian: the essential requirement of a good political and economic order is that it protect, promote, and respond to the free choices of individuals" (p. 260). Stein was among those, including Martin Bronfenbrenner, D. Gale Johnson, and Don Patinkin, who studied at Chicago after Friedman was a graduate student but before he began to teach there. Stein coined the term "supply-side" economics.

The October 1993 edition of the *Journal of Political Economy* is a memorial issue containing ten articles on Stigler, including articles by Friedman, Wallis, Becker, and Sowell. In a longer memorial essay on Stigler for the National Academy of Sciences, Friedman writes: "I never knew him to do a mean or hurtful or unworthy thing to anyone. . . . George was an extremely valuable colleague. He provided much of the energy and drive to the interaction among members of the Chicago economics department, business school, and law school that came to be known as the Chicago School." This would indicate that Friedman himself sometimes expresses the view that the phrase "Chicago school" was not used much before the middle to late 1950s.

H. Laurence Miller, "On the 'Chicago School of Economics,'" *Journal of Political Economy* (February 1962), sees a major division between Friedman and earlier Chicago economists: "The way in which Friedman and other modern Chicagoans concentrate their attack on government interference with the market represents a major departure from the earlier Chicago position" (p. 67). Also see in the same issue Stigler's "Comment" and Martin Bronfenbrenner's "Observations on the 'Chicago School(s).'" Bronfenbrenner humorously wrote:

> I never heard of any "Chicago School" until I left Chicago. . . . Shortly after leaving the Midway . . . I encountered the term full force. It was usually used pejoratively, especially when I was included in the membership. On the banks of Lake Mendota [the University of Wisconsin at Madison] . . . "the Chicago School" meant Pangloss plus Gradgrind, with touches of Peachum, Torquemada, and the Marquis de Sade thrown in as "insulter's surplus."

Bronfenbrenner, at the University of Wisconsin from 1947 to 1957, wrote more seriously: "There are not one but two Chicago Schools; the departure of Jacob Viner and the passing of Henry Simons are the watersheds between them" (pp. 72–73). Bronfenbrenner later provided more background in "A Conversation with Martin Bronfenbrenner," *Eastern Economic Journal* (January-March 1987). A. W. Coats, "The Origins of the 'Chicago School(s)'?" *Journal of Political Economy* (October 1963), provides further discussion. Coats holds: "There is no doctrinal continuity between the initial period . . . and more recent circumstances." He writes as well: "In retrospect, it appears that the dominant intellectual influences upon Chicago economics in the 1890's and early 1900's were Veblen and John Dewey rather than Laughlin" (pp. 487 and 492), although he notes that Laughlin early on gave economics a reputation for conservatism at Chicago.

Don Patinkin, *Essays on and in the Chicago Tradition* (Durham, N.C.: Duke University Press, 1981), is a noteworthy and provocative collection of articles. Patinkin was a student at Chicago from 1941 to 1947. This work contains a great deal of information on the history of economics there. Patinkin commences with personal reminiscences and continues with essays on Knight. After articles of his own work, Patinkin returns to historical topics in "The Chicago Tradition, the Quantity Theory, and Friedman," originally published in 1969, in which he challenges Friedman's presentation of an "oral tradition" in the quantity theory of money at Chicago before Friedman began to teach there. This article includes important correspondence between Patinkin and Jacob Viner with respect to the Chicago school of economics. William J. Baumol, *Journal of Political Economy* (December 1983), wrote in reviewing Patinkin's work that "Chicago in the 1930s, 1940s, and 1950s . . . adhered to no party line in political philosophy or analytic approach. It welcomed pure theory, empirical analysis, literary writing, and mathematical economics; libertarians, neutrals, and socialists. . . . [I]t was hardly of a piece with what has come to be called the Chicago School" (p. 1082).

J. Ronnie Davis, *The New Economics and the Old Economists* (Iowa State University Press, 1971), is an informative presentation of the views of largely Chicago economists during the Great Depression. Gordon Tullock writes in the foreword that Davis "ably demonstrates that the point of view held by almost all leading economists in the United States during . . . the Great Depression was a view which most modern laymen would denominate 'Keynesian'" (p. x).

Melvin Reder has written two valuable articles on the history of the Chicago school, "Chicago Economics: Permanence and Change," *Journal of Economic Literature* (March 1982), and the entry on "Chicago School" in *The New Palgrave: A Dictionary of Economics*, vol. 1 (London: Macmillan, 1991). He writes in the former: "In retrospect, the Chicago economics of the 1930s may appear as the precursor of what it was to become in the 1960s and 1970s. But in prospect this did not seem the only possible course of development, or even the most likely," and "The remarkable success of the Chicago School during the third quarter of this century was due in large part to the fact that it was able to take a leading role both in scientific research and in providing a rationale for political conservatism" (pp. 2 and 35). In the latter article, he divides the school's history into three periods: "(1) a founding period, in the 1930s; (2) an interregnum, from the early 1940s to the early 1950s; and (3) a modern period, from the 1950s to the present" (p. 413).

Warren J. Samuels, *The Chicago School of Political Economy* (New Brunswick, N.J.: Transaction Publishers, 1993), is a collection of articles that originally appeared in the December 1975 and March 1976 editions of the *Journal of Economic Issues*. Samuels writes: "Whether the success of the School is due to the merit of its ideas, the hard work . . . or personality of its members, or the spirit of the age . . . , the School is arguably the most successful in economics since World War II." He includes Buchanan and Coase, as well as Friedman, Stigler, and Becker, in the Chicago school. Several of the contributors emphasize Knight as opposed to Viner in the creation of the school.

Robert H. Nelson, *Economics as Religion: From Samuelson to Chicago and Beyond* (Pennsylvania State University Press, 2001), is an investigation into the role of economics in society—akin, in the author's view, to theology—with much consideration of Chicago economists. "From the 1960s onward," Nelson writes, "a new school of economics based at the University of Chicago took center stage in American intellectual life. . . . Chicago has also promoted a new libertarian trend within economics," and "the impact of the Chicago school not only on American economics but on all American social science and on government is nothing short of astonishing" (pp. 17–18 and 117).

Mary S. Morgan, *The History of Econometric Ideas* (Cambridge University Press, 1990); R. J. Epstein, *A History of Econometrics* (Amsterdam: North-Holland, 1987); and Clifford Hildreth, *The Cowles Commission in Chicago, 1939–1955* (Berlin: Springer-Verlag, 1986)—in addition to providing more general histories—have information on the Cowles Commission at Chicago and its interaction with the economics department and Friedman. Also see Carl F. Christ, "The Cowles Commission's Contributions to Econometrics at Chicago, 1939–1955," *Journal of Economic Literature* (March 1994), for the perspective of a participant.

Daniel Bell and Irving Kristol (eds.), *The Crisis in Economic Theory* (New York: Basic Books, 1981), is an excellent snapshot of where the economics profession was at that time. Contributors include, in addition to the editors, Kenneth Arrow, Peter Drucker, and Allan Meltzer. Friedman, though he does not contribute an essay, is the most discussed contemporaneous economist. James Dean notes in his essay that behind Friedman's idea of a fixed rule for monetary growth is a "fundamental premise of pre-Keynesian laissez faire economics, namely that the private sector is self-stabilizing. Real-world instability results primarily from the fiscal, monetary, and regulatory actions of government. Keynes, of course, suggested just the opposite," and changes in economists' thinking might be attributed to the "steady gains made by Chicago-style economic philosophy, roughly coincident with the progress of Milton Friedman's career" (pp. 25 and 30).

Arjo Klamer (ed.), *Conversations with Economists: New Classical Economists and Opponents Speak Out on the Current Controversy in Macroeconomics* (Totowa, N.J.: Rowman & Allanheld, 1984), is another early 1980s consideration of the state of economics, more exclusively by academics. Of contemporary economists, the focus is more on Robert Lucas than on Friedman, but Friedman is likely second in the number of references. There is less consideration of radical change in academic economics than there is in Bell and Kristol's collection. Klamer writes in his introduction that during the 1950s and 1960s, the influence of monetarists was "minimal. Milton Friedman . . . was considered a heretic. . . . But Friedman and others persisted. . . . The resulting monetarist debate would dominate macroeconomic discourse in the early 1970s" (p. 7).

Klamer had this exchange with James Tobin:

Interviewer: You are brilliant, but so is he. Still, it seems to be hard for the both of you to come to any form of agreement. Why is that?

Tobin: . . . [O]ne reason it didn't work is that Friedman always replied that he didn't say what I said he had said. And I was simply saying what everybody believed Friedman had been saying.

Interviewer: Do you think that such a problem of communication is typical among economists?

Tobin: No, I don't think so. But I believe that Friedman had a crusade that he was pushing all over the world, not just in the profession. He saw the big picture, and the big picture was right for him. He didn't really want to be bothered by these little technical problems. [p. 106]

Franco Modigliani made these comments: "Friedman is driven by the idea that whatever the government does is bad. He has a mission and seems to be willing to sacrifice some intellectual honesty for that"; he also called Friedman a "tough . . . very fast and dangerous" (p. 120) debater. Karl Brunner, who was at Chicago in the 1950s, said that Friedman was "very important for me. I never really developed a close personal contact with him, but I learned much from him and also from the whole group around him. . . . They really alerted me to price theory and its potential application to the problems of the world." Brunner had these recollections of other Chicagoans:

Frank Knight was a very impressive, knowledgeable person. We had all kinds of discussions over luncheon and on occasional Sunday afternoons. I remember one afternoon that he began to talk about the wandering of Germanic tribes at the end of the Roman Empire. . . . He also probed, with an inquisitive and searching mind, many ideas in philosophy and theology. . . . Knight was a rare intellectual, one of the great ones of this century. Let me also add to my list Aaron Director, who conveyed a remarkable insight how to use price theory to understand our world. [pp. 180–181]

Randall E. Parker (ed.), *Reflections on the Great Depression* (Cheltenham, U.K.: Edward Elgar, 2002), is a solid collection of interviews on the depression, including interviews with Friedman, Samuelson, Tobin, Abramovitz, Hart, Schwartz, and Stein. Samuelson comments: "You haven't heard Milton Friedman talk about 100 percent money for a long time. Gary Becker I think converted him out of it. He said they'll just grow up a system of credit *outside* the banking system" (p. 32). Friedman says in response: "At the time I was pressing 100 percent money there was some possibility of moving in that direction because the banking system was heavily invested in government securities. . . . Since then the situation has changed drastically. . . . [W]hile I still think in principle it would be good reform, the particular difficulties that it is designed to remedy are not as serious as they were earlier" (Friedman-Ebenstein correspondence, June 21, 2005).

Warren J. Samuels and Jeff Biddle (eds.), *Research in the History of Economic Thought and Methodology,* vol. 10 (Greenwich, Conn.: JAI Press, 1992), contains a symposium on Friedman's methodology. Of particular value is Daniel Hammond's interview with Friedman, one of the best. Friedman comments: "I have to confess, that in reading what all you people write, I get tremendous insight into what I thought. (Laughter) . . . [P]ersonally, I have never been very introspective" (p. 95).

Juan Gabriel Valdés, *Pinochet's Economists: The Chicago School in Chile* (Cambridge University Press, 1995), is an even-handed account of its subject. Valdés provides no evidence for direct Friedman involvement in the Chilean regime of Augusto Pinochet, other than his and Harberger's trip to Chile. Valdés notes that during the second half of the 1970s when much of the rest of academia condemned Chile for its political abuses, Friedman and other free market economists praised it for its economic reforms.

Elton Rayack, *Not So Free to Choose: The Political Economy of Milton Friedman and Ronald Reagan* (New York: Praeger, 1987), is a negative appraisal of Friedman's participation in public policy. Rayack writes that Friedman is an "ideologue—often simplistic in his presentation of economic analysis, frequently cavalier in his treatment of history, citing data that tend to confirm a hypothesis he is defending while conveniently ignoring other data that are obviously inconsistent with his analysis" (p. 8). Rayack also says that Friedman's

first association with a major political victory . . . came with enactment of California's Proposition 13. The statute imposed severe restraints on . . . tax increases, particularly with respect to taxes on property. Friedman played a key role in its passage, as he appeared in an influential television commercial in support of the cap on taxes. Proposition 13 not only touched off a tax revolt that spread to a number of other states, it also contributed to the political momentum of Ronald Reagan. [p. 6]

Friedman is discussed in many histories of economic thought. Ben Seligman, *Main Currents in Modern Economics* (New York: Free Press, 1962), has a section on Friedman, "Theory as Ideology." Here Seligman writes (without referring to a "Chicago school"), after discussing the Keynesianism of Alvin Hansen: "The viewpoint represented by . . . Hansen was not . . . well received in certain academic circles. This has been especially so at the University of Chicago where Frank Knight, Jacob Viner, Henry Simons, Lloyd Mints, George Stigler, and Milton Friedman have built with great vigor and forcefulness a tradition emphasizing the virtues of pure competition. . . . One of the sharpest exponents of this outlook has been Milton Friedman." Seligman makes the perceptive comments, paraphrasing Friedman in the first instance, that "[t]he quantity theory of money now was heading the counter-revolution against Keynes" and Friedman sees "economic instability . . . as basically monetary instability" (pp. 673, 678, and 681).

Henry Spiegel, *The Growth of Economic Thought*, 3rd edition (Durham, N.C.: Duke University Press, 1991; first edition, 1971), is a classic work. Spiegel did not discuss Friedman much in the first edition. Later he added these comments: "The monetarists, ably led by Milton Friedman, constitute a reaction against the emphasis on investment, fiscal policy, and the consumption function as it prevailed under the influence of the Keynesian revolution, whose followers were not overly impressed with the importance of monetary changes" (p. 668).

Todd Buchholz, *New Ideas from Dead Economists* (New York: Plume, 1999; first edition, 1990), has a chapter, "The Monetarist Battle against Keynes," largely on Friedman. Buchholz writes that a "titanic struggle took place between Keynesians and monetarists from the 1950s through the 1970s. . . . No one was better suited by temperament or intellect to lead the monetarist counterrevolution. . . . Friedman was not intimidated by conventional wisdom." Buchholz offers a critique of Friedman's proposal for increasing money supply by a set amount each year: "A fixed monetary rule . . . might have been disastrous," when, as during the 1980s, velocity fell." Buchholz notes that in the wake of monetarism in the 1980s, "more than 50 countries cut their top [tax] rates" (pp. 227, 235, 243, and 245).

John Kenneth Galbraith, *Economics in Perspective* (Boston: Houghton Mifflin, 1987), presents a flattering picture of Friedman's place in twentieth-century economics. Friedman is "perhaps the most influential economic figure of the second half of the twentieth century." Galbraith provides this description:

> A small, vigorously spoken man, uniquely determined in debate and discussion, entirely free of the doubt that on occasion assails intellectually more vulnerable scholars, Friedman was, as he remains, the leading American exponent of the classical competitive market, which he held still to exist in substantially unimpaired form except as it had suffered from ill-advised government intrusion. Monopoly, oligopoly and imperfect competition played no important part in his thinking. Friedman was a powerful opponent of government regulation and government activity in general. Freedom, he held, was maximized when the individual was left free to deploy his own income as he wished. [p. 271]

Paul Samuelson, "Milton Friedman," *Newsweek*, October 25, 1976, provides these thoughts on Friedman's influence on the occasion of Friedman's receipt of the Nobel Prize: "MIT, Harvard, Oxford and every topnotch economics department would today feel deprived and one-sided if the fruitful Chicago viewpoint were not represented on its faculty. This new fact is a tribute to one great leader." Samuelson also comments on Friedman's "bounce and gaiety, his rapier intelligence, his unfailing courtesy in debate. The world admires him for his achievements. His intimates love him for himself" (p. 89).

William Breit and Roger Ransom, *The Academic Scribblers*, 3rd edition (Princeton, N.J.: Princeton University Press: 1998; first edition, 1971), has a chapter on Friedman, "Classical Liberal as Economic Scientist." The authors emphasize that "no single event in the history of the United States had more sweeping impact on economic thought than the Great Depression." They write that the

> movement away from the monetary implications of neoclassical economics was . . . brought to a standstill by the empirical research and theoretical arguments of this brilliant economist. No one testifying before congressional committees was listened to with more respect. . . . Friedman's most powerful means of persuasion has been the force of his personality that has allowed his heretical and radical ideas in defense of market capitalism to capture the imagination of scores of economists and legislators. . . . Today, he challenges Keynes as the twentieth century's most influential economist. [pp. 223–226]

Breit and Ransom call attention to the tie between Friedman's and Mill's thought. They compare Mill's line in *On Liberty*, "The only freedom which deserves the name is that of pursuing our own good in our own way, so long as we do not attempt to deprive others of theirs, or impede their efforts to obtain it," with Friedman's line in *Capitalism and Freedom*, "the goal of liberalism is 'to pre-serve the maximum degree of freedom for each individual separately that is compatible with one man's freedom not interfering with other men's freedom'" (pp. 254–255). Breit and Barry T. Hirsch's *Lives of the Laureates*, 4th edition (Cambridge, Mass.: MIT Press, 2004), is a collection of autobio-graphical lectures by Nobel laureates in economics, including Friedman. Several of the essays, includ-ing those by Becker, Lucas, and James Heckman, include significant discussion of Friedman.

Mark Skousen, *The Making of Modern Economics: The Lives and Ideas of the Great Thinkers* (Ar-monk, N.Y.: M. E. Sharpe, 2001), contains a chapter on Friedman, "Milton's Paradise: Friedman Leads a Monetary Counterrevolution." Skousen writes: "If anyone could take on the Keynesians and restore classical economics, it was Milton Friedman. . . . In many ways, Adam Smith is his mentor. . . . [Friedman] has done more than any other economist to reverse the Keynesian tide and reestablish the virtues of neoclassical economics" (pp. 380 and 397). Skousen (ed.), *Dissent on Keynes: A Critical Appraisal of Keynesian Economics* (N.Y: Praeger, 1992), includes a chapter by Roger Garrison, "Is Milton Friedman a Keynesian?" Skousen has written extensively on Friedman in a column for the *Freeman*. Articles of particular interest include "Friedman Challenges Hayek" (March 1995), "Friedman vs. the Austrians, Part II: Was There an Inflationary Boom in the 1920s?" (April 1995), "Vienna and Chicago: A Tale of Two Schools" (February 1998), and "Milton Friedman, Ex-Keynesian" (July 1998). Skousen has most recently completed a volume comparing Austrian and Chicago economics, *Vienna and Chicago: Friends or Foes? A Tale of Two Schools of Free-Market Economics* (Washington, D.C.: Capital Press, 2005).

Many chapters have been written on Friedman in books on economists. J. R. Shackleton and Gareth Locksley (eds.), *Twelve Contemporary Economists* (New York: John Wiley & Sons, 1981), in-cludes "Positively Milton Friedman," by John Burton, which commences: "Attempting to portray the work of Milton Friedman in 5000 words is an impossible assignment. It is like trying to catch the Ni-agara Falls in a pint pot," and concludes that: "Milton Friedman is the Adam Smith of this century" (pp. 53 and 69).

Robert Sobel, *The Worldly Economists* (New York: Free Press, 1980), is an excellent book, styl-ishly written. Sobel concentrates on economists who have served in government and who are in the public eye. His description of the personal sources of Arthur Burns's influence in the chapter on Burns is excellent. Sobel's chapter on Friedman is perhaps the best brief introduction to his life and career through the 1960s. Sobel writes: "In a period when a large majority of economists accepted Keynesianism . . . , Friedman led the counterattack. . . . Witty, often eloquent, and supremely logical, he is the most important critic of the new economics" (p. 144). Sobel provides a particularly good discussion of Friedman's early career, writing that those who remember Friedman when he was at the National Bureau of Economic Research in the late 1930s "speak of his constant insistence upon schol-arly detachment, and a few reflect that this usually appeared in his criticisms of liberal economists who were sympathetic with . . . the New Deal. Economists should strive for objectivity, he thought, and seek to make the discipline as value-free and scientific as possible" (p. 152). Sobel speculates that the source of Friedman's emphasis on value neutrality was Mitchell. He notes that some of Fried-man's World War II advocacy of fiscal policy to control inflation stems from the circumstance that the policy alternative at the time was wage and price controls.

Henry Spiegel and Warren J. Samuels (eds.), *Contemporary Economists in Perspective* (Green-wich, Conn.: JAI Press, 1984), contains a chapter on Friedman by Niels Thygesen. Thygesen, from the University of Copenhagen, writes: "Friedman's influence ranges well beyond the academic. To an ex-tent unprecedented in the age of specialization, his ideas have become a matter for debate in much wider circles. It is doubtful whether any other economist has had a comparable impact on the public debate on a major policy issue," and "The most surprising aspect of Friedman's achievements is that he has not to a greater extent earned the gratitude of the profession" (pp. 218 and 244).

George H. Nash's, *The Conservative Intellectual Movement in America: Since 1945* (Wilmington, Del.: Intercollegiate Studies Institute, 1996; first edition, 1976) remains the authoritative work in the field. Nash writes that the "conservative case for the free society needed a fresh practical restatement in the 1960s. Fortunately for the movement, it was forthcoming—from the irrepressibly brilliant economist Milton Friedman and the rising Chicago School of economics." Nash also writes: "The publication of *Capitalism and Freedom* and Friedman's emergence as a preeminent economist among conservatives constituted a major landmark in the evolution of the postwar Right. . . . [B]y the end of the 1960s he was probably the most highly regarded and influential conservative scholar in the country, and one of the few with an international reputation" (pp. 267 and 270). Nash's work is invaluable for describing the evolution of postwar conservative (including libertarian) intellectual thought in the United States through 1976.

Jim Powell, *The Triumph of Liberty* (New York: Free Press, 2000), contains a chapter on Friedman, where he writes: "Friedman ranks as the greatest champion of liberty during the twentieth century. He worked in more media on more issues than anyone else, for more than fifty years. His influence extended around the world. . . . He inspired millions to help carry the torch of liberty on its next lap" (p. 386). Powell, who roomed with David Friedman in college and occasionally visited the Friedmans' home as a young man, adds in *FDR's Folly: How Roosevelt and His New Deal Prolonged the Great Depression* (New York: Crown Forum, 2003): "Milton Friedman kindly went over the manuscript twice, offering many corrections and suggestions. . . . Ever since I first met him and began to follow his work almost forty years ago, he has inspired me as a scholar and as a defender of individual liberty" (p. 323).

Alan Walters, "Milton Friedman," in John Eatwell, Murray Milgate, and Peter Newman (eds.), *The New Palgrave: A Dictionary of Economics*, vol. 2 (London: Macmillan, 1991), is a good introduction to Friedman's career in economics. Walters calls attention to Friedman's early work, emphasizes *A Theory of the Consumption Function*, and concludes: "The success of his advocacy has by any objective standard been enormous. . . . In effectiveness, breadth and scope, his only rival among the economists of the 20th century is Keynes" (p. 427).

Charles K. Rowley and Anne Rathbone, "Milton Friedman, 1912: Harbinger of the Public Choice Revolution," in Charles K. Rowley and Friedrich Schneider, *Encyclopedia of Public Choice*, vol. 1 (Kluwer Academic Publishers, 2004), is an excellent summary of Friedman's thought. Friedman is "arguably the most influential economist of the twentieth century" (p. 146).

Charles Murray writes in *What It Means to Be a Libertarian: A Personal Interpretation* (New York: Broadway Books, 1997) of those who have inspired him: "I haven't the temerity to call Milton Friedman a colleague, but his advice over the years has been as wise as his critiques have been acute" (p. 177). In *In Our Hands: A Plan to Replace the Welfare State* (Washington, D.C.: AEI Press, 2006), Murray revives Friedman's idea of a negative income tax.

Martin Anderson says in *Impostors in the Temple: American Intellectuals Are Destroying Our Universities and Cheating Our Students of Their Future* (New York: Simon & Schuster, 1992) that Friedman is an "archetype of what an academic intellectual should be. Beyond his brilliant mind and his influential research and writing, he has a natural instinct for teaching. He teaches naturally . . . whether in front of a lecture hall or in personal conversation. He loves the play of ideas, loves challenging people, making them think, pursuing the truth wherever it leads. About him is an aura of pure intellectual integrity" (pp. 37–38).

William E. Simon, in *A Time for Reflection: An Autobiography* (Washington, D.C.: Regnery, 2004), wrote: "There is no better modern book on economic freedom . . . than Milton's Friedman's *Capitalism and Freedom*" (p. 72).

Julian Simon, *A Life against the Grain: The Autobiography of an Unconventional Economist* (New Brunswick, N.J.: Transaction, 2002), said: "It is quite amazing how often Milton Friedman has touched my thinking or my imagination, even though I've only been together with him on perhaps four occasions." He also tells the anecdote of once, after having recommended overbooking on airlines in the 1970s, which Friedman opposed and which proved successful, writing to Friedman "roughly as follows: 'About the airline oversales scheme: I'm not given to I-told-you-so's, but . . . I told you so.' And he replied . . . : 'Many thanks for your "I told you so"; you are entitled to it.' . . . Friedman himself . . . told the story . . . at a large banquet, and then wrote me as follows: 'There is no reason why [it] should be kept private. It is something that actually happened'" (pp. 214 and 296).

Daniel Yergin and Joseph Stanislaw, *The Commanding Heights: The Battle Between Government and the Marketplace that Is Remaking the Modern World* (New York: Simon & Schuster, 1998), provides these thoughts on Friedman: "He emerged from among the Chicago faculty as an iconoclastic and controversial thinker and leader of what was, by the late 1950s, an all-out assault on virtually every aspect of Keynesian economics. . . . He believed his ideas could transform the world—and, arguably, they did." The authors also quote Lawrence Summers, Clinton's secretary of the treasury, Harvard president, nephew of Paul Samuelson and Kenneth Arrow, and John Bates Clark medal recipient: "As for Milton Friedman, he was the devil figure in my youth. Only with time have I come to have large amounts of grudging respect. And with time, increasingly ungrudging respect" (pp. 147–151).

David Boaz, *Libertarianism: A Primer* (New York: Free Press, 1997), is an excellent comprehensive introduction to its subject, covering all areas from history to current public policy to a vision of a libertarian future. Boaz writes that "through *Capitalism and Freedom,* his long-running *Newsweek* column, and the 1980 book and television series *Free to Choose,* he became the most prominent American libertarian of the past generation" (p. 56). William Niskanen, in *Policy Analysis and Public Choice* (Northhampton, Mass.: Edward Elgar, 1998), writes that, on reading *Capitalism and Freedom,* "one is struck by the sense of optimism about the ultimate power of ideas—a faith that closely reasoned argument, an accumulation of evidence, and a leavening of wit will persuade most people and that our governmental processes will be responsive to their preferences" (p. 307). Also see Boaz (ed.), *The Libertarian Reader: Classic and Contemporary Writings from Lao-tzu to Milton Friedman* (New York: Free Press, 1997).

Anna Jacobson Schwartz has written on Friedman on several occasions, including a September 1998 review of *Two Lucky People* in the Federal Reserve Bank of Minneapolis periodical *The Region.* She observes that Friedman has changed the popular mind-set with respect to government's appropriate role in the economy: "He did so by radically altering the popular understanding of the Great Depression. He highlighted the one-third fall in the quantity of money. . . . The Federal Reserve System produced the economic collapse, not the failings of a market economy." She also says that in a "broader sense, the collapse of collectivist regimes in the past decade underscored his celebration of free market economics." Also see Schwartz's introduction to Kurt R. Leube (ed.), *The Essence of Friedman* (Stanford, Calif.: Hoover Institution Press, 1987).

Warren J. Samuels, "Rose Friedman and Milton Friedman's *Two Lucky People,*" in Warren J. Samuels and Jeff E. Biddle (eds.), *Research in the History of Economic Thought and Methodology,* vol. 18-A (New York: JAI, 2000), holds that "Friedman is a very rigorous economic theorist. His thinking on matters of political economy, however, is not as rigorous. One should not expect memoirs such as these to be . . . deep or seriously self-critical. But the memoirs continue lines of reasoning found in his/their previous polemical books . . . which, in my view, leave much to be desired" (p. 243) and that "[t]he memoirs reveal two very different Milton Friedmans: Friedman the rigorous economic scientist and Friedman the activist but nonrigorous ideological high priest of 'free markets,' 'limited government,' and 'free enterprise'" (p. 242). Samuels (ed.), "Notes on Frank H. Knight's Course on the History of Economic Thought . . . ," *Research in the History of Economic Thought and Methodology,* vol. 22-B (San Diego: Elsevier, 2004), quotes Taylor Ostrander, who took Knight's history of economic thought class, from 2003 correspondence: "When I went to Chicago in 1933 there was *no* Chicago school. It was really the New Deal, and especially Henry Simons' reaction to it, plus the two strong student personalities Stigler and Friedman, that began to build a Chicago School"—with respect to which Samuels comments, "This is a valuable point. The designation 'School' came later" (p. 272).

Eric Schliesser, "Galilean Reflections on Milton Friedman's 'Methodology of Positive Economics,'" *Philosophy of the Social Sciences* (March 2005), writes: "Milton Friedman's essay 'The Methodology of Positive Economics' is the most influential methodological statement within economics and the most widely discussed paper by philosophers and methodologists of economics in the secondary literature of the twentieth century" (pp. 50–51). David Reisman, *Conservative Capitalism: The Social*

Economy (1999), remarks: "Friedman argues that accurate predictions are the economist's proper study, that full explanations, however illuminating in themselves, are simply not needed for the task in hand" (p. 135).

Bruce Caldwell, *Beyond Positivism: Economic Methodology in the Twentieth Century* (London: George Allen & Unwin, 1982), contains a chapter on Friedman's "methodological instrumentalism." Caldwell correctly comments: "Though many parts of Friedman's essay ['The Methodology of Positive Economics'] are consistent with the logical empiricism of his time, his preoccupation with prediction and his insistence that the 'realism of assumptions' is immaterial are not" (pp. 173 and 184). For an exchange between Caldwell and this writer featuring considerable discussion of Friedman's methodological views, see the January 2005 inaugural edition of the *NYU Journal of Law & Liberty*.

This writer's *Friedrich Hayek: A Biography* (New York: Palgrave, 2001) and *Hayek's Journey: The Mind of Friedrich Hayek* (New York: Palgrave, 2003) contain chapters on Friedman and the Chicago school of economics. The August 2005 edition of *Liberty* has an article by this writer, "Milton Friedman's Legacy." William Ebenstein and Alan Ebenstein, *Great Political Thinkers*, 6th edition (Fort Worth, Tex.: Harcourt, 2000), contains a chapter on libertarianism with discussion of Friedman.

NOTES

ABBREVIATIONS

CF	Milton Friedman, *Capitalism and Freedom,* 40th anniversary edition (Chicago: University of Chicago Press, 2002)
EPE	Milton Friedman, *Essays in Positive Economics* (Chicago: University of Chicago Press, 1953)
Essence	Milton Friedman, *The Essence of Friedman* (Stanford, Calif.: Hoover Institution Press, 1987)
FA	Friedman Archive, Hoover Institution on War, Revolution and Peace, Stanford, California
Frazer	William Frazer, *Power and Ideas: Milton Friedman and the Big U-Turn,* 2 vols. (Gainesville, Fla.: Gulf/Atlantic Publishing, 1988)
FTC	Milton and Rose Friedman, *Free to Choose* (New York: Avon, 1981)
Lives	William Breit and Roger W. Spencer (eds.), *Lives of the Laureates,* 2nd ed. (Cambridge, Mass.: MIT Press, 1990)
Memoirs	Milton and Rose Friedman, *Two Lucky People: Memoirs* (Chicago: University ofChicago Press, 1998)
MHUS	Milton Friedman and Anna Jacobson Schwartz, *A Monetary History of the United States, 1867–1960* (Princeton University Press, 1963)
Shils	Edward Shils, *Remembering the University of Chicago: Teachers, Scientists, and Scholars* (Chicago: University of Chicago Press, 1991)

INTRODUCTION

1. *Memoirs,* 32.
2. R. H. Inglis Palgrave (ed.), *Dictionary of Political Economy,* vol. 2 (London: Macmillan, 1896), 704.
3. *FTC,* 29.

CHAPTER 1

1. Friedman-Ebenstein interview (2000).
2. Ibid.
3. Emma Lazarus, "The New Colossus" (1883).
4. *Memoirs,* 20.
5. *Lives,* 81.
6. Milton Friedman, "Autobiography of Milton Friedman," Nobel e-Museum, Nobel Foundation Web site (1976, 2000).

7. *Memoirs*, 21.
8. Ibid., 262.
9. Friedman comment on "Milton Friedman: A Biography," draft manuscript (2004).
10. *Memoirs*, 22.
11. Friedman-Ebenstein interview (2000).
12. *Memoirs*, 23.
13. Ibid.
14. Friedman-Ebenstein email correspondence (September 25, 2006).
15. *Lives*, 79–80.
16. Friedman-Ebenstein interview (2002)
17. Ibid.
18. *Memoirs*, 24.

CHAPTER 2

1. Friedman-Ebenstein interview (2002).
2. Milton Friedman, "Autobiography of Milton Friedman," Nobel e-Museum, Nobel Foundation Web site (1976, 2000).
3. *Memoirs*, 617.
4. Ibid., 25.
5. Ibid., 28.
6. Ibid., 27.
7. Ibid., 29.
8. Milton Friedman, "My Five Favorite Libertarian Books," *FEE Today* (April 2002), 1.
9. *Memoirs*, 29.
10. Milton Friedman, "Homer Jones: A Personal Reminiscence," *Journal of Monetary Economics* 2 (1976), 434, 436.
11. "Wallis Years at the University of Rochester," transcript of interviews with William H. Meckling (University of Rochester Library, Rochester, N.Y., June 1982), 54.
12. In Justin Martin, *Greenspan: The Man Behind Money* (Cambridge, Mass.: Perseus Publishing, 2000), 30.
13. Friedman-Ebenstein interview (2003).
14. In *Memoirs*, 30.
15. In Martin, *Greenspan*, 29.
16. In Brian Snowdon and Howard R. Vane, *Conversations with Leading Economists: Interpreting Modern Macroeconomics* (Cheltenham, U.K.: Edward Elgar, 1999), 124–125.

CHAPTER 3

1. *Memoirs*, xi.
2. Wesley C. Mitchell (ed.), *What Veblen Taught* (New York: Viking Press, 1947), xiii.
3. In Shils, 543.
4. Edward Shils, *Portraits: A Gallery of Intellectuals* (Chicago: University of Chicago Press, 1997), 31–32.
5. FA, box 5, folder 13.
6. Ibid.
7. *Memoirs*, 34–35.
8. Ibid., 621.
9. In Brian Snowdon and Howard R. Vane, *Conversations with Leading Economists: Interpreting Modern Macroeconomics* (Cheltenham, U.K.: Edward Elgar, 1999), 128.
10. "Wallis Years at the University of Rochester," transcript of interviews with William H. Meckling (University of Rochester Library, Rochester, N.Y., June 1982), 58.

11. *Memoirs,* 52.
12. In Henry C. Simons, *Economic Policy for a Free Society* (Chicago: University of Chicago Press, 1948), v.
13. Milton Friedman, "The Monetary Theory and Policy of Henry Simons," *Journal of Law and Economics* (October 1967), 1.
14. *Memoirs,* 44.
15. Kenneth J. Arrow, "Harold Hotelling," in John Eatwell, Murray Milgate, and Peter Newman (eds.), *The New Palgrave: A Dictionary of Economics,* vol. 2 (London: Macmillan, 1991), 670.
16. *Memoirs,* 44.
17. Milton Friedman, "Autobiography of Milton Friedman," Nobel e-Museum, Nobel Foundation Web site (1976, 2000).
18. In Frazer, vol. 1, 19.
19. *Memoirs,* 48.
20. FA, box 37, folder 1, 1.
21. Ibid., 1–2.
22. Ibid., 41.
23. Ibid., 44 (second paragraph is crossed out in original).
24. Ibid., 53.

CHAPTER 4

1. *Memoirs,* 9.
2. Ibid., 14.
3. Milton Friedman, "Autobiography of Milton Friedman," Nobel e-Museum, Nobel Foundation Web site (1976, 2000).
4. *Memoirs,* 42.
5. W. Allen Wallis, "George J. Stigler: In Memorium," *Journal of Political Economy* (October 1993), 775.
6. *Memoirs,* 35.
7. Ibid., 618.
8. Ibid., 38.
9. Ibid., 55.
10. Ibid., 60–61.
11. "Wallis Years at the University of Rochester," transcript of interviews with William H. Meckling (University of Rochester Library, Rochester, N.Y., June 1982), 53.
12. Frazer, vol. 1, 151.
13. Leonard Silk, *The Economists* (New York: Basic Books, 1976), 40.
14. In Richard Parker, *John Kenneth Galbraith: His Life, His Politics, His Economics* (New York: Farrar, Straus and Giroux, 2005), 31.
15. Milton Friedman and George J. Stigler, *Roofs or Ceilings? The Current Housing Problem* (Irvington-on-Hudson, N.Y.: Foundation for Economic Freedom, 1946).
16. *EPE,* 134.
17. *Memoirs,* 618.
18. Ibid., 54.
19. Rose Friedman 2003 comment on "Milton Friedman: A Biography," draft manuscript.
20. Milton Friedman, review of Ralph Blodgett, *Cyclical Fluctuations in Commodity Stocks, Journal of Political Economy* (October 1936): 842–843.
21. In J. Daniel Hammond, "An Interview with Milton Friedman on Methodology," in Warren J. Samuels and Jeff Biddle (eds.), *Research in the History of Economic Thought and Methodology,* vol. 10 (Greenwich, Conn.: JAI Press, 1992), 106.
22. Milton Friedman, "Autobiography of Milton Friedman," Nobel e-Museum, Nobel Foundation Web site (1976, 2000).

23. *Memoirs,* 81.
24. Ibid., 80.
25. *Lives,* 82.
26. *Memoirs,* 81.

CHAPTER 5

1. Frazer, vol. 1, 165.
2. *Memoirs,* 104.
3. Carl Shoup, Milton Friedman, and Ruth P. Mack, *Taxing to Prevent Inflation* (New York: Columbia University Press, 1943), 111.
4. *Memoirs,* 110.
5. Ibid., 112.
6. FA, box 37, folder 17.
7. Robert Sobel, *The Worldly Economists* (New York: Free Press, 1980), 154.
8. W. Allen Wallis, "The Statistical Research Group, 1942–1945," *Journal of the American Statistical Association* (June 1980), 322.
9. In Frazer, vol. 1, 156.
10. James Berger, "Sequential Analysis," in John Eatwell, Murray Milgate, and Peter Newman (eds.), *The New Palgrave: A Dictionary of Economics,* vol. 4 (London: Macmillan, 1991), 313.
11. Wallis, "Statistical Research Group," 329.
12. *Memoirs,* 125.

CHAPTER 6

1. May 19, 1945, letter from Friedman to George Stigler (in the possession of Stephen Stigler).
2. George Stigler, *Memoirs of an Unregulated Economist* (New York: Basic Books, 1988), 24.
3. *Lives,* 97.
4. Milton Friedman, "George Stigler: A Personal Reminiscence," *Journal of Political Economy* (October 1993), 772.
5. In Leonard Silk, *The Economists* (New York: Basic Books, 1976), 71.
6. Robert Bangs, *American Economic Review* (June 1947): 482–483.
7. *Memoirs,* 85.
8. Frazer, vol. 1, 139.
9. Robert Leeson, *The Eclipse of Keynesianism: The Political Economy of the Chicago Counter-Revolution* (New York: Palgrave, 2000), 132.
10. Stigler, *Memoirs,* 40.
11. In Alan Ebenstein, *Friedrich Hayek: A Biography* (New York: Palgrave, 2001), 175.
12. In Shils, 470.
13. Friedman, "Stigler: Reminiscence," 769.
14. *Memoirs,* 183.

CHAPTER 7

1. http://reason.com/9506/FRIEDMAN.jun.shtml.
2. *Memoirs,* 183.
3. Lester Telser–Ebenstein interview (2004).
4. *Lives,* 23.
5. *Memoirs,* 197; Friedman-Ebenstein interview (2004).
6. Friedman-Ebenstein interview (2004).
7. FA, box 7, folder 4.

8. In Carl F. Christ, "The Cowles Commission's Contributions to Econometrics at Chicago, 1939–1955," *Journal of Economic Literature* (March 1994), 46.

9. Robert M. Solow, "Cowles and the Tradition of Macroeconomics," in Alvin K. Klevorick (ed.), *Cowles Fiftieth Anniversary Volume* (1983).

10. Melvin W. Reder, "Chicago School," in John Eatwell, Murray Milgate, and Peter Newman (eds.), *The New Palgrave: A Dictionary of Economics*, vol. 1 (London: Macmillan, 1991), 415.

11. Frazer, vol. 2, 706.

12. In Christ, "Cowles Commission's Contributions," 34–35.

13. Ibid., 35.

14. Milton Friedman, "James Laurence Laughlin," in John Eatwell, Murray Milgate, and Peter Newman (eds.), *The New Palgrave: A Dictionary of Economics*, vol. 3 (London: Macmillan, 1991), 140.

15. Friedman-Ebenstein interview (2004).

16. Milton Friedman, "Schools at Chicago," *The University of Chicago Record* (1974), 7, 6.

CHAPTER 8

1. *EPE*, 3.

2. Ibid.

3. Ibid., 289.

4. Ibid., 7.

5. Ibid., 6–7.

6. Ibid., 9.

7. In J. Daniel Hammond, "An Interview with Milton Friedman on Methodology," in Warren J. Samuels and Jeff Biddle (eds.), *Research in the History of Economic Thought and Methodology*, vol. 10 (Greenwich, Conn.: JAI Press, 1992), 100.

8. *Memoirs*, 215.

9. Frazer, vol. 1, 3.

10. *EPE*, 283.

11. Ibid., 277.

12. Ibid., 15.

13. Frazer, vol. 1, 160.

14. In Hammond, "Interview," 109.

15. In Don Patinkin, *Essays on and in the Chicago Tradition* (Durham, N.C.: Duke University Press, 1981), 16.

16. FA, box 36, folder 8 (letter to Alan Coddington [October 8, 1979]).

17. Milton Friedman and L. J. Savage, "The Expected-Utility Hyypothesis and the Measurability of Utility," *Journal of Political Economy* (December 1952), 465.

18. Milton Friedman, *Dollars and Deficits* (Englewood Cliffs, N.J.: Prentice-Hall, 1968), 44.

19. In Eamonn Butler, *Milton Friedman: A Guide to His Economic Thought* (New York: Universe Books, 1985), 227.

20. Hammond, 107.

21. *EPE*, 134.

22. FA, box 36, folder 5 ("Economic Policy: Intentions vs. Results," 18).

23. In Robert Leeson, "Patinkin, Johnson, and the Shadow of Friedman," *History of Political Economy* (Winter 2000), 733–734.

24. *EPE*, 47.

25. Ibid., 56–57.

26. *Memoirs*, 189.

27. John Stuart Mill, *On Liberty* (1859), chapter 2.

28. George Stigler, *Memoirs of an Unregulated Economist* (New York: Basic Books, 1988), 161.

29. *CF*, 73.

30. *EPE,* 264.
31. Ibid.
32. Peter Newman, *Economica* (back cover of *EPE*).
33. William J. Baumol, *Review of Economics and Statistics* (back cover of *EPE*).
34. C. S. Soper, *Economic Record* (November 1954), 326.
35. Friedman-Ebenstein correspondence (September 26, 2001).

CHAPTER 9

1. *Memoirs,* 108.
2. Ibid., 126–127.
3. Ibid., 162.
4. Ibid., 176.
5. In Arjo Klamer (ed.), *Conversations with Economists* (Totowa, N.J.: Rowman & Allanheld, 1984), 135.
6. *CF,* xvi.
7. Frazer, vol. 1, 183; David Friedman–Ebenstein e-mail correspondence (July 27, 2004); David Friedman–Ebenstein interview (2004).
8. Janet Martel–Ebenstein interview (2004).
9. David Friedman–Ebenstein e-mail correspondence.
10. Alan Porter–Ebenstein interview (2005).
11. *CF,* 12.
12. Ibid., 33.
13. Milton Friedman, *The Optimum Quantity of Money and Other Essays* (Chicago: Aldine, 1969), vi.
14. *CF,* iv.

CHAPTER 10

1. *Memoirs,* 75.
2. FA, box 91, folder 4 (letter to Anna J. Schwartz [December 10, 1963]).
3. Milton Friedman, *Milton Friedman's Monetary Framework: A Debate with His Critics,* edited by Robert J. Gordon (University of Chicago Press, 1974), 164.
4. Shils, 446–447.
5. Milton Friedman, "The Monetary Theory and Policy of Henry Simons," *Journal of Law and Economics* (October 1967), 8.
6. *Lives,* 172, 175.
7. In J. Daniel Hammond (ed.), *The Legacy of Milton Friedman as Teacher* (Cheltenham, U.K.: Edward Elgar, 1999), xv.
8. Milton Friedman, *Price Theory,* 2nd ed. (Chicago: Aldine, 1976), 1–2.
9. Hammond, *Legacy,* xii.
10. Gary Becker–Ebenstein interview (2004).
11. Shils, 141.
12. Ibid.
13. D. Gale Johnson–Ebenstein interview (2001).
14. Lester Telser–Ebenstein interview (2004).
15. Ibid.
16. Larry Sjaastaad–Ebenstein interview (2004).
17. Thomas Sowell–Ebenstein interview (2002).
18. William Breit and Barry T. Hirsch, *Lives of the Laureates,* 4th edition (Cambridge, Mass.: MIT Press, 2004), 280–281.

19. Brian Snowdon and Howard R. Vane, *Conversations with Leading Economists: Interpreting Modern Macroeconomics* (Cheltenham, U.K.: Edward Elgar, 1999), 136.
20. In Hammond, *Legacy,* xxiii.
21. Ibid., xxiii.
22. Ibid., xxv.
23. Snowden and Vane, *Conversations,* 136.
24. Larry Wimmer–Ebenstein interview (2003).
25. Ibid.
26. Hammond, *Legacy,* xii.
27. In ibid., xxvi.
28. Ibid.
29. Ibid.
30. Ibid., xxiv.
31. Ibid., xxv.
32. FA, box 76, folder 1.
33. FA, box 7, folder 4.
34. John Turner–Ebenstein interview (2003).
35. Paul Samuelson-Ebenstein correspondence (June 30, 2005).
36. *Memoirs,* 157.
37. Ibid., 212.

CHAPTER 11

1. "The Economists," *Fortune* (December 1950), 112.
2. John Maynard Keynes, *The General Theory of Employment, Interest, and Money* (1936), 96.
3. Ibid., 97.
4. Ibid., 100.
5. Ibid., 373.
6. Alvin H. Hansen, *A Guide to Keynes* (New York: McGraw-Hill, 1953), 72.
7. Joseph A. Schumpeter, *Ten Great Economists* (London: George Allen, 1956), 290.
8. In *Memoirs,* 224.
9. Ibid., 165.
10. Milton Friedman, *A Theory of the Consumption Function* (Princeton, N.J.: Princeton University Press, 1957), 3, 6.
11. Ibid., 21.
12. Charles K. Rowley and Anne Rathbone, "Milton Friedman, 1912: Harbinger of the Public Choice Revolution," in Charles K. Rowley and Friedrich Schneider (eds.), *The Encyclopedia of Public Choice,* vol. 1 (Kluwer Academic Publishers, 2004), 153.
13. Friedman, *A Theory of the Consumption Function,* 237.
14. Friedman-Ebenstein correspondence (May 30, 2006).

CHAPTER 12

1. John Kenneth Galbraith, *Economics in Perspective: A Critical History* (Boston: Houghton Mifflin, 1987), 274.
2. "Theorizing for Goldwater?" *Business Week* (November 23, 1963), 106.
3. David Asman interview with Milton Friedman (May 15, 2004).
4. *Lives,* 139.
5. In Richard Parker, *John Kenneth Galbraith: His Life, His Politics, His Economics* (New York: Farrar, Straus and Giroux, 2005), 53.
6. *EPE,* 268.

7. Robert Leeson, *The Eclipse of Keynesianism: The Political Economy of the Chicago Counter-Revolution* (New York: Palgrave, 2000), 98.
8. John Maynard Keynes, *The Economic Consequences of the Peace* (1919), 11–12.
9. In Frazer, vol. 1, 11–12.
10. Keynes, *Economic Consequences,* 254.
11. John Maynard Keynes, *The General Theory of Employment, Interest, and Money* (1936), 379–380.
12. Milton Friedman, in Geoffrey E. Wood, *Explorations in Economic Liberalism* (London: Macmillan, 1996), 3.
13. Ibid., 3, 8.
14. In Frazer, vol. 2, 551.
15. Ibid.
16. Friedman-Ebenstein interview (1995).

CHAPTER 13

1. *CF,* 37, 50.
2. In J. Daniel Hammond, *Theory and Measurement: Causality Issues in Milton Friedman's Monetary Economics* (Cambridge University Press, 1996), 1.
3. Brian Snowdon and Howard R. Vane, *Conversations with Leading Economists: Interpreting Modern Macroeconomics* (Cheltenham, U.K.: Edward Elgar, 1999), 134.
4. *Memoirs,* 50.
5. FA, box 75, folder 5.
6. *EPE,* 139.
7. Henry C. Simons, *Economic Policy for a Free Society* (Chicago: University of Chicago Press, 1948), 175.
8. Milton Friedman, "The Monetary Theory and Policy of Henry Simons," *Journal of Law and Economics* (October 1967), 4.
9. Hammond, *Theory and Measurement,* 62–63.
10. *MHUS,* 3.
11. Mark Skousen, *Vienna and Chicago: Friends or Foes?* (Washington, D.C.: Capital Press, 2005), 74.
12. Ibid.
13. *MHUS,* 299.
14. Skousen, *Vienna and Chicago,* 38.
15. *MHUS,* 313.
16. Karl Marx and Friedrich Engels, *The Communist Manifesto* (1848).
17. In Randall E. Parker (ed.), *Reflections on the Great Depression* (Cheltenham, U.K.: Edward Elgar, 2002), 50–51.
18. Gene Smiley, *Rethinking the Great Depression* (Chicago: Ivan R. Dee, 2002), 165.
19. Jim Powell, *FDR's Folly: How Roosevelt and His New Deal Prolonged the Great Depression* (New York: Crown Forum, 2003), back cover.
20. In Allan H. Meltzer, "*A Monetary History* as a Model for Historians," *Cato Journal* (Winter 2004), 357.
21. Harry Johnson, *Economic Journal* (back cover of *MHUS*).
22. James Tobin, "The Monetary Interpretation of History: A Review Article," *American Economic Review* (June 1965), 85.
23. In Parker, *Reflections,* 109.
24. In Robert Leeson, "Patinkin, Johnson, and the Shadow of Friedman," *History of Political Economy* (Winter 2000), 60.
25. Anna Jacobson Schwartz–Ebenstein e-mail correspondence (February 7, 2005).
26. In Parker, *Reflections,* 117.

27.   Milton Friedman, "Reflections on *A Monetary History*," *Cato Journal* (Winter 2004), 349.

CHAPTER 14

1.   Paul Samuelson–Ebenstein correspondence (June 30, 2005).
2.   Friedman-Ebenstein interview (2000).
3.   George Stigler, *Memoirs of an Unregulated Economist* (New York: Basic Books, 1988), 148.
4.   Edward Chamberlin, *Toward a More General Theory of Value* (New York: Oxford University Press, 1957); cited in Stigler, *Memoirs,* 150.
5.   Stigler, *Memoirs,* 148.
6.   In Don Patinkin, *Essays on and in the Chicago Tradition* (Durham, N.C.: Duke University Press, 1981), 266.
7.   In Ronald Coase, "Law and Economics at Chicago," *Journal of Political Economy* (April 1993), 244–245.
8.   In J. Daniel Hammond, "An Interview with Milton Friedman on Methodology," in Warren J. Samuels and Jiff Biddle (eds.), *Research in the History of Economic Thought and Methodology,* vol. 10 (Greenwich, Conn.: JAI Press, 1992), 110.
9.   Gary S. Becker, "George Joseph Stigler," *Journal of Political Economy* (October 1993), 761.
10.   Mark Skousen, *Vienna and Chicago: Friends or Foes?* (Washington, D.C.: Capital Press, 2005), 62.
11.   D. Gale Johnson–Ebenstein interview (2001).
12.   Henry Spiegel, "Jacob Viner," in John Eatwell, Murray Milgate, and Peter Newman (eds.), *The New Palgrave: A Dictionary of Economics,* vol. 4 (London: Macmillan, 1991), 814.
13.   In *Memoirs,* 160.
14.   Stigler, *Memoirs,* 150–151.
15.   Melvin W. Reder, "Chicago Economics: Permanence and Change," *Journal of Economic Literature* (March 1982), 10, 32.
16.   Milton Friedman, "Schools at Chicago," *The University of Chicago Record* (1974), 3.

CHAPTER 15

1.   William Breit and Barry T. Hirsch, *Lives of the Laureates,* 4th edition (Cambridge, Mass.: MIT Press, 2004), 224–225.
2.   Friedman-Ebenstein interview (1995).
3.   John Turner–Ebenstein interview (2003).
4.   Robert Lucas, in Breit and Hirsch, *Lives,* 279.
5.   Shils, 140.
6.   *CF,* iii.
7.   Ibid., 1–2.
8.   Jeremy Bentham, *An Introduction to the Principles of Morals and Legislation* (London: Methuen, 1982), 12.
9.   *CF,* 195.
10.   Ibid., 4.
11.   John Stuart Mill, *On Liberty* (1859), chapter 3.
12.   *CF,* 93, 95–96.
13.   Ibid., 4.
14.   Mill, *On Liberty,* chapter 3.
15.   *CF,* 4.
16.   Mill, *On Liberty,* chapter 5.
17.   *CF,* 12.
18.   Mill, *On Liberty,* chapter 3.
19.   *CF,* 33.

20. Mill, *On Liberty,* chapter 1.
21. *CF,* 2.
22. John Stuart Mill, *Utilitarianism* (1861), chapter 2.
23. *CF,* 2.
24. Friedrich Hayek, *The Road to Serfdom* (London: Routledge, 1944), 100.
25. *CF,* 11.
26. Hayek, *Serfdom,* 53.
27. *CF,* 2.
28. James Madison, *The Federalist,* no. 51.
29. *CF,* 8–9.
30. In Alan Ebenstein, *Hayek's Journey: The Mind of Friedrich Hayek* (New York: Palgrave, 2003), 168–169.
31. Milton Friedman, "Economic Freedom, Human Freedom, Political Freedom," lecture delivered at Smith Center (November 1, 1991).
32. *CF,* xii.

CHAPTER 16

1. *Memoirs,* 283.
2. Ibid., 293.
3. Ibid., 303.
4. Milton Friedman, *Dollars and Deficits: Inflation, Monetary Policy and the Balance of Payments* (Englewood Cliffs, N.J.: Prentice-Hall, 1968), 39.
5. Ibid., 57.
6. Ibid., 67.
7. *Memoirs,* 332.
8. Milton Friedman, introduction to *New Individualist Review* (Indianapolis: Liberty Press, 1981), xiii.
9. Barry Goldwater, *The Conscience of a Conservative* (Washington, D.C.: Regnery Gateway, 1990), 17.
10. In Annelise Anderson and Dennis L. Bark, *Thinking about America: The United States in the 1990s* (Stanford: Hoover Institution Press, 1988), 464.
11. Milton Friedman interview for PBS "Commanding Heights," http://www.pbs. org/wgbh/commandingheights/shared/minitext10/int_miltonfriedman.html (October 1, 2000).
12. "Right Face," *Newsweek* (January 13, 1964), 73.
13. "Theorizing for Goldwater?" *Business Week* (November 23, 1963), 106.
14. Milton Friedman, "The Goldwater View of Economics," *New York Times Magazine* (October 11, 1964), 35.
15. *Memoirs,* 374.
16. Martin Anderson, *Impostors in the Temple: American Intellectuals Are Destroying Our Universities and Cheating Our Students of Their Future* (New York: Simon & Schuster, 1992), 37.
17. Milton Friedman, "Schools at Chicago," *The University of Chicago Record* (1974), 6–7.

CHAPTER 17

1. Franco Modigliani, *Adventures of an Economist* (New York: Texere, 2001), 57.
2. Paul A. Samuelson, *Economics,* 10th ed. (New York: McGraw-Hill, 1976), 848.
3. In Mark Skousen, "The Perseverance of Paul Samuelson's *Economics,*" *Journal of Economic Perspectives* (Spring 1977), 142.
4. Ibid.
5. Ibid.

6. Todd G. Buchholz, *New Ideas from Dead Economists* (New York: Plume, 1999), 241.
7. In J. Daniel Hammond, "An Interview with Milton Friedman on Methodology," in Warren J. Samuels and Jiff Biddle (eds.), *Research in the History of Economic Thought and Methodology,* vol. 10 (Greenwich, Conn.: JAI Press, 1992), 104.
8. Ibid, 105.
9. Milton Friedman, *Friedman on Galbraith* (Vancouver: Fraser Institute, 1977), 12, 15, 23–24, 30.
10. Robert Leeson, "Patinkin, Johnson, and the Shadow of Friedman," *History of Political Economy* (Winter 2000), 142.
11. John Kenneth Galbraith, *The New Industrial State* (Boston: Houghton Mifflin, 1967), 124.
12. Milton Friedman, *Milton Friedman's Monetary Framework: A Debate with His Critics,* edited by Robert J. Gordon (University of Chicago Press, 1974), 77, 88.
13. In Henry Spiegel and Warren J. Samuels, *Contemporary Economists in Perspective* (Greenwich, Conn.: JAI Press, 1984), 246.
14. Friedman, *Monetary Framework,* 143.
15. Milton Friedman, *The Counter-Revolution in Monetary Theory* (London: Institute of Economic Affairs, 1970), 22–3.
16. In *Santa Barbara News-Press* (June 11, 2004), A9.
17. In Leeson, "Patinkin, Johnson, and the Shadow," 98.
18. In Daniel Bell and Irving Kristol, *The Crisis in Economic Theory* (New York: Basic Books, 1981), 66.
19. *Essence,* 389.
20. Ibid., 393–394.
21. Friedman-Ebenstein correspondence (May 18, 2005).
22. Ibid.
23. *CF,* xvi.
24. In Don Patinkin, *Essays on and in the Chicago Tradition* (Durham, N.C.: Duke University Press, 1981), 284–285.
25. Harry G. Johnson, "The Keynesian Revolution and the Monetarist Counter-Revolution," *American Economic Review* (May 1971), 9–11.
26. Leeson, "Patinkin, Johnson, and the Shadow," 746–747.
27. In ibid., 753.
28. In Robert Leeson, *Keynes, Chicago and Friedman,* vol. 1 (London: Pickering & Chatto, 2003), x.
29. Leeson, "Patinkin, Johnson, and the Shadow," 735–738.
30. Ibid., 736.
31. Friedman-Ebenstein correspondence (May 5, 2005).
32. Lester Telser–Ebenstein interview (2004).
33. R. M. Hartwell, *A History of the Mont Pelerin Society* (Indianapolis: Liberty Fund, 1995), 161–162.
34. In Frazer, vol 1, 179–180.
35. Milton Friedman, introduction to *New Individualist Review* (Indianapolis: Liberty Press, 1981), ix.
36. "Right Face," *Newsweek,* January 13, 1964, 73.
37. George H. Nash, *The Conservative Intellectual Movement in America: Since 1945* (Wilmington, Del.: Intercollegiate Studies Institute, 1996), 169.
38. In William E. Simon, *A Time for Reflection: An Autobiography* (Washington, D.C.: Regnery, 2004), xv, 73.
39. Melvin W. Reder, "Chicago Economics: Permanence and Change," *Journal of Economic Literature* (March 1982), 7.
40. Ronald Coase, "Law and Economics at Chicago," *Journal of Law and Economics* (April 1993), 247.

41. George J. Stigler, *The Economist as Preacher and Other Essays* (University of Chicago Press, 1982), 170.
42. *Essence*, 401–402.

CHAPTER 18

1. Milton Friedman, "Social Responsibility: A Subversive Doctrine," *National Review* (August 24, 1965), 705.
2. Milton Friedman, "Minimum-Wage Rates," *Newsweek* (September 26, 1966), 96.
3. Milton Friedman, "Inflationary Recession," *Newsweek* (October 17, 1966), 92.
4. Milton Friedman, "Politics and Violence," *Newsweek* (June 24, 1968), 90.
5. Milton Friedman, "The Draft," *Newsweek* (March 11, 1968), 82.
6. Milton Friedman, "Oil and the Middle East," *Newsweek* (June 26, 1967), 63.
7. Milton Friedman, "Current Monetary Policy," *Newsweek* (January 8, 1967), 59.
8. Milton Friedman, "Inflation and Wages," *Newsweek* (September 28, 1970), 77.
9. In Steven F. Hayward, *The Age of Reagan* (New York: Random House, 2001), 524.
10. *CF*, 35–36.
11. Ibid., 36.
12. Richard Nixon, *The Memoirs of Richard Nixon*, vol. 1 (Norwalk, Conn.: Eaton Press, 1978), 428.
13. Milton Friedman, "Higher Taxes? No," *Newsweek* (August 7, 1967), 86.
14. Milton Friedman, "Spend, Tax, Elect," *Newsweek* (July 15, 1968), 72.
15. Milton Friedman, "End the Surtax," *Newsweek* (February 10, 1969), 74.
16. Milton Friedman, "Fiscal Responsibility," *Newsweek* (August 7, 1967), 68.
17. Milton Friedman, "The Limitations of Tax Limitation," *Policy Review* (Summer 1978).
18. Rich Thomas, "The Magic of Reaganomics," *Time* (December 26, 1988).
19. *Memoirs*, 354.
20. Milton Friedman, "Regressive Income Tax," *Newsweek* (April 22, 1968), 86.
21. "Productivity: Two Experts Cross Swords," *Newsweek* (September 8, 1980), 68–69.
22. Friedman, "Regressive Income Tax," 86.
23. Milton Friedman, "Monetary Policy Dominates," *Wall Street Journal* (January 8, 1999), A18.
24. In Justin Martin, *Greenspan: The Man Behind Money* (Cambridge, Mass.: Perseus, 2000), 79.
25. In Mark A. Wynne, Harvey Rosenblum, and Robert L. Formaini (eds.), *The Legacy of Milton and Rose Friedman's* Free to Choose (Dallas, Tex.: Federal Reserve Bank, 2004), xi.
26. *Memoirs*, 380.
27. Paul Samuelson, "The New Economics," *Newsweek* (November 25, 1968), 96.
28. Milton Friedman, "After the New Economics," *Newsweek* (December 9, 1968), 83.
29. In *Memoirs*, 410.
30. "The Intellectual Provocateur," *Fortune* (December 19, 1969), 71.
31. Milton Viorst, "Friedmanism," *New York Times Magazine* (January 25, 1970), 22.
32. In J. Daniel Hammond, "An Interview with Milton Friedman on Methodology," in Warren J. Samuels and Jiff Biddle (eds.), *Research in the History of Economic Thought and Methodology*, vol. 10 (Greenwich, Conn.: JAI Press, 1992), 96–97.
33. FA, box 40, folder 2, "Comment on Katona and Fisher" (August 28, 1949), 1–2.
34. Ibid., 3.
35. *Memoirs*, 359.

CHAPTER 19

1. *Memoirs*, 375.
2. Milton Friedman, "A Dollar Is a Dollar," *Newsweek* (May 15, 1967), 86.
3. *Memoirs*, 376.

4. Ibid., 387.
5. In ibid., 382.
6. In Richard Reeves, *President Nixon: Alone in the White House* (New York: Simon & Schuster, 2001), 51.
7. *Memoirs,* 383–284.
8. "Three Views of Nixonomics and Where It Leads," *Newsweek* (January 31, 1972), 74.
9. Milton Friedman, *Bright Promises, Dismal Performance: An Economist's Protest* (New York: Harcourt Brace Jovanovich, 1983), 9–10.
10. "President Honors Milton Friedman for Lifetime Achievements," www.whitehouse.gov/news/releases/2002/05/20020509-1.html.
11. In *Memoirs,* 401.
12. Ibid.
13. Ibid.
14. Ibid., 601–602.
15. Robert Skole, "En-Nobeling Milton Friedman," *Nation* (January 22, 1977), 68.
16. *Memoirs,* 445–446.
17. Ibid., 596.
18. Ibid., 597.
19. "Things as They Are," *Nation* (October 30, 1976), 419.
20. Melville J. Ulmer, "Friedman's Currency," *New Republic* (November 6, 1976), 8–9.
21. "A Nobel for Friedman," *Newsweek* (October 25, 1976), 86.
22. In *Memoirs,* 444.
23. Ibid.
24. FA, box 6, folder 3.
25. www.nobel.se/economics/laureates/1976/press.html.
26. *Essence,* 347–348.
27. *Memoirs,* 452.
28. Ibid.
29. FA, box 7, folder 1.
30. *CF,* 49.
31. Ibid., 57.
32. *MHUS,* 10.
33. Ibid., 12.
34. Ibid., 133.
35. Ibid., 270.
36. Milton Friedman, in Geoffrey E. Wood, *Explorations in Economic Liberalism* (London: Macmillan, 1996), 7.
37. *Memoirs,* 74.
38. Ibid., 313.
39. Ibid., 352.
40. Ibid., 374.
41. Friedman-Ebenstein correspondence (November 22, 2004).
42. *Memoirs,* 190.

CHAPTER 20

1. Milton Friedman, *Why Government Is the Problem* (Stanford: Hoover Institution, 1993), 6.
2. *Memoirs,* 563.
3. Ibid., 471.
4. Ibid., 473.
5. John Stuart Mill, *On Liberty* (1859), Introduction.
6. *FTC,* xv.

7. Adam Smith, *An Inquiry Into the Nature and Causes of the Wealth of Nations*, vol. 1 (Indianapolis: Liberty Classics, 1976), 456, 426.
8. *Memoirs*, 480.
9. *FTC*, i.
10. Ibid.
11. Ibid.
12. *Memoirs*, 605.
13. Ibid., 503.
14. Ibid., 504.

CHAPTER 21

1. *Memoirs*, 209–210.
2. Martin Anderson, *Revolution* (New York: Harcourt Brace Jovanovich, 1988), 164.
3. Ronald Reagan, *Reagan: In His Own Hand* (New York: Free Press, 2001), 267.
4. Ronald Reagan, *Speaking My Mind: Selected Speeches* (New York: Simon and Schuster, 1989), 96.
5. Milton Friedman, "The Path We Dare Not Take," *Reader's Digest* (March 1977), 110.
6. Milton Friedman, "What Is America?" *Saturday Evening Post* (October 1978), 16.
7. Milton Friedman, "Will Freedom Prevail?" *Newsweek* (November 19, 1979), 142.
8. Milton and Rose Friedman, *The Tyranny of the Status Quo* (New York: Harcourt Brace Jovanovich, 1984), 1.
9. *Memoirs*, 390.
10. Edwin Meese–Ebenstein interview (1996).
11. Martin Anderson, *Revolution* (New York: Harcourt Brace Jovanovich, 1988), 172.
12. Edwin Meese III, *With Reagan: The Inside Story* (Washington, D.C.: Regnery Publishing, 1992), 127.
13. Donald T. Regan, *For the Record: From Wall Street to Washington* (New York: Harcourt Brace Jovanovich, 1988), 157.
14. William E. Simon, *A Time for Reflection: An Autobiography* (Washington, D.C.: Regnery, 2004), 72.
15. Rich Thomas, "The Magic of Reaganomics," *Newsweek* (December 16, 1988), 33.
16. *FTC*, i.
17. *Memoirs*, 396.
18. In Annelise Anderson and Dennis L. Bark, *Thinking about America: The United States in the 1990s* (Stanford, Calif.: Hoover Institution Press, 1988), 559.
19. Milton Friedman, "Freedom's Friend," *Wall Street Journal* (June 11, 2004).
20. In Alan Ebenstein, *Friedrich Hayek: A Biography* (New York: Palgrave, 2001), 285.
21. Richard Cockett, *Thinking the Unthinkable: Think-Tanks and the Economic Counter-Revolution, 1931–1983* (London: Fontana, 1995), 149, 152, 154.
22. In Ebenstein, *Hayek*, 389.
23. In Cockett, *Thinking the Unthinkable*, 154.
24. Milton Friedman, "Monetary Policy Dominates," *Wall Street Journal* (January 8, 1999), A18.
25. Erik Guyot, "Hong Kong's Stock Intervention Is 'Insane,' Milton Friedman Says," *Wall Street Journal* (September 3, 1998), A19.
26. Margaret Thatcher, *The Downing Street Years* (London: HarperCollins, 1995), 804.
27. In Daniel Yergin and Joseph Stanislaw, *The Commanding Heights: The Battle Between Government and the Marketplace that Is Remaking the Modern World* (New York: Simon & Schuster, 1998), 149.

CHAPTER 22

1. Hayek Archive, Hoover Institution on War, Revolution and Peace, box 73, folder 40.

2. Ibid.
3. Friedrich Hayek, *Denationalisation of Money*, 3rd ed. (Great Britain: Institute of Economic Affairs, 1990), 80; Friedrich Hayek, *New Studies in Philosophy, Politics, Economics and the History of Ideas* (London: Routledge, 1990), 208.
4. "The Road from Serfdom," *Reason* (July 1992), 32.
5. David Boaz (ed.), *Toward Liberty: The Idea that Is Changing the World* (Washington, D.C.: Cato Institute, 2002), 23.
6. David Dimbleby, "A Half-Term Report on Mrs. Thatcher's Progress by Hayek and Friedman," *Listener,* March 12, 1981, 331–332.
7. Fritz Machlup (ed.), *Essays on Hayek* (Hillsdale, Mich.: Hillsdale University Press, 1976), xxi.
8. Milton Friedman, *National Review* (April 27, 1992), 35.
9. Larry Sjaastaad–Ebenstein interview (2004).
10. In Annelise Anderson and Dennis L. Bark (eds.), *Thinking About America: The United States in the 1990s* (Stanford, Calif: Hoover Institution Press, 1988), 455–456.
11. Ibid., 456, 459, 463.
12. Ibid., 467.
13. Friedman-Ebenstein interview (1995).
14. March 5, 1996, letter from Friedman to Mark Skousen (in the possession of Skousen).
15. *Essence,* 465.
16. Milton Friedman, *Why Government Is the Problem* (Stanford: Hoover Institution Press, 1993), 15–16.

CHAPTER 23

1. Milton Friedman, "Free to Choose," *Wall Street Journal* (June 9, 2005).
2. John Stuart Mill, *On Liberty* (1859), chapter 5.
3. *CF,* 85.
4. Ibid., 87.
5. Milton Friedman and Thomas Szasz, *On Liberty at Drugs* (Washington, D.C.: 1992), 76.
6. Ibid., 3.
7. Friedman-Ebenstein correspondence (May 30, 2006).
8. Friedman and Szasz, *On Liberty at Drugs,* 65.
9. In ibid., 39.
10. Friedman-Ebenstein correspondence (June 1, 2005).
11. Milton Friedman, "Is Welfare a Basic Human Right?," *Newsweek* (December 18, 1972), 67.
12. Friedman-Ebenstein correspondence (June 1, 2005).
13. Ibid.
14. *Memoirs,* 628.
15. Friedman-Ebenstein correspondence (May 5, 2005).
16. Milton Friedman, "Public Schools: Make Them Private," *Washington Post* (February 19, 1995).

CHAPTER 24

1. *CF,* xiii-xiv.
2. Milton and Rose Friedman, *The Tyranny of the Status Quo* (New York: Harcourt Brace Jovanovich, 1984), 8.
3. FA, box 33, folder 3.
4. Friedman-Ebenstein interview (2005).
5. *Essence,* 421.
6. Friedman-Ebenstein correspondence (November 22, 2004).
7. Milton Friedman, *Money Mischief: Episodes in Monetary History* (New York: Harcourt Brace Jovanovich, 1992), x, 261, 264–265.

8.   Milton Friedman, letter to the editor, *Wall Street Journal* (February 9, 1994), A15.
9.   Milton Friedman, "How to Cure Health Care," *The Public Interest* (Winter 2001), 22.
10. Milton Friedman, "Making Philanthropy Out of Obscenity," *Reason* (October 2005), 33.
11. *CF*, ix.
12. *Memoirs*, xii.
13. Milton Friedman, *Money Mischief: Episodes in Monetary History* (New York: Harcourt Brace Jovanovich, 1992), v.
14. In David Boaz (ed.), *Toward Liberty: The Idea that Is Changing the World* (Washington, D.C.: Cato Institute, 2002), 55.
15. Milton Friedman, extemporaneous talk, Cato Institute 25th Anniversary Dinner, May 9, 2002.
16. "President Honors Milton Friedman for Lifetime Achievements," Office of the Press Secretary, the White House, May 9, 2002.
17. Donald Rumsfeld, "Changing the Course of History," *Cato Policy Report* (July/August 2002), 11.
18. George F. Will, "Milton Friedman at 90: Man of the Century," *Hoover Digest* (Fall 2002).
19. Gary Becker, "Happy Birthday, Milton Friedman," *BusinessWeek* (July 1, 2002).
20. Arnold Schwarzenegger, "My Economics," *Wall Street Journal* (September 24, 2003).
21. Milton Friedman, "A Natural Experiment in Monetary Policy Covering Three Episodes of Growth and Decline in the Economy and the Stock Market," *Journal of Economic Perspectives* (Fall 2005), 149.
22. Ben Bernanke, in Mark A. Wynne, Harvey Rosenblum, and Robert L. Formaini (eds.), *The Legacy of Milton and Rose Friedman's Free to Choose: Economic Liberalism at the Turn of the 21st Century* (Dallas, Tex.: Federal Reserve Bank, 2004), 208, 214.
23. Alan Greenspan, in "The Power of Choice: The Life and Ideas of Milton Friedman" (Eirie: Penn.: Free to Choose Media, 2006).
24. Friedman-Ebenstein correspondence (September 26, 2001).
25. Friedman-Ebenstein correspondence (September 16, 2005).
26. *FTC*, xxi.
27. *EPE*, 43.

INDEX

Abramovitz, Moses, 27
agriculture support programs, 171–72
Allende, Salvador, 189
all-volunteer army, 173, 176–80, 187
American Economic Association (AEA), 23, 27,
   44, 55, 60, 156, 158, 160, 164, 238
American Enterprise Institute (AEI), 165–67,
   197
Anderson, Martin, 153–54, 198, 206, 208
Angell, James, 27
Arrow, Kenneth, 26, 56

balanced budget, 176–77
Balcerowicz, Leszek, 214
Baltimore, David, 191–92
Banfield, Ed, 168
Banfield, Laura, 168
Bangs, Robert, 51–52
bank failures, 120–23
Bank of the United States, 120, 121
Baroody, William, 166
Bauer, Peter, 236
Begin, Menachem, 213
Berger, James, 45
Bernanke, Ben, 161, 238
"Black Tuesday," 114, 119
Blodgett, Ralph, 37
Boaz, David, 235
Boorstin, Daniel, 168
Boorstin, Ruth, 168
Bork, Robert, 168
Borts, George, 164
Brady, Dorothy, 100
Bronfenbrenner, Martin, 39
Buchholz, Todd, 156–57
Buckley, William F., 151, 166, 186, 226
Burns, Arthur, 15–17, 38, 57, 59, 113, 179,
   185–86, 208
Burns, Helen, 78

Bush, George W., 176, 189, 198, 236, 237

Campbell, Glenn, 197
capitalism, 69, 103, 107, 114, 118, 124–25, 144,
   203, 206, 210, 239
Capone, Al, 10–11
Carter, Jimmy, 178
Cato Institute, 166, 235–36
Chamberlain, Edward, 87
Cheney, Richard, 237
"Chicago Boys," 189
Chicago-Chilean study program, 189–90
"Chicago school of economics," 129–32, 162,
   214. *See also* University of Chicago:
   Department of Economics
"Chicago schools," 130
Chitester, Robert, 200
Chodorov, Frank, 165
Clark, John Bates, 26. *See also* John Bates Clark
   Medal
Clark, Maurice, 26
Clinton administration, 198
Coase theorem, 167
Coase, Ronald, 167–68
Cockett, Richard, 211
Columbia University, 25–30, 38, 48, 50, 127
   MF's graduate studies at, 25–27, 31–32
   MF a visiting professor at, 151
Colwell, Ernest, 51
Committee on Social Thought, 54, 136, 216
communism, 54, 69, 109, 114, 148, 190, 203,
   213–14, 21, 232
Cowles Commission of econometricians, 51,
   54–59, 67, 158
Cowles Foundation, 158
Crane, Ed, 235, 241

Davenport, John, 132
de Soto, Hernando, 236

279

Declaration of Independence, 201
Deng Xiaoping, 213–14
Dewey, John, 229
Dicey, A. V., 138, 142, 220
Director, Aaron, 24, 32, 53, 54, 60, 130, 136, 167–70, 216
    on MF's marriage to Rose, 39
Dorfman, Joseph, 132
Douglas, Paul, 22–23, 54, 137

Eccles, Marriner, 43
economic data collection, 35–36
economics:
    cyclical fluctuations and, 37, 88, 115, 117
    empirical approach to, 1, 26–27, 38, 39, 63–67, 75, 101, 114, 131, 133, 217, 238–39
    institutional approach to, 26, 27
    history of, 20
    mathematical approach to, 51, 55
    positive, 63–75, 119, 217, 234, 239–40
    prediction in, 55, 64–68
Eisenhower, Dwight D., 17, 185
European Coal and Steel Community, 80
exchange rates, 72–73, 100, 171, 173, 185–86, 213, 227

Family Assistance Program, 174
Federal Reserve:
    Great Contraction and, 18, 117–18, 120, 122–23, 128
    MF's briefings to, 136–37
    stabilization policy and, 156
    See also Bernanke, Ben; Burns, Arthur; Eccles, Marriner; Greenspan, Alan; Jones, Homer
Federal Communications Commission, 171–72
Federalist, The, 143
Ferguson, David, 125
Feulner, Ed, 166
fiscal policy, 23, 73–74, 103, 108, 110, 115, 156–57, 175, 177–78, 181, 198, 211–212
Fisher, Irving, 23, 110, 115
flexible international exchange rates, 72–73, 100, 171, 173, 185–86, 213, 227
Ford, Gerald, 167, 200
Foundation for Economic Education, 51, 140
Frazer, William, 35, 50, 58, 66, 217
free market, 3, 17, 20–21, 60, 73, 109, 144, 149, 151, 166, 189, 206, 213

Friedman, David Director (MF's son), 46, 53, 77–78, 80–83, 147, 148, 150, 181, 197, 203, 228, 232
Friedman, Helen, (MF's sister), 7
Friedman, Janet (MF's daughter), 44, 53, 77–78, 80–83, 147, 148, 150, 197, 203, 228
Friedman, Jeno Saul (MF's father), 5–8, 11, 13
Friedman, Milton, personal life and traits:
    agnosticism, 9, 11, 82
    birth of, 5, 7
    in Boy Scouts, 9
    California residence, 199–200
    Capitaf (Vermont residence), 182, 200
    Chicago residence, 53, 78–79
    childhood and youth, 7–11
    childrearing philosophy, 82
    death of, 241
    decision to become an economist, 18
    enjoyment of debate, 106–107
    family history, 5–7
    family life, 77–83
    summer vacations, 80–81
    father's death, 11, 13
    friendships, 16, 27, 32, 44, 47, 50, 52, 62, 148, 157, 164, 168, 181, 216
    grandchildren, 203
    Fortune magazine article, 180–81
    Judaism, 9, 11–12
    libertarian views, 1, 3, 55, 72, 75, 132–38, 151, 156, 165–66, 215, 218, 232, 239
    love of mathematics, 11
    marriage to Rose, 39–41
    as "moral example," 93
    move to San Francisco, 197
    New York Times Magazine cover, 181
    open heart surgery, 188–89
    pessimism, 206
    physical appearance, 7
    political views, 34–35, 135, 187, 237
    precocity, 8, 10
    professorial temperament, 187
    sense of humor, 1, 90, 181, 194–95
    television appearances, 181, 235
    visit to Chile, 189–90
    as word extremist, 85–87
    Wanderjahr (wandering year), 147–48
Friedman, Milton, career:
    advisor to Goldwater, 152–53, 169, 185
    advisor to Nixon, 185–88
    advisor to Reagan, 185, 208–210
    AEA president, 160–61, 164, 168
    Center for Advanced Study, 81

Committee on Social Thought, 136
Congressional testimony of, 43, 113–14,
    135–38, 174
criticism of, 137–38, 162–64, 190–92,
    216–17
development of views, 175–76
economic theorist, 2
empiricist, 1, 26–27, 38, 39, 63–67, 75, 101,
    114, 131, 133, 217, 238–39
entrepreneurial ventures, 14
Fulbright recipient, 80
Hoover Institution, 197–98
influence, 1–2, 46, 73, 88, 159, 210–214, 238
monetarist, 115–17
Mont Pelerin Society president, 164
National Bureau of Economic Research, 37
National Resources Committee, 33–37, 101,
    135, 167
New Individualist Review advisor, 165, 216
Newsweek column, 169–71, 180, 181, 183,
    185–86
Nobel laureate, 190–95
offered job at Stanford, 153
positivism and, 217
predictions, 150, 170, 179, 199
price theory course of, 59, 86–90, 94, 105,
    147
professional organization involvement,
    164–67
professorship at Chicago (1946–76), 51–52,
    53, 85–95, 129–33
professorship at Chicago (1963–1964), 151
professorship at Madison, 41–42, 115
professorship at University of Minnesota,
    47, 51
public intellectual, 1, 74, 139, 147, 181, 183,
    237
public policy advocate, 135–37
Saturday Evening Post essays, 207
statistician, 14, 35, 50–51, 66, 97
supply-sider, 178
"teacher of economics," 1, 93
theory of permanent and transitory income,
    90, 101–104
visiting fellow at Cambridge, 80–81
visiting professor at Columbia (1964–1965),
    153
visiting scholar at Federal Reserve Bank of
    San Francisco, 200
Volker lectures, 139–40
Wesley Clair Mitchell Research
    Professorship in Economics, 153

Friedman, Milton, education:
    elementary school, 8–9
    graduate school at Chicago, 19–25
    graduate school at Columbia, 25–27, 31–32
    high school, 10–12
    receives masters degree from Chicago, 25
    receives Ph.D. from Columbia, 48
    research assistant to Knight, 36
    research assistant to Kuznets, 38
    research assistant to Schultz, 32–33
    undergraduate at Rutgers, 13–18, 19
Friedman, Milton, influences:
    Burns, 15–17
    childhood, 34
    father's death, 11, 13
    founding fathers, 143
    Hayek, 142–43, 144
    Hotelling, 26
    Jones, 15–17
    libertarian, 15–16, 34, 141–42
    Mill, 140–42
    Mints, 162
    Mises, 144
    Simons, 70, 116
    Viner, 20–21
Friedman, Milton, opinions and commentary:
    on balanced budgets, 177
    on capitalism, 239
    on *Capitalism and Freedom*, 145
    on communism, 214
    on Cowles Commission, 56–57
    on critics, 68, 70, 159
    on democracy and economics, 144
    on equality, 35
    on his family, 7
    on fiscal policy, 178, 181, 212
    on flat tax, 178
    on foreign policy, 231–32
    on free market, 109, 234
    on freedom, 140–42, 152–53
    on Galbraith, 157–58
    on Goldwater, 152–53
    on graduate school at Chicago, 19, 22–23, 27
    on graduate school at Columbia, 26, 27
    on the Great Depression, 125
    on Hayek, 219
    on Hotelling, 26
    on immigrants, 6
    on importance of early career, 55
    on individualism, 140, 142–43, 204
    on inflation, 42, 43, 73–74, 107, 115–16, 149,
        218

on influence, 144–45
on international exchange, 73
on limited government, 143
on Keynes, 24, 107, 160
on "lucky accidents," 11
on Mises, 221
on MIT, 157
on *A Monetary History of the United States,*
    127–28
on monetary policy, 108, 115–16, 232–33
on Mont Pelerin Society, 164
on his mother, 11
on New Deal Washington, 33–34
on Nixon, 185, 188
on Nobel prize, 191
on Phillips Curve, 160
on planned economic development, 150
on positive economics, 75, 87–88, 240
on prediction in economics, 64–66
on price stabilization, 116
on public policy, 233–34
on Reagan, 210
on rent control, 35, 49–50, 136, 171
on Rose, 32, 101, 140, 204
on Schultz, 33
on Simons, 25
on Stigler, 47
on taxation, 175–77
on teaching, 92, 95
on undergraduate experience, 14
on the University of Chicago, 22–23, 53,
    60–61, 131, 133
on unjustified government activities, 171–73
on writing for public audiences, 182–83
Friedman, Milton, works:
    Capitalism and Freedom, 118, 147, 151, 162,
        178, 181–82, 210, 223, 225
    as better than *Free to Choose,* 145
    dedicated to Janet and David, 83
    development of, 137–143
    excerpts from, 114, 141, 142–43, 194, 221,
        231, 235
    political philosophy in, 140–43
    praise for, 156
    Reagan's having read, 206
    unjustified government activities listed
        in, 171–72
    use of "destiny" in, 73
    "The Case for Flexible Exchange Rates," 68,
        72, 80
    "Comments on Monetary Policy," 68,
        73–74

"The Counter-Revolution in Monetary
    Theory," 110, 211–212
Dollars and Deficits, 149–50
"The Expected Utility Hypothesis and
    Measurability of Utility," 68
Free to Choose (book), 118, 141, 145, 199,
    201–204, 205, 207, 209–210
Free to Choose (television series), 200–204,
    205, 207, 210–211
"The Goldwater View of Economics," 152–53
*Income from Independent Professional
    Practice* (dissertation), 48–49, 101
"Inflation and Unemployment" (Nobel
    lecture), 193
"Liberalism, Old Style," 139
"The Marshallian Demand Curve," 68, 70
"The Methodology of Positive Economics,"
    63–69, 72, 100, 193, 239
"A Monetary and Fiscal Framework for
    Economic Stability," 68–71, 74, 116
*A Monetary History of the United States,
    1867–1960,* 49, 88, 135, 147, 151–52,
    173, 181
    development of, 113–18
    importance of, 2, 123, 125–26
    MF on, 127
    reception of, 126–27
*Money Mischief: Episodes in Monetary
    History,* 233, 235
*The Optimum Quantity of Money and Other
    Essays,* 83
Price Theory: A Provisional Text, 87, 147
"Professor Pigou's Method for Measuring
    Elasticities of Demand from Budgetary
    Data," 37
"The Role of Monetary Policy," 160–61, 168
"Social Responsibility: A Subversive
    Doctrine," 169
Taxing to Prevent Inflation, 42
A Theory of the Consumption Function, 83,
    97, 100–103, 113, 235
"The Tide in the Affairs of Men," 198,
    219–20
"The Tide Is Turning," 198
Tyranny of the Status Quo, 199, 231
    "The Utility Analysis of Choices
        Involving Risk," 68
"Why Government Is the Problem," 198
Friedman, Rose Director (MF's wife):
    birth and childhood, 31–32
    birth of daughter, Janet, 44, 77
    birth of son, David, 46, 78

in Chicago, 53, 77–79, 94–95, 97
desire to return the West Coast, 153, 197
engagement to MF, 36–37, 39
family of, 31–32
in France, 80
graduate student at Chicago, 31, 32–33, 36, 232
Hoover Institution office, 198
making of *Free To Choose*, 200–204
marriage to MF, 39–41
meets MF, 31
in Minnesota, 51
religion, 31
research assistant to Knight, 36
in San Francisco, 197–200
sister to Aaron, 24, 32, 151
stillborn childbirth, 42
support for school vouchers, 228–29
undergraduate at Chicago, 32
Wanderjahr (wandering year), 147–51
in Washington, 36, 42, 44
White House lunch, 236–37
in Wisconsin, 41–42
Friedman, Rose Director, opinions and
        commentary:
    on the AEA, 165
    on *Free To Choose*, 200, 204
    on Knight and Viner, 33
    on MF, 32
    on MF's Nobel prize, 191, 193
    on MF's teaching, 94–95
    on New York, 50
    on Samuelson, 156
Friedman, Rose Director, works of:
    author of "Poverty: Definition and
        Perspective," 167
    coauthor of "The Tide in the Affairs of
        Men," 198, 219–20
    coauthor of "The Tide Is Turning," 198
    coauthor of *Studies in Income and Wealth*,
        100–101
    coauthor of *Two Lucky People*, 235
    coauthor of *Tyranny of the Status Quo*, 231
    coauthor on *Free to Choose*, 199
    role in *A Theory of the Consumption
        Function*, 101
    role in *Capitalism and Freedom*, 140
Friedman, Ruth (MF's sister), 7, 83
Friedman, Sarah Ethel Landau (MF's mother),
        5–8, 11, 18, 27, 46, 82–83, 153
Friedman, Tilllie "Toots" (MF's sister), 82–83,
        153

Gaidar, Yegor, 214
Galbraith, John Kenneth, 105–106, 152, 155,
        157–58, 180, 200
Gandhi, Mohandas, 159
Gates, Tom, 179
Goldwater, Barry, 151–53, 169, 170, 181, 185,
        232
Gordon, Donald, 72
Great Contraction (1929–1933), 18, 118–28, 238
Great Depression, 2, 18, 34, 69, 85, 113–27, 135,
        162, 177
    Keynes' causation theory of, 123–24
    Marxism and, 124
    MF's causation theory of, 2, 113, 119–23
    MF's lessons on, 125
    myths surrounding, 119–23
Greenspan, Alan, 161, 179, 208, 237, 238
gross national product (GNP), 119, 234

Hall, Thomas, 125
Hammond, Daniel, 93
Hansen, Alvin, 99
Harberger, Arnold, 62,189–90
Harrington, Michael, 202
Harris, Seymour, 139
Harrod, Roy, 110–11
Hawley-Smoot tariff, 121
"Hayek Tide," 220
Hayek, Friedrich, 51, 86, 87, 136, 139, 140,
        142–45, 151
Hazlitt, Henry, 206
Heller, Walter, 42, 180
Heritage Foundation, 166
Hitler, Adolf, 41
Hoffman, Nicholas von, 202
Homan, Paul, 132
Hoover Institution, 90, 167, 197–99, 208, 210,
        233
Hoover, Herbert, 114, 123, 197
Hotelling, Harold, 25–26, 38, 50
housing, government built, 172
Hume, David, 65
Humphrey, Hubert, 188
Hutchins, Robert Maynard, 51, 79

income, theory of permanent and transitory, 90,
        101–103
income tax:
    flat-rate, 177–78
    negative, 173–74, 187, 227–28
    progressive, 70, 99–100, 175
indexation of taxation, 173–74

inflation, 17, 127, 150, 160–62, 170–75, 179–81,
193, 199
average annual world consumer price index,
238
causes of, 233
MF on, 42, 43, 73–74, 107, 115–16, 149, 216,
218
monetary phenomenon, 1, 42, 171, 204, 213,
237
intellectual tides, 220
Intercollegiate Society of Individualists (ISI),
165–66, 216

Jefferson, Thomas, 125, 201
John Bates Clark Medal, 60, 156
Johnson, D. Gale, 60, 89, 131–32
Johnson, Harry, 126, 162–64
Johnson, Lyndon B., 42, 180
Jones, Homer, 15–17, 18, 36, 38

Kennedy, David, 125
Kennedy, John F., 42, 152, 180, 185
Keynes, John Maynard, 39, 57, 80, 85, 97–103,
113, 123–24
influence of, 105–112
MF on, 23–24, 107, 160
as quantity theorist, 24
Keynes, John Neville, 63
Keynesianism, 59, 69, 99, 106–111, 157
emphasis on demand, 178
empirical, 213
MF's challenges to, 80, 97, 100–103, 133, 211
Kirk, Russell, 139, 206
Klaus, Vaclav, 214
Klein, Lawrence, 57
Knight, Frank, 2, 16, 21–26, 33, 36, 38, 54, 58,
60, 87, 88, 129, 136, 162, 167
Koopmans, Tjalling, 55, 57
Korean War, 111
Kuznets, Simon, 38–39, 48–49

Laar, Mart, 236
Laird, Melvin, 167, 187
Landon, Alf, 34
Lange, Oskar, 54–55, 65–66
Laughlin, James Laurence, 20, 59, 129
Lazarus, Emma, 6
Leeson, Robert, 50, 58, 108, 158, 162–63
legalization of drugs, 225–27
Lekachman, Robert, 202
Leland, Simeon, 54
Lerner, Abba, 35

Levi, Edward, 168
Levi, Kate, 168
Lewis, Anthony, 190
Lewis, H. Gregg, 60
liberalism, 22, 131, 138–39, 166
libertarian movement, 3, 73, 131–32, 139, 151,
165–66, 215, 224, 235. See also
Friedman, Milton: libertarian
influences on; libertarian views of
licensure provisions, 172
Lucas, Robert, 91, 130, 138
Luria, S. E., 192

Machlup, Fritz, 27
Mack, Ruth P., 42
macroeconomics, 47, 88, 175, 176, 198, 211–12
Madison, James, 143
Marschak, Jacob, 51, 54
Marshall, Alfred, 70–72, 87, 99, 157
Martin, William McChesney, 202
Marx, Karl, 3, 114, 124, 213, 214
Marxism, 2, 123–24
Massachusetts Institute of Technology (MIT),
157
McCracken, Paul, 208
Meese, Edwin, 208–209
Meltzer, Allan, 126
microeconomics, 21, 47, 48, 88, 131, 175
military conscription, 172, 173, 179–80
Mill, John Stuart, 15, 20, 34, 54, 72, 140–42, 201,
223–24
Millis, Harry A., 22, 54
Milton and Rose D. Friedman Foundation, 228,
229
Milton Friedman Prize for Advancing Liberty,
236
minimum wage, 64, 170–72
Mints, Lloyd, 22–23, 54, 62, 115, 162
Mises, Ludwig von, 139, 142, 144, 218, 221, 206
Mitchell, Wesley Clair, 2, 17, 20, 26, 38–39, 49,
57, 85, 113
Modigliani, Franco, 155, 157
monetary theory and policy, 23–24, 38, 86–90,
107–110, 156, 162–63
during the Great Contraction, 118–28
MF on, 87–88, 148, 170, 212, 232–33
MF's influence on, 73–74, 238
MF's teaching of, 86, 105
money supply and, 115–28
monetary velocity, 23–24, 110, 161
money supply, 160–61, 168, 171, 211, 213, 218
decline in, 18, 113, 119–22

Great Contraction and, 117–23
   inflation and, 1, 42
   prices and, 16, 17, 110
   published statistics of, 117
Mont Pelerin Society, 132, 136, 148, 164–66,
   215–16, 219
Morgenthau, Henry, 42–43
Moynihan, Daniel Patrick, 171
Mundell, Robert, 90

NAIRU (nonaccelerating inflation rate of
   unemployment), 161
Nash, George, 166
National Bureau of Economic Research, 2, 16,
   17, 26, 27, 36, 37–38, 135, 232
national parks, 172, 173
Nef, John, 23, 54
New Deal, 33–35, 39, 114, 118, 125–26, 135, 187
New Economics, 180
Newman, Peter, 74
Neils Bohr Institute of Physics, 56
Niskanen, David, 235
Nixon, Richard, 17, 73, 174, 179–80, 185–89,
   198, 206, 207, 232
Nobel laureates in economics:
   Arrow, Kenneth, 26, 56
   Becker, Gary, 88
   Buchanan, James, 87
   Coase, Ronald, 167
   Heckman, James, 91
   Kuznets, Simon, 39
   Lucas, Robert, 91
   Markowitz, Harry, 91
   Modigliani, Franco, 155
   Samuelson, Paul, 21
   Scholes, Myron, 91
   Solow, Robert, 57
   Stigler, George, 33, 48
   Tobin, James, 158
   Friedman, Milton, 190–93, 210
Nobel laureates from University of Chicago, 19,
   55
Nobel laureates from English-speaking
   countries, 210
Nobel prize, competition for, 163
Nordhaus, William, 156–57

output, government control of, 171–72

Palgrave, Sir Robert Harry Inglis, 3
Patinkin, Don, 67, 70, 162–64
Perlman, Mark, 158, 164

Philadelphia Society, 165–66
Phillips curve, 100, 160
Phillips, A. W., 160
Pinochet, Augusto, 189
Piven, Frances Fox, 202
Popper, Karl, 68
Porter, Alan, 83
positive economics, 63–75, 119, 217, 234,
   239–40
Powell, Jim, 125–26
price theory, 59, 86–90, 94, 105, 147
prohibition against carrying mail for profit, 172,
   173
prohibition, alcohol, 10, 226, 227

quantity theory, 17, 23–24, 100, 107, 110, 114,
   131, 133, 136, 161–62, 213

Rand, Ayn, 151
Rathbone, Anne, 103
Reagan, Ronald, 153, 175–78, 185, 198, 205–210,
   213, 220, 232, 235
Reder, Melvin, 57–58, 133, 167
Regan, Donald, 209
rent control, 35, 49–50, 136, 171, 172
Ricardo, David, 36
Robbins, Lionel, 85
Rockefeller, John D., 19
Roosevelt recession, 121
Roosevelt, Franklin D., 23, 34, 35, 114, 121, 123
Rosten, Leo, 37
Rowley, Charles, 103
Rumsfeld, Donald, 167, 202, 236
Rutgers University, 13–18, 19, 34, 36, 38, 50, 122

Samuelson, Paul, 21, 49, 94–95, 130, 138,
   155–57, 160, 169, 180, 216, 241
Savage, Jimmie, 46, 60, 68, 85–86
school choice, 225, 228
school vouchers, 3, 173, 204, 223–29, 234
Schultz, Henry, 22, 24, 25, 32–33, 35, 37, 50, 54
Schultz, Theodore, 60
Schuman Plan, 80
Schumpeter, Joseph, 99, 132
Schwartz, Anna Jacobson, 1, 113, 117–18, 120,
   125–26, 173, 186, 232, 238
Schwarzenegger, Arnold, 237
Seldon, Arthur, 211, 232
sequential analysis, 45, 47
Shanker, Albert, 202
Shils, Edward, 21–22
Shoup, Carl, 42

Shultz, George, 73, 167, 181, 186, 197, 207–209, 226, 237
Silk, Leonard, 35
Simon, William, 208–209
Simons, Henry, 22, 24–25, 54, 68, 70, 116, 131, 142, 162, 175
Sjaastaad, Larry, 90, 219
Skole, Robert, 191
Skousen, Mark, 117, 131, 156, 241
Slutzky, Eugen, 115
Smiley, Gene, 125–26
Smith, Adam, 20, 187, 192, 193–94, 200–202, 220, 237
Sobel, Robert, 44
social security, 171–72
socialism, 3, 34, 69, 109, 144
Socrates, 65
Solow, Robert, 57, 80, 157, 159
Soper, C. S., 74
Sowell, Thomas, 90, 94, 198, 202, 225
Spiegel, Henry, 132
Sprinkel, Beryl, 208
Statistical Research Group (SRG), 44–46, 47, 50, 66–67, 77, 86
Stein, Herb, 208
Stigler, George, 60, 81, 130, 158, 162, 209
    coauthor with MF of "Roofs of Ceilings?" 35, 49, 136
    death of, 232
    friendship with MF, 32–33, 47–52
    on MF, 48, 73, 132–33, 168
Stigler, Stephen, 51, 78
stock market, 114, 119, 121–22
"stock of money in the United States," 117. See also money supply
Sunday, Billy, 227

tariffs, 121, 171, 172
Tax Reduction Act, 175
Telser, Lester, 56
Thatcher, Margaret, 210–211, 214, 218, 220, 241
Thomas, Norman, 34
Thomas, Rich, 209
tides, intellectual, 221
Tobin, James, 126, 155, 158–59, 163, 216
Tolkien, J. R. R., 83
toll roads, publicly owned, 172, 173
Triffin, Robert, 66
Turner, John, 94, 138

Ulmer, Melville, 192

unemployment, 18, 64, 98–100, 103, 118–19, 126, 160, 170, 206
    natural rate of, 161–62
University of Chicago, 16, 79, 105, 162, 164, 165, 168
    Chilean student program 189–90
    MF associated with, 2
    MF's graduate studies at, 19–25, 135
    MF's teaching at, 53, 86–95, 105, 129, 151–52
    Round Table radio program, 72, 82, 136
    student protests at, 190
University of Chicago, Department of Economics, 20, 22–23, 25, 51, 53–61, 129–33, 237
    "Chicago School of Economics" and, 129–33
    distinctiveness of, 131–33
    MF's influence on, 132–33
    periods of development of, 129–30
    songs written by graduate students at, 60–61

Valentine, Gloria, 199
Veblen, Thorstein, 20, 106
Versailles Peace Treaty, 41, 105
Vietnam War, 151, 165–66, 170, 180, 187, 232
Viner, Jacob, 2, 20–24, 26, 31, 33, 35, 38, 54, 59, 70, 86, 88, 129, 131–32
voting rights, 143
vouchers. See school vouchers

Wald, Abraham, 45
Wald, George, 191
Wallis, Allen, 16, 27, 32–33, 44, 58, 60, 167, 179, 208
    arranges for MF to meet with Nixon, 185
    death of, 232
    on MF, 24, 33, 34, 45, 85–86
    recommends MF to Chitester, 200
Walters, Alan, 211
Wanderjahr (wandering year), 147–48
welfare state, 2, 123–24, 220
Westmoreland, William, 180
Will, George, 236–37
Wimmer, Larry, 92–93
Witte, Edwin, 42
World War II, 41–46, 50–51, 105, 114, 121, 123, 127, 130, 136, 150, 187, 231
Wright, Chester, 54

Yeltsin, Boris, 214
Yntema, Theodore, 54

Zhao Ziyang, 190, 213–14